Verge

STUDIES IN GLOBAL ASIAS

Volume 2, Issue 2
Fall 2016

Verge (ISSN 2373-5058) is published twice a year in the spring and fall by the University of Minnesota Press, 111 Third Avenue South, Suite 290, Minneapolis, MN 55401-2520. http://www.upress.umn.edu

Postmaster: Send address changes to *Verge,* University of Minnesota Press, 111 Third Avenue South, Suite 290, Minneapolis, MN 55401-2520.

Essays (between 6,000 and 10,000 words) should be prepared using parenthetical documentation with a list of works cited. Authors' names should not appear on manuscripts; instead, please include a separate document with the author's name and address and the title of the article with your electronic submission. Authors should not refer to themselves in the first person in the submitted text or notes if such references would identify them; any necessary references to the author's previous work, for example, should be in the third person. Submissions and editorial queries should be sent to verge@psu.edu.

Books for review should be addressed to

Verge: Studies in Global Asias
c/o Department of Asian Studies
102 Old Botany
University Park, PA 16802

Address subscription orders, changes of address, and business correspondence (including requests for permission and advertising orders) to *Verge,* University of Minnesota Press, 111 Third Avenue South, Suite 290, Minneapolis, MN 55401-2520.

Subscriptions: Regular rates, U.S.: individual, 1 year, $35; libraries, 1 year, $100. Other countries add $5 for each year's subscription. Checks should be made payable to the University of Minnesota Press. Back issues are $17.50 for individuals, $50 for libraries (plus $6 shipping for the first copy, $1.25 for each additional copy inside the U.S.; $9.50 shipping for the first copy, $6 for each additional copy, outside the U.S.). *Verge* is available online through the JSTOR Current Scholarship Program at http://jstor.org/r/umnpress. A subscription to *Verge* is a benefit of attending Penn State's biennial Global Asias conference.

Verge Studies in Global Asias **2.2**

■ ASIAN EMPIRES & IMPERIALISM   FALL 2016

Essays

Editors' Introduction

ERICA BRINDLEY AND ON-CHO NG

Asian Empires Revisited: Decentering Imperialism

WHILE EMPIRES IN ASIA, such as the mighty Mauryan and Qin, have admittedly existed since ancient times, the concept of empire has largely been defined according to Western history and historiography. To be sure, various Asian states throughout history might legitimately be defined and conceived in terms of the elements and attributes known to have been shared by empires in world history, but the almost exclusive use of Western historical experiences as the criteria of intelligibility tends to flatten the particularities of imperial regimes that laid outside of the ambit of Europe. The unfortunate result has been that even though many governing entities could indeed have been understood as "empires" in premodern world history, the notion of "empire" in much existing scholarship has a propensity to retain the imprint of a historical pattern that begins with the Roman *imperium* and extends to the Byzantine and Holy Roman empires in the premodern period. This paradigm, presumed to be of universal applicability, is then appropriated as the working definition of the modern empires of Portugal, Spain, the Netherlands, Great Britain, America, and Japan, notwithstanding the fact that the new technological prowess of these latter-day imperial versions is duly acknowledged. In brief, the study of world empires has been dominated by this patently Eurocentric, and thus relatively static, conception of empire, which has served as the basic model for understanding the nature and effects of various megaterritorial governing structures throughout world history.

Our conception and use of the term *empire* in this special issue loosens the term (and indeed the entire nomenclature) of *empire* from the dominion of a single historical trajectory largely projected by the Roman–Byzantine–European models. The authors featured in the following pages, especially those who work on premodern Asian empires, describe imperial regimes in terms of some well-known and generally accepted general features of empire. Most notably, they see empire as a colossal state that possesses military, economic, cultural, ideological, juridical, bureaucratic, and administrative controls and claims over a substantial, multiethnic region or territory in the world. But by treating premodern Asia as a unique mega-region that was distinct from European homeland cultures and histories, and by paying due attention to its particular methods of imperial growth and development, these authors offer new definitions of empire that dislocate it from the culturally parochial and essentialized baggage of more European-derived discussions of empire dominant in general, contemporary academic circles.

Specifically, Pamela Kyle Crossley and Peter K. Bol both urge us to exercise caution when applying the concept and term of "empire" to some of the premodern East Asian mega-states. In fact, they argue that we might serve historical realities better if we refrain from labeling these mega-states as "empires" at all, unless we can establish a far more precise means of distinguishing distinct levels and types of military, ideological, and administrative control across the East–West divide. As far as Crossley and Bol are concerned, the premodern empires they discuss did not maintain tight, homogenous, supraregional control throughout. Rather, they exercised administrative, legal control most directly through their civil governments in the "inner" realms and only nebulous, ephemeral control via military structures in their "outer," colonial realms. Such manifestations do not neatly fit the patterns of imperial rule often imputed to Roman and Byzantine empires, patterns that stress the clear and systematic transformation of a state into a fully centralized regime with major reach in terms of both administrative and military control.

This special issue also provides a discursive arena for the vast concept of "Asian imperialisms," which covers a conceptual ground even more massive than that of "Asian empires" to the extent that imperialism is a putative historical phenomenon abstracted from the workings of a conglomeration of empires. Current models of imperialism tend to take the concept itself for granted, presenting it as a naturalized analytic category that describes a particular power relationship or structure of authority, the pattern of which is based on relatively recent examples, drawing from the British, American, European, and Japanese realms. In a general way, these imperialist experiences and examples do display the leitmotif of the sanctioned use of force and other coercive or administrative measures to express, assert, impose, propagate, and promote the interests of a dominant superpower in and beyond the formal, territorial boundaries of its state. But the actual exercising of imperialist powers takes many forms at different levels. There is no simple conceptual umbrella under which various strands of Asian imperialisms can be adequately fit. Thus, taken in toto, this special issue offers a shifting of emphases and a decentering of commonly understood manners of interpreting imperialism in global history, introducing Asian imperialisms from a host of perspectives that seek to reveal more than the coercive power of the modern imperialist regimes armed with their military, bureaucratic, and technological apparatuses.

Our special issue operates on the methodological premise that empires and imperialisms should not only be defined, discussed, and understood at the macroscopic level but also explored, examined, and explained at the microscopic level by laying bare the generative and constructive possibilities of individual agency. Of key importance in many of the works included here is the creative link between identity construction and imperial authority and control. Imperialism in this context is often presented in terms of a structured relationship of power, one that defines a dominant–subordinate (the Hegelian master–slave) relationship maintained not only through military might and administrative measures but also through the imagined realms of perception, memory, and even fantasy.

In this imagined realm, the self-construction of individual agents—their perceived identities and the identities of those around them—is constantly being negotiated and reified through generative acts that respond to the relationship in which they find themselves. Thus, for example, in this volume, we see pro-independence activists in Taiwan resisting claims emanating from mainland China on their sovereignty by proclaiming their belonging to an abstract "American empire"; we learn how contemporary Korean Americans might gain a sense of community through the ritual performance of moments in a shared history; and we witness how Filipino intellectuals come to terms with their self-identities in light of American, Japanese, and Russian czarist powers. These examples and more help illustrate the fact that the very perception of imperialist structures of power is often a mechanism through which behaviors and ways of thinking are influenced and change, especially when it comes to one's identity, or sense of self, within the imperial domain.

As a main engine driving history, the imperialist power dynamic thus provides both the framework and the fuel not just for creating states and facilitating various forms of transnational and interregional exchange but also for forging and preserving individual identities. As individuals encounter the hard and soft powers of empire and imperialism, the existential question of identity—that of defining the master and the subject—comes to the fore. Whether an imperial subject is part of the dominant group or a member of the subaltern, the imperialist power dynamic shapes and defines one's sense of the self.

Various grassroots and local perspectives on imperialism provide specific examples of how subjects and subaltern alike, as transformative historical agents, accept, reject, and alter imperial authority in the process of creating individual, group, and state identities. We see how these identities exert an effect over conceptions of the self and human behavior, in daily life at home as well as in faraway colonies, and in the form of policies, threats, or political stances that stake out variable and alternate claims to power. Although this phenomenon is present in the bulk of the analyses that follow, it is especially noticeable in the collaborative review of Yoshimi Yoshiaki's *Grassroots Fascism* published as a *Codex* feature in this issue's **Convergence** section, which reveals the insidious nature of fascism as it plays out in various individuals' psyches and memories; in Charlotte Eubanks's *Portfolio* contribution on Japanese board games, which outlines a process through which children learn to experience the fruits of colonial conquest; and in contributions by Derek Sheridan, Sony Coráñez Bolton, and David S. Roh on independence activists in Taiwan, postcolonial disability in the Philippines, and the racialization of Korean Americans, respectively.

As this brief sketch makes clear, this issue's main concerns are distributed evenly across the journal's **Convergence** and **Essays** sections. The issue's opening **Convergence** section exhibits a wide array of techniques, angles, and approaches with which to interrogate and highlight the themes of Asian empires and imperialisms. Its four special features—*A&Q*, *Codex*, *Portfolio*, and *Interface*—constitute vastly different modes of exploration. Collectively, these features offer wide-ranging perspectives on empires and imperialisms at both the macroscopic and microscopic levels, helping to illustrate and explain large trends in statehood and history as well as local responses at the grassroots and individual levels.

Our first feature, an *A&Q* contribution by Crystal Mun-hye Baik on the performance art of Dohee Lee, a contemporary Korean American artist in the Bay Area, shows how an artist may use performance rituals and cosmological symbols reminiscent of a specific place (Jeju Island) as a "decolonial tactic" to conjure a sense of community and a deep relationship to Korean history. The creation of an identity in the imagined realm serves as a type of response to perceived imperialisms in both the past and present. Our second feature, *Codex,* consists of commentaries by Ethan Mark, Aaron William Moore, and Sheldon Garon and a meta-commentary by Reto Hofmann, who collaboratively assess Yoshimi Yoshiaki's impactful book *Grassroots Fascism* in the larger context of imperialism, total war, and the Japanese war experience. What is striking about this discussion is its emphasis on individuals' experience of imperialism as it works through memory and weaves itself into the cloth of their lives in drastically different ways.

In our third feature, *Portfolio,* Charlotte Eubanks imparts fresh insights into the lived experiences of empire and imperial consciousness through her analysis of the *sugoroku* board game. This feature locates a new site for imperialism, fashioned through children's fantasies of conquest, the possession of new and exotic territories, and the obtainment of a good life in a glorious transnational sphere. Last, in our fourth feature, *Interface,* two separate teams of Chinese historians and scholars show us how they use digital technologies to explore the history of Chinese empires through spatialized data and special user interfaces. By sharing their work on a European Research Council–sponsored project on "Communication and Empire: Chinese Empires in Comparative Perspective," Hilde De Weerdt, Chu Ming-kin, and Ho Hou-Ieong show us how digital methods can make possible a more accurate study of how political communication and elite networks affected the creation and maintenance of empires and other kinds of polities. Similarly, Peter K. Bol demonstrates how the China Historical Geographic Information System project, currently a collaboration of the Harvard University Center for Geographic Analysis and the Fudan University Center for Chinese Historical Geography, enables the spatialization of data throughout the so-called imperial realms, which in turn reveals new insights into how control and authority were exerted in premodern times.

All our **Convergence** features demonstrate the importance of examining the lived experiences and shared communities that make up imperial mind-sets, imperial geographies, imperial structures, and imperial cultures. Each of the contributing authors explores some facet of imperialism by looking at sites, spaces, and individuals not normally examined in discussions of empire that are focused on the center or top echelons of government. The pieces as a whole draw our attention to the vast panorama and even psychological realms of imperialism, defining imperialism in terms of a distinctive power dynamic involving occupation, possession, acquisition, suppression, military coercion, and subjugation, on one hand, and repentance, group unity, rebellion, defiance, fantasy, and creative uses of memory, on the other.

The five **Essays** included in this volume range from a big-picture discussion of the act of creating notions of empire and civilization in Eurasian history to individual, ethnographic interventions taken in contemporary

Taiwan to a discussion of imperial or postcolonial mentalities in contemporary Filipino and American Korean literature and to bonds of solidarity formed among Chinese contract laborers in nineteenth-century Cuba. Despite the myriad differences among these articles in scope, discipline, topic, time period, and place, they intriguingly find common ground in the main points that they make. Indeed, each of these **Essays** shows how the act of positing or creating a group identity involves recourse to a certain conception of empire as well as an imperial power dynamic. The formation of self or group identity thus hinges on a perceived notion of an imperial landscape in the world outside the self, and one's responses to such a landscape are critical to the further propagation of such imperial notions in the lived world of dominant and subordinate subjects alike. This self-fashioning occurs even in cases where there is no actual juridical, territorial, or military expression of empire, as is the case in Derek Sheridan's ethnography of Taiwan.

This issue's lead **Essays** contribution, Pamela Kyle Crossley's "The Imaginal Bond of 'Empire' and 'Civilization' in Eurasian History," is a magisterial, comparative account of so-called Eurasian empires as seats of civilizational, cultural, or moral influence. Crossley's incisive argument—that these latter notions of "empire" are largely fictive, later concoctions that overemphasize ideological (cultural and ethical) forces in history—will no doubt serve as a springboard for much future discussion on the topic. Tracing state types through three historical stages of continental empires across Eurasia: (1) classical (Han and Roman), (2) confessional (Byzantine, Sassanian, Central Asian, and Tang), (3) and monarchical (Mongol, Ming-Qing, Russian, and Ottoman), Crossley persuasively shows how the notion of empire as a strong, civilizational force was often a rhetoric deployed by later elites to propagate a unified sense of identity. Most of the continental empires in the history of Eurasia, Crossley argues, were actually only "imperial" to the extent that they had a robust, coercive military infrastructure or apparatus that controlled far-flung populations. It is entirely appropriate that the issue's **Essays** section begins with a massive, comparative provocation that questions the very core of the notion of "empire" through a comparative analysis of imperial reach and control throughout the ages and across Eurasia.

Derek Sheridan's **Essays** contribution, based on the author's fieldwork in Taiwan in 2012, traces the emergence of epistemological claims for belonging to empire—the American empire—by certain independence activists in Taiwan. It is an astute account of a group's origins and its relationships to other groups, one that also takes into account Taiwan's historical position among a variety of empires ranging from the Qing to the Dutch, Japanese, and, now, American. Significantly, this work shows how the very conception of an empire is an act of mapping out a political cosmology, and it does so by pointing to the performance of imperial claims in local political struggles.

Sony Coráñez Bolton explores the meanings and import of a 1908 travel journal, *Hacia la Tierra del Zar*, written by the towering Filipino statesman, literary figure, and *ilustrado* intellectual Teodoro Kalaw. Bolton reads Kalaw's travel writing as a map that shows the circulation of transnational capital in American transpacific expansion, Japanese military–economic imperialism, and the abortive imperial turpitude of czarist Russia. The essay canvasses a variety of theoretical approaches to come to terms with the cultural and nationalist self-identities of the new Filipino intellectuals who came of age in the years just following the Philippine wars for independence.

David S. Roh offers a fresh reading of the famous novel *GO* by Kaneshiro Kazuki by focusing on the question of *zainichi* (Korean Japanese) selfhood and identity. Roh reveals the ways in which the American empire manifested itself in territorial and political form as the SCAP and in cultural forms via popular culture and racial discourse. He also shows how the *zainichi*, as historical agents, appropriated and exploited the cultural and intellectual resources afforded by the empire, throwing into sharp relief a psychology of the workings of the American empire and the *zainichi*'s quest for authentic personhood and effective citizenship.

Margaret Mih Tillman's **Essays** contribution sheds new light on the coolie trade, an integral part of the geoeconomic workings of the Spanish–American empires, by offering an in-depth study of the Chinese laborers and migrants in Cuba, tapping into hitherto unused archival resources. Tillman documents how Chinese contract laborers in Cuba exhibited agency and solidarity in the face of economic and political exploitation. Their painstaking efforts to forge new identities and statuses for themselves demonstrate the limits of the claim that contract labor could serve as an intermediary step in the transition from slave labor to free labor. In the process of plumbing vertically the actions and circumstances of the Cuban Chinese laborers, Tillman reveals the horizontal historical dynamics of the intersections of the Chinese, Spanish, and American empires, especially those of nascent global capitalism.

As the multidisciplinary assemblage of works here shows, empires and imperialisms are far more than diplomatic maneuvering, application of brute force, and territorial aggrandizement. The argument for the primacy of empire and imperialism as a historical force is an argument for the intrication of geopolitical events with culturo-ideological imaginings. Just as empire is a site of military conquest, bureaucratic management, and juridical oppression, so too is it an ideational domain of identity formation, existential adaptation, and intellectual invention. If imperialism is the phenomenon of the extension of the power of militarily and technologically powerful countries over weaker ones, it is also a framework in which the subaltern exercise agency to engender change. To disengage empire and imperialism from the conventional moorage to territorial domain, military power, and juridical authority is not to minimize the historical significance of these forces; it is to broaden our interpretive gaze at empire and imperialism as complex conceptual entities with multifarious micro and macro dimensions. Needless to say, what we do in this issue can only be a beginning, just as all intellectual endeavors are beginnings to the extent that they will be refined, enriched, and even superseded. But our job is well started if we are here able to reconstruct empires in Asia as theaters of human action that have hitherto been understudied and overlooked.

Convergence

A&Q
—

CRYSTAL MUN-HYE BAIK

MAGO and Communal Ritual as Decolonial Praxis: An Exchange with Dohee Lee

IN SEPTEMBER 2015, Crystal Baik conducted an interview with the Korean American choreographer and visual artist Dohee Lee in San Francisco. The initial in-person exchange focused on Lee's spectacular performance, *MAGO,* and unexpectedly expanded into a three-month-long e-mail correspondence between Baik and Lee. As part of the interview process, Lee and Baik also selected a series of images to reflect the vibrant spirit of their collaboration. The following *A&Q* feature is based on this continuing dialogue and curated visual archive.

▓ PRELUDE
In her epic performance *MAGO,* Dohee Lee—a Korean diasporic choreographer, musician, and artist based in the San Francisco Bay Area— imagines an otherworldly environment that engulfs the audience into its reverberating folds. Premiering at the Yerba Buena Center for the Arts in November 2014 following a four-year gestation period, *MAGO* is a multigenre, multimedia work organized into six chapters. Juxtaposing Korean traditional dance, percussion, and live opera *(pansori)* with elements of modern dance, electronica, and imagery, *MAGO* commences in the center's lobby before traveling to the main stage and looping back to the lobby for the finale. Accompanying Lee through the center's voluminous structure, the audience enacts a series of kinesthetic, verbal, and affective exchanges with the artist. Through this interactive, if not intensive process, the audience becomes an integral component of *MAGO.*

Though a vacillating and unpredictable encounter, *MAGO* is also firmly anchored in a rich corpus of Korean cosmologic symbols, mythologies, and shamanic rituals affiliated with *Jeju-do* (Jeju Island). Located off the

Figure 1. Dohee Lee encounters the audience in *MAGO*. Photograph by Pak Han.

coast of the Korean Peninsula and the place of Lee's birth, Jeju Island embodies a complicated history of colonial conquest and militarized occupation. Yet, rather than understanding mythical formations as whimsical folk traditions or totalizing gestures that reference a foregone past, Lee approaches cultural practices as subjugated knowledges that unhinge the official narrative of Korean liberation crafted by the South Korean and U.S. states. By mobilizing Mago, the Korean goddess of creation and cosmic sound, as the pivotal figure of her performance, Lee interrogates the multiple iterations of militarized and imperial violence that have gripped Jeju Island. Through the interlacing of cultural mythologies with personal memories of Jeju, Lee alludes to the somber silence surrounding her maternal grandparents' grievous pasts of horror and survival—experiences that she sensed as a child but could not articulate or give words to until she was a young adult:

> I was born in Jeju and had to move out [to the Korean Peninsula] when I was seven years old. But every summer and winter vacation, I went to Jeju to see my grandparents and my relatives. So it's my home. . . . One thing I really noticed was this thick silence—this silence among ourselves and

our neighbors. I didn't know what it was, but something was strange about it. . . . Later, when my grandparents passed away—that was 2006—I was so regretful that I never ever asked my grandparents about their history.

Here the intimacies of home, kinship, and family secrets are ensnared within Jeju's histories of multiple colonialisms. Jeju was once the independent kingdom of Tamna with an indigenously distinct culture but was absorbed into the Goryeo Dynasty in the twelfth century and became a tributary of the Joseon Dynasty in the fourteenth century (Eckert et al. 1990). Following centuries of considerable tension with Korean monarchial rule, Jeju was transformed into a Japanese imperial colony between 1910 and 1945. With the collapse of the Japanese empire in 1945, Jeju Island was then jointly reoccupied by the U.S. and South Korean militaries. Prominently known for anticolonial activism and the only province that resisted separate presidential elections in the northern and southern halves of Korea in 1948, Jeju was openly characterized by the United States as a "red" (communist) colony in need of state discipline (Kwon 2010). Between 1948 and 1955, this directive led to the U.S.–South Korean military-backed massacre of up to eighty thousand civilians, or nearly one-third of the island's population—an onslaught that Lee's grandparents survived but continued to relive in its aftermath (Kim 2000, 161–62). As a microcosm of and precursor to the ferocity unleashed during the Korean War (1950–53), the Jeju massacre is now commonly referred to as the April Third Incident, or simply 4.3 (Kim 2009; 2012; Suh 2010; Kim 2010). Calculated by the South Korean and U.S. governments as a martial action necessary to ensure democracy in the island, 4.3 condenses into an unsettling presence (Kim 2000). In fact, survivors and their kin continue to live, side by side, with perpetrators of the terrifying massacre, including members of the anticommunist paramilitary youth group the Northwest Youth League and aging civilians who silently colluded with the U.S.–South Korean military (Kim 2003, 309–12). However, with the recent construction of a state-of-the-art naval base in the small fishing village of Gangjeong, the brutal memories of the April Third Incident resurface in more blatant ways. Under the auspices of the U.S. government, which maintains wartime control of the South Korean military, the Gangjeong base symbolizes the American "pivot" toward Asia or the rechanneling of U.S. military, economic, and political resources into this targeted geographical area (Lee and Hong 2013).[1]

Lee's *MAGO* confronts these histories of violence not as discrete phenomena but as entwined developments indicative of an underlying logic: the state's rendering of Jeju as a disposable outpost crucial to the state's inter/national security interests (Baik 2015). Drawing from her position in an ever-shifting Korean diaspora, Lee troubles fixed renderings of South Korean and U.S. official history. That is, by conceptualizing her performative works as transnational feminist formations, Lee critiques patriotic and patriarchal practices of national memorialization that eclipse the contradictions and differences underlying everyday life. In that sense, I situate Lee within a transnational feminist milieu constituted by Korean diasporic artists and cultural practitioners, such as Jane Jin Kaisen, kate-hers RHEE, Minouk Lim, Erica Cho, and Eunji Cho. Though these different artists refer to the significance of earlier social and aesthetic movements originating in South Korea and the United States (e.g., the Minjung social movement and the Fluxus movement, respectively), their works also break from these formal practices by critiquing their racialized, gendered, and heteronormative dimensions.[2] Lee, therefore, grapples with the militarized imperial enfiguration of contemporary Korea through a diasporic feminist standpoint. Indeed, as discussed throughout this essay, Lee reconfigures Korean shamanistic practices to produce cross-racial affiliations and solidarities that exceed the material borders of Jeju Island and the Korean Peninsula.

How, then, does Lee's utilization of cultural practices and mythologies contend with the interlocking forms of militarized imperial violence that continue to reverberate in the present day? By framing *MAGO* as a communal ritual, how does Lee attend to a community of listeners who share, albeit momentarily, in the complicated process of recognizing those disappeared by the U.S. and South Korean states? Finally, how might we understand Lee's reinterpretation of mythology and ritualistic tradition as a decolonial praxis?

These are but a handful of questions that surfaced during a recent in-person interview with Dohee Lee in San Francisco (September 2015), which extended into a three-month-long e-mail exchange between Lee and me.[3] Throughout our expansive correspondence, Lee touches on an array of interrelated issues, ranging from her own relationship to Jeju to her use of ritualistic practices as modes of radical critique. Following our dynamic exchange, I asked Lee to choose a selection of images that best captures, for her, the spirit of our conversation and, in a more general sense, the rhythmic unfolding of *MAGO*. Taking these images as initial entry points or cues, the following acts build around this curated visual archive. As intimated in the remainder of this essay, my discussion with Lee continues in surprising ways, destabilizing the fixed temporality and answer-and-volley schema of the formal interview—reflective, perhaps, of the shape-shifting form of *MAGO* itself.

Figure 2. "Myths are not just tales from long ago. They are launching points for taking stories into you. They are transformed into new personal myths." Photograph by Pak Han.

■ ACT I. MYTHOLOGY

In the opening sequence of *MAGO,* Lee appears from the shadows, adorned in a traditional Korean mask and delicate layers of translucent paper. Embodying the Korean mythic deity Mago, Lee slowly walks through an aisle and intermittently pauses to interact with captivated audience members. Dragging tentacles of tapering cloth behind her, Lee mouths indecipherable sounds that are remixed into a cacophony of breaths, songs, and guttural pronunciations. In juxtaposing these jarring echoes with unexpected moments of silence, the immersive soundscape is as intriguing as it is baffling. What is sounded is not merely aural; it is so palpable, so thick, that the felt vibrations sink into the skin. Yet, Mago's utterances remain encrypted and a cipher. For the remainder of the performance, the audience listens closely to Lee as they attempt to decode Mago's whispered stories.

Taking both tranquil and ferocious forms throughout the performance, Lee's embodiment of Mago transforms into the heart and through-line of her spectacular work. When I press her about the development and production of *MAGO,* Lee carefully responds by describing her fantastical encounter with a mysterious figure (whom she later identifies as Mago) in a hazy dream in 2008:

> This woman came to me and said something that I couldn't really under-stand. She was blurry. . . . She dropped these bells into my hands that were ringing so loudly. All of these vibrations! My body was really shaking. I said, "Oh, I have to find this woman." . . . I said, "I have to pay attention to this." I started searching for this woman—the woman that I found was Mago.

In an uncanny sense, Mago's spectral appearance occurred at a tumul-tuous moment: Lee's dream dovetailed with the South Korean govern-ment's abrupt announcement of the construction of a new naval base in Gangjeong. When Lee became aware of this development, she found the news alarming yet strangely familiar—or, as stated by Lee, "like déjà vu." In many ways the remilitarization of the island stokes unmitigated fears and unforgotten atrocities affiliated with the bloody 4.3 massacre. As shared by Lee, her grandparents miraculously survived the April 3 atrocities. However, close friends, neighbors, and other family members were not so fortunate. Even as the South Korean government publicly broached and apologized for the "incident" on national television in 2003, the devastating Cold War history of Jeju is rarely discussed among South Koreans or Korean diasporans. In that sense, Lee's pairing of the April Third Incident with the Gangjeong naval base construction gestures to the politics of silence affixed to Jeju's history. While these military ac-tions are visibly marked, recorded, and documented, many choose to disengage with or disavow this history. Today, thousands of deaths remain unacknowledged or unaccounted for by the South Korean state. Amid the government's silence, Jeju's inhabitants continually speak of the uneasy presence of ancestral ghosts who restlessly wander across *Halla-san*'s, or Mount Halla's, hamlets and meadows. Subsequently, for many survivors and their loved ones, the Gangjeong naval base symbolizes a structural continuation of 4.3 and obstructs efforts for intergenerational healing. As offered by anthropologist Kim Seong-nae (2013, 236), the untether-ing of 4.3 from a linear, chronological timeline generates a circuitous sense of time, or "durational time," that indefinitely binds survivors and their families to an undying past. For Lee, the militarization of Ganjeong is "the same story [as the April Third Incident] but it's happening at a different time":

My eyes traveled back to the ocean, where new military development is once again destroying the land and people. Drills cut into ancient volcanic stone and families, neighbors, and villages are divided again. Sixty years. It still continues.

Situated within this historical context, Lee's invocation of Mago provides an alternative pathway to make meaning of horrific killings that remain unheard in the "real" world. Transmitted across generations and retold during moments of calamity, cultural mythologies transform into profound wells of accrued memories, fears and hopes, and collective lessons. Lee's summoning of Mago, then, indexes a critical genealogy of knowledge that intervenes in ahistorical articulations of the here and now: contemporary acts of state-inflicted violence, intrusion, and dispossession are placed along an established path of militarized imperial desires. For Lee, this understanding of mythology constitutes the very backbone of *MAGO*. By enabling public narrations of past injustices, the performance imagines and images a just future. Lee's imagistic use of Mago is especially impactful because the deity shares a unique relationship with Jeju Island. Affiliated with the vast expanse of the ocean, Mago is summoned by those who depend on the ocean's generosity for their livelihood. For instance, the *haenyeo,* or Jeju's lineage of female divers (including Lee's own grandmother), looks to the goddess as the protector and restorer of health, healing, and justice. Among those who continue to endure and witness, firsthand, the ramifications of a militarized agenda in modern-day Jeju, Mago is continually evoked as a potent symbol of fierce resistance and stubborn survival.

■ ACT II. RITUAL

In the segment "Waterways," Lee sits center stage as slow-moving imagery of Jeju's rocky shores and an elderly woman's face pierce two screens placed in the background. Dressed in gauzy garments, with Hangul-filled scrolls draped across her shoulders and chest, Lee carefully enumerates the names of those killed during the April Third Incident. As Lee enunciates each name in a steady and deliberate tone, *soombi-sori*—or the high-pitched whistling noises made by the *haenyeo* as they come up for air—fills the lofty forum. Intermittently, Lee lifts her head to look at and acknowledge the felt presence of the audience.

For Lee, the audience is a crucial and constitutive element of *MAGO.* By calling on the audience as active participants rather than passive consumers of the performance, Lee reconceptualizes communal ritual through *MAGO.* Here Lee's understanding of performance-as-ritual deserves some

Figure 3. "Ritual has a purpose to it. You have a reason to do it. I'm calling out, I'm evoking stories that others might feel connected to: to each other, to spaces, to ancestors.... We need this in our society. It's not only my story, it's also your story.... Rituals are encounters." Photograph by Pak Han.

unpacking. Lee does not define or understand the communal ritual as an essentialized set of prescribed rites recited in a mechanized manner; rather, the ritual is a conduit for communication, recognition, and negotiation. Hence, through intentional exchanges with audience members, a collaborative and shared performance takes shape. These poignant yet transient relations produce specific roles and obligations: by initiating and maintaining connectivity with the audience, Lee becomes the facilitator of the emergent interactions. In return, Lee asks the audience to become attentive witnesses open to all that unfolds before them. This playful notion of the audience, of course, does not universally appeal to all participants. Yet, for Lee, the "negative" feelings of anxiety, discomfort, and unease are productive insofar as they challenge and push the boundaries of her artistic praxis:

> Many are unprepared to be engaged . . . and yes, something happens, some people are uncomfortable, some people hate it. But for me, that's great! [I

ask people,] "Why do you hate it? Why are you happy to be a part of it?" It's so interesting to me. . . . It's all about discovery. . . . It's about understanding the connection, the moment of exchange.

Lee's adept mediation of these improvisational interactions hints at her expansive knowledge of Korean ancestral rituals, such as the *gut*, a form of ancestor worship involving ceremonial offerings, sacrifices, prayers, oracles, and rhythmic movements (Kendall 2009).[4] In a more general sense, Lee's reference to the ritual as form and practice emphasizes the political significance of shamanic traditions among Koreans (Kwon 2010).[5] Throughout Korea and the diaspora, shamans occupy a powerful role in the realm of political resistance and protest. Mediating between the spiritual and mundane worlds, the shaman, or *mudang* (female) and *baksu* (male), does not merely communicate the lamentations of the dead to the living. Instead, by literally inhabiting the historical experiences of those who have passed away from unnatural acts, shamans give fleshed form to the memories and testimonies of the dead. Thus, as agents who facilitate public processes of mourning amid intentional acts of silencing and obscuration, shamans actualize innovative approaches to sensing inconceivable experiences of pain.

Understood as such, Lee's summoning of the deceased in "Waterways" is a ritual of representational continuity. By intentionally naming and situating the disappeared in a genealogy of kin among a community of witnesses, Lee produces an "othered" space of radical alterity coinhabited by the living and disappeared. Resonating, in some ways, with Diana Taylor's description of the mnemonic practice of "DNA"—or the symbolic performance of unbroken ties and social affiliations among an assemblage of conscientious participants—the dead are assured that they "are neither forgotten nor 'surrogated'" and that "no one else will take their place" (Taylor 2003, 187). For Lee, these ritualistic practices of publicly and explicitly naming the dead accentuate presence over absence and memory over erasure.

Lee's engagement with embodied memory, presence, and the audience becomes even more palpable in "Invited Ritual: Crow." In this segment, Lee personifies yet another quality of Mago: the omniscient trickster who moves at a frenzied pace as she visualizes social traces and scenes evacuated from plain sight. With tufts of feather framing her angular face, Lee takes the animated form of the crow, an ominous figure in Korean mythology. Ubiquitous in Jeju, crows hold especially portentous meanings among the older generations of islanders. For instance, survivors of and bystanders to 4.3 often refer to the crow as the sole witness of mass

Figure 4. Dohee Lee embodies the crow in *MAGO*. Photograph by Pak Han.

executions that took place in the forests and foothills of Mount Halla.

Yet, the figure of the crow is also meaningful in the sense that it links the past with the present and gestures to the unquelled spirits that inhabit Jeju's landscape:

> Visiting these massacre sites, including Halla Mountain, I constantly found myself in the company of a murder of crows. It seemed to me that they were witnesses and protectors of the land and lost souls. Watching me, piercing me with their gaze, and asking, "What did you see?" "What did you hear?"

On stage, these troubled spirits take material form as a choir of performers, donning eerie white masks, takes center stage. Lee then addresses the audience through the following inquires: *What did you see? What did you hear?* As she shifts her gaze to those in the forum, Lee continues to press the audience. *What did you see? What did you hear?* Slowly, participants yell out a range of answers: "bombs on my grandmother's house," "racism," "air strikes in Gaza."[6] As Lee continues with her line of questioning, the audience's simultaneous responses accumulate, overlap, and wash over the space. For Lee, this reciprocated practice of listening and responding

Figure 5. A circle of witnesses in *MAGO*. Photograph by Pak Han.

enacts moments of self-reflexivity by allowing the audience to identify distinct modes of racialized and gendered violence that stretch beyond the borders of Jeju. These recounted incidences—the terrifying experiences of militarized warfare, racial oppression, and settler occupation—are not isolated, nor are they exceptional. Rather, they point to the "darker side of [Western] modernity" or the ways in which militarized imperialism generates dense concentrations of pain that disproportionately affect specific communities and bodies.[7] Through this powerful recollection, Jeju's history of militarized warfare is placed within a global map of unevenly distributed violence affiliated with Western (primarily U.S.) colonial rule and mechanisms of extraction:

> It's not only Jeju—it's other places too. Different countries [such as the United States] have immense power to take away land. . . . They do what they want to do. So people realize that they are not only talking about [Jeju's] history, but about the present moment: we experience, see, hear all of these things, but we never talk about it. We never talk about it. So by asking people, "What did you see? Can you tell what you saw?" I don't want to lecture to people. I just want them to listen and speak to each other.

Figure 6. "I just hope this will help the younger generation search for and find ways to connect to different pasts, to their land, to others. . . . I think art can do this. It can create these different routes of understanding, it can generate conversations so that we might share information and imagine together. So yes. I want [younger generations] to imagine and speak up." Photograph by Pak Han.

Punctuated by a moment of silence, Lee draws "Invited Ritual" to a close with two final phrases: *Open your eyes. Open your ears.*

■ ACT III. PURI/RELEASE

In her recent talk given at the University of California, Riverside, Michelle M. Jacob, an associate professor of ethnic studies at the University of San Diego and a member of the Yakama Nation, offered a succinct definition of decolonization (Jacob 2015). Drawing from and citing the work of Waziyatawin Angela Wilson and Michael Yellow Bird, Jacob referred to decolonization as "the intelligent, calculated, and active resistance to the forces of colonialism that perpetuate the subjugation and/or exploitation of our minds, bodies, and lands" (Jacob 2013, 5). Jacob continued by stating,

"Decolonization is about reclaiming traditions . . . to move [forward] in the complex social, political, and economic realities colonization brought to our peoples and homelands" (6).

Though Jacob applies this definition to describe the specific struggles of the Yakama people, her broad configuration of decolonization as a material, discursive, and ontological process—one that is difficult, ongoing, and structural—is tremendously helpful for my own understanding of the decolonial. Specifically, I draw on Jacob's articulation to unpack the ways in which Lee's *MAGO* engages with decolonization in relationship to Jeju and Korea. In many ways, Lee's intentional use of cultural symbols, ancient mythologies, and shamanic mediation privileges local ways of knowing and vernacular forms of knowledge in Jeju Island. In other words, Lee's embracing of suppressed ancestral histories and alternative systems of thought is a decolonial tactic because it labors toward the dismantling of the state's narrative of national progression and practices of disposability. Lee creates routes and relations that ineluctably link, even if momentarily, disparate temporalities, communities, and generations by treating cultural practices as malleable discursive tools. Hence, in stark contrast to the suffocating silence enforced by the U.S.–South Korean military alliance in Jeju, Lee's artistic praxis fosters intergenerational and transnational communities of listeners and witnesses. *MAGO,* therefore, does not merely challenge dominant narrations. Rather, the performance-as-ritual permits us to encounter and sit with submerged socialities that are not immediately legible to the human eye.

Perhaps, what is most compelling about *MAGO* is Lee's skilled ability to translate an ethics of care toward and commitment to Jeju in ways that are meaningful to an expansive audience. Identifying herself and others from Jeju as caretakers of the island's land, water, animals, and people, Lee renders perceptible the unbearable grief that has accumulated across space and time. These fleeting moments do not definitively resolve or rectify the devastation endured by Jeju's people. Instead, by producing *puri,* a shamanic term referring to intentional moments of physical, emotional, and spiritual release, Lee recognizes the "spirits that hold this land" and initiates processes of healing:

> How can we remember the songs of our ancestors, the words that they spoke, their care of the land, people and spirits? I believe that art has the power to creatively confront these struggles. . . . That is why my creative journey is centered in ritual. I dedicate my performance as a ritual to not only discover my own history, but also invite others to discover their own.

Crystal Mun-hye Baik is assistant professor in the Department of Ethnic Studies at the University of California, Riverside. She is completing her first full-length book manuscript, tentatively titled *Demilitarized Futures: Korean Transnational Artists and a Poetics of Division.*

■ **NOTES**

My sincere gratitude to Tina Chen, Leland Tabares, and the editorial staff at *Verge* for this opportunity to share Dohee Lee's important body of work. Thank you, as well, to the anonymous reader for the detailed and tremendously helpful feedback. Finally, thank you to Cristiana Baik, for her stupendous reading of earlier drafts of this essay, and to Dohee Lee, for sharing her work and poetry with me.

1. Former U.S. secretary of state Hillary Clinton (2011) first offered the United States's "pivot" toward Asia.

2. Here I would like to emphasize that my understanding of Lee's work, as part and parcel of a Korean transnational feminist milieu, is my own theorization and conceptualization. My current book project, tentatively titled *Demilitarized Futures: Korean Transnational Artists and a Poetics of Division,* elaborates on this critical genealogy of Korean transnational feminist artists and cultural practitioners.

3. The initial interview with Lee took place at the ODC Theater in San Francisco, California, on September 21, 2015, and continued in follow-up exchanges via e-mail on September 24 and 27 and November 20 and 21, 2015. All quotations included in this essay are excerpts from the interview transcript and our correspondence.

4. To clarify, the *gut* or *kut* (굿) is an ornate ritual performed by shamans, which involves offerings and sacrifices as ancestor worship, rhythmic movements, songs, oracles, and prayers. Refer to Kim (2013).

5. For a thorough reading concerning the political uses and importance of shamanic traditions within South Korean society, refer to chapter 5, "The Democratic Family," in Kwon (2010).

6. Some of these responses from the audience are documented by Ravine (2014).

7. The phrase the "darker side of [Western] modernity" is attributed to Mignolo (2011).

■ **WORKS CITED**

Baik, Crystal Mun-hye. 2015. "Unfaithful Returns: *Reiterations of Dissent,* U.S.–South Korean Militarized Debt, and the Architecture of Violence Freedom." *Journal of Asian American Studies* 18, no. 1: 41–72.

Clinton, Hillary. 2011. America's Pacific Century. *Foreign Policy,* October 11. http://foreignpolicy.com/2011/10/11/americas-pacific-century/.

Eckert, Carter J., Ki-Baik Lee, Young Ick Lew, Michael Robinson, and Edward W. Wager. 1990. *Korea: Old and New, a History.* Cambridge, Mass.: Harvard University Press.

Jacob, Michelle. 2013. *Yakama Rising: Indigenous Culture Revitalization, Activism, and Healing.* Tucson: University of Arizona Press, 2013.

———. 2015. *Yakama Rising: Indigenous Culture Revitalization, Activism, and Healing, a Book Talk.* November 25. University of California, Riverside.

Kendall, Laurel. 2009. *Shamans, Nostalgias, and the IMF: South Korean Popular Religion in Motion.* Honolulu: University of Hawai'i Press.

Kim, Bong-Jin. 2003. "Paramilitary Politics under the USAMGIK and the Establishment of the Republic of Korea." *Korea Journal* 43, no. 2: 289–322.

Kim, Dong-Choon. 2010. "The Long Road toward Truth and Reconciliation: Unwavering Attempts to Achieve Justice in South Korea." *Critical Asian Studies* 42, no. 4: 525–52.

Kim, Hun Joon. 2009. "Seeking Truth after Fifty Years: The National Committee for Investigation of the Truth about the Jeju 4.3 Events." *International Journal of Transitional Justice* 3, no. 3: 406–23.

———. 2012. "Local, National, and International Determinants of Truth Commission: The South Korean Experience." *Human Rights Quarterly* 34, no. 3. 726–750.

Kim, Seong-nae. 2000. "Mourning Korean Modernity in the Memory of the Cheju April Third Incident." *Inter-Asia Cultural Studies* 1, no. 3: 461–76.

———. 2013. "The Work of Memory: Ritual Laments of the Dead and Korea's Cheju Massacre." In *A Companion to the Anthropology of Religion,* edited by Janice Boddy and Michael Lambek, 222–38. Malden, Mass.: John Wiley.

Kwon, Heonik. 2010. *The Other Cold War.* New York: Columbia University Press.

Lee, Hyun, and Christine Hong. 2013. "Lurching towards War: A Post-Mortem on Strategic Patience." *Foreign Policy in Focus,* February 13. http://fpif.org/lurching_towards_war_a_post-mortem_on_strategic_patience/.

Mignolo, Walter. 2011. *The Darker Side of Western Modernity: Global Futures, Decolonial Options.* Durham, N.C.: Duke University Press.

Ravine, Jai Arun. 2014. "Undercurrent: A Review of Dohee Lee's MAGO." November 18. http://jaiarunravine.com/undercurrent-a-review-of-dohee-lees-mago/.

Suh, Jae-Jung. 2010. "Truth and Reconciliation in South Korea: Confronting War, Colonialism, and Intervention in the Asia Pacific." *Critical Asian Studies* 42, no. 4: 503–24.

Taylor, Diana. 2003. *The Archive and the Repertoire: Performing Cultural Memory in the Americas*. Durham, N.C.: Duke University Press.

Codex
———

A Collaborative Review of *Grassroots Fascism: The War Experience of the Japanese People* by Yoshimi Yoshiaki

Grassroots Fascism, Greater Asianism, and the Centrality of the Sino-Japanese War

ETHAN MARK

I first encountered *Grassroots Fascism* in the context of a Japanese history graduate seminar at Columbia University way back in 1991. At the time, I was gearing up for a dissertation project on the Japanese occupation of Indonesia during World War II. Yoshimi's book immediately caught my attention, as I had never seen anything like it: a sober, nuanced, and profoundly engaged account of Japan's war as seen from below, examining the evolving experiences, motivations, and views of a whole range of ordinary Japanese—at home, on the front lines, and in between—as reflected in their own words, drawing largely on wartime sources and consistently concerned with the fascinating but also extremely challenging issue of popular war participation. From the first pages, one is confronted with unforgettable images: the hundreds of postcards sent to the newspapers in support of parliamentarian Saitō Takao, who spoke out in defense of democracy and against military rule in the wake of the young officers' coup attempt in February 1936; happy diary entries of peasant army conscripts for whom army life turned out to hold a range of appeals that had little to do with the emperor-centered ideology so often assumed to have been governing Japanese thoughts at the time. Yoshimi writes, "From the moment they joined the army, peasant soldiers were liberated from time-consuming and arduous farming chores. With 'a daily bath,' 'fairly good' food, and 'fine shoes,' they led more privileged lives than they had in their farming villages. They received salaries that they could save or send to their families. They were able to enjoy 'equal' treatment without regard to their social status, wealth or poverty. They received education

17

and were able to improve their social standing through their own talents" (Yoshimi [1987] 2015, 50). Equally refreshing and memorable was Yoshimi's revelation of the wide and varied appeal of empire and empire building among Japanese rank-and-file soldiery—again as documented in their own wartime words. With characteristic nuance, Yoshimi observed of such popular imperial dreams, "These were the attempts of some men to find a way to live in the war's midst after it had shattered their life prospects. It must be said that soldiers were cornered into this situation. At the same time, we cannot overlook this aspect: that the desire to get as much profit as possible out of the war transcended their unhappiness at being conscripted, and that soldiers supported the war in earnest" (Yoshimi [1987] 2015, 51).

Two aspects of *Grassroots Fascism* particularly struck me at the time and have had a profound impact on my own understanding of and thinking on the war in Asia ever since. The first was the *historicity* of Yoshimi's narrative: the evolution of popular experience and views in tandem with the twists and turns of the war's evolution, expansion, and ultimate implosion. The range and depth of popular critical responses to the young officers' coup attempt in Tokyo in February 1936 is one example. Another is the extent of popular malaise on the eve of the Pacific War, as the Sino-Japanese War entered its fifth year. I was already familiar with some of the strategic reasons for the bold Japanese move against the Western powers at Pearl Harbor and southward into Southeast Asia in 1941. I also knew of Japanese frustration and confusion at their inability to crush Chinese resistance in the period leading up to it. But only from *Grassroots Fascism* did I gain an understanding of the depth and degree of the *crisis* precipitated in Japanese society by the bloody stalemate in China: a crisis at once political, social, economic, cultural, and moral. The seeds of Japanese fascism, it turns out, were sown in the battlefields of China, as an increasingly brutal and brutalized soldiery and an increasingly desperate and deprived home front population came to place a disastrous faith in the authoritarian state to engineer a "decisive breakthrough"— and resolved to make whatever sacrifices that state deemed necessary to that end.

The second, related lesson of *Grassroots Fascism* is the centrality of the China experience to Japan's larger war—the implications, and interdependence, of China developments to developments elsewhere—in Japan proper, in Japan's wartime empire, and indeed in the Second World War as global conflict. I discuss this in some detail in my translator's introduction to the book, but here I'd like to emphasize the particular relevance of this centrality of the China War to subsequent developments in the area that I know best—that is, in the Southeast Asian theater, in particular in occupied Indonesia.

In my ongoing research on the Japanese occupation of Indonesia, I have sought to approach and understand the encounter between Indonesians and Japanese as a transnational cultural interaction. From the very beginning, I was struck by the energy, passion, and radicalism of the Japanese side in occupied Indonesia. The Japanese arrived in Indonesia proclaiming the revolutionary arrival of an Asian empire that could transcend imperialism, an Asian brotherhood that could transcend capitalism, and an Asian modernity that could transcend modernity. In seeking to understand where this came from, I found Yoshimi's study absolutely invaluable, because it makes clear that Japanese ideology and propaganda in Southeast Asia, like that on the home front, can only be understood in light of its highly charged and contested northeast Asian formative context. As Yoshimi so vividly documents, during the four and a half years of total war that preceded Pearl Harbor, continued mobilization of the Japanese populace as well as the elusive "pacification" of the "inscrutably" resistant Chinese demanded an ideological cause that transcended the old, worn-out justifications for Japan's empire—ideally, a cause that might even seem to transcend empire itself. What had started as a relatively straightforward imperialist mission *had* to become, in the eyes of many Japanese, something much more noble, profound, and radical. When subsequent international developments created an opportunity for Japan to strike out against the long-resented Western colonial powers in Southeast Asia, the Japanese were thereby more than ready to embrace this "world-historical" opportunity with both hands, with profound implications both for the Japanese and for the Southeast Asians in the path of this hurricane-force ideological (and military) whirlwind.

The fascinating, variegated responses to the Japanese and their propaganda among the indigenous population, in an Indonesian social and historical context that was profoundly different from that of occupied China, are too complex to explore in any detail here. But put simply, Java's population proved much more open than their Chinese counterparts to ideas of a Japanese-sponsored "Asian" alternative to Western rule and Western modernity. In turn, many Japanese responded with an almost religious sense of redemption and relief for themselves, for their nation, and for its imperial project. As Yoshimi illustrates, Japan's occupation of Indonesia, as elsewhere, proved ultimately and inevitably disastrous for the local population and for many Japanese as well. Yet, however ambiguous in its effects and implications, the ideological storm unleashed by the Sino-Japanese conflict was to have impacts that extended not only throughout Asia but across the globe.

Seventy years since that war's end, in a time of unprecedented polarization regarding Japan's wartime history and its legacies, Professor Yoshimi's classic study offers irrefutable confirmation of the nature of this history in the words of the people who lived it. In placing the rise of Japanese fascism in an imperial frame of reference via a narrative acutely attuned to social and historical nuance, I would argue that *Grassroots Fascism* also represents an essential contribution to a global field that even now—twenty-nine years since the book's first appearance in Japanese—is still in many ways in its infancy: the study of fascism as global history.

Ethan Mark is university lecturer in modern Japanese and Asian history in the Japanese and Asian Studies programs at Leiden University, Netherlands. He is translator of Yoshimi Yoshiaki's *Grassroots Fascism: The War Experience of the Japanese People* (2015) as well as author of essays in the *American Historical Review* and *Journal of Asian Studies*.

■ **WORK CITED**

Yoshimi Yoshiaki. (1987) 2015. *Grassroots Fascism: The War Experience of the Japanese People*. Translated by Ethan Mark. New York: Columbia University Press.

Mirror, Mirror: *Grassroots Fascism* and the Global Mobilization for Total War

AARON WILLIAM MOORE

Yoshimi Yoshiaki's *Grassroots Fascism*, which has now been ably translated by Ethan Mark, continues to be an important intervention in our discussion of Japan's "total war" experience from 1937 to 1945. In particular, Yoshimi's emphasis on individual life writing by ordinary Japanese citizens, as opposed to the commanding heights of the state, ponderous intellectual leaders, and large, inchoate cultural forces like the mass media, has been crucial; until recently, this perspective was lacking in the Anglophone Japanese historiography when compared to fields like British and German history, despite it being a strong trend in Japanese works and the existence of rich archival collections in Japan.[1] By foregrounding the importance of personal documents, Yoshimi exposed the social dynamics that enabled devastating warfare in the 1930s and 1940s. I was inspired by his methodology, but I also saw the need to compare the Japanese materials with Chinese, Russian, American, and British documents. In comparison, the Japanese experience seems less unique than it might first appear, and a transnational convergence of social, economic, and military forces exposes the emergence of a global system of total war mobilization.

One of Yoshimi's most significant contributions to the social history of the war was documenting the extent to which the radicalization of policy was driven by the Japanese people and not simply directed by an impersonal state apparatus; what I found in the diaries of soldiers, which I outline at length in my book *Writing War* (Moore 2013), was that this was also a transnational problem in the 1930s and 1940s. Many servicemen disciplined themselves in anticipation for the battlefield, using the plentiful patriotic and pro-war cultural and discursive tools they had at their disposal (Young 1999; Orbaugh 2015). This process was very similar for Chinese servicemen, which I have argued made the conflict there even more brutal than it would have been if Japan had been conducting a garden-variety colonial war or a Clausewitzian "real war" with clearly defined outcomes.[2] Incessant self-mobilization had dire consequences: in what must now be considered an orthodox historical view, Yoshimi insisted that the 1937 China quagmire enabled Japanese aggressions elsewhere in Asia and the Pacific.[3] Though Yoshimi was careful to note that the battlefields on the mainland produced many divergent reactions among Japanese soldiers, many in fact returned to Japan with a powerful "resolve" to finish the war in China (and then in the Pacific) by any means necessary. Research (including my own) on U.S. servicemen's accounts shows how unexceptional this "resolve" was when societies were in a state of war mobilization, even while wartime propaganda averred that the East and West were irreconcilably different and essentially unique (Schrijvers 2002).[4] Despite the importance of religion, literature, and social ritual as determinative forces in how we view ourselves and others, during mobilization, soldiers' diaries often reveal striking similarities from Japan to China, Britain, the United States, and the Soviet Union.

Historians, like Sheldon Garon in this volume, are now working to show how these convergences could be the product of intentional design: wartime leaders studied global practices to stay on top of the best methods for defending airspace, rationing food, policing discontent, and other "total war" necessities. So Yoshimi's observation of the repeated surveys and high anxiety in wartime Japan, particularly regarding potential antiwar sentiment among the people, reminds us of, for example, the British context; it was the Ministry of Information wherein, as

Angus Calder ([1969] 2008, 471) put it in his classic study, the "advertising industry was nationalised for the duration." National, local, and even nongovernmental organizations (e.g., Mass Observation) were constantly measuring, policing, and mobilizing the citizenry, and even in countries with radically different political systems, these activities took on a remarkably similar character.[5] While cultivating and managing women and youth, for example, was a concern for wartime authorities in Japan and its "fascist" allies, Germany and Italy, it was also a concern in the Soviet Union and Great Britain (Stargardt 2007; de Grazia 1993; Kucherenko 2011; Summerfield 1989). One important difference from one national context to the other was the state's capacity and effectiveness. In Britain and Japan, officials had many tools at their disposal to discipline their subjects; in Nationalist China, particularly after the 1937 invasion, this capability was dramatically diminished. Nevertheless, efforts to "rationalize" daily life, militarize society, police sexuality, prepare for air wars, control commodity prices, and manipulate the press (to name just a few areas) were important for the Nationalist Party under Chiang Kai-shek. In any case, the Japanese wartime systems exposed by Yoshimi through his use of personal documents show us how the empire was part of a global movement toward mass organization and mobilization in the 1930s and 1940s, even if some governments were more effective than others in achieving this.

Reading *Grassroots Fascism* with the benefit of many years of research on personal documents, I have slightly different questions from when I first launched my doctoral dissertation. First, how should we explain similarities that are *not* the obvious product of mimetic state practices? If young people in wartime Japan, Russia, China, and Britain all seemed to experience a political awakening at around the same time—fourteen to sixteen years old—but do not share exactly the same culture, educational system, labor laws, family structure, political discourse, or social systems, are we to turn to developmental psychology, or some other field, to understand the phenomenon? *Grassroots Fascism* showed how battlefield experience was largely eclipsed by stories of civilian suffering after 1945, which came to dominate the memory of World War II in Japan. In Russia and the Soviet Union, in Great Britain, and, above all, in China, the suffering and perseverance of ordinary citizens have been emphasized in recent popular discourse but, in all of these cases, did not lead to a renunciation of war (Thurston and Bonwetsch 2000; Calder [1969] 2008; Lary 2010). Did the voices for peace in postwar Japan achieve their victory merely because the military had failed, and was subsequently destroyed by the Allied powers, or must we also give credit to the organized efforts by the

Japanese people, such as the peace and labor movements that were so often closely intertwined?[6]

Grassroots Fascism, by its focus on Japan, thus begs some important questions about the global history of World War II and its long aftermath. The book's most important achievement, however, has been to inspire a generation of historians of Japan to use research on personal documents as a means of understanding popular views of the war effort. Yoshimi taught us to see those views, in an era when democracy and imperialism were not mutually exclusive but mutually reinforcing, as absolutely essential to our narrative of the period, and this may be one of Japanese history's most important contributions to a truly global history of World War II.

Aaron William Moore is senior lecturer (associate professor) at the University of Manchester. He is the author of *Writing War: Soldiers Record the Japanese Empire* (2013) and of the forthcoming *Bombing the City: Civilian Narratives of the Air War in Britain and Japan, 1939–1945.*

■ NOTES

1. There has been work in oral history, such as Cook and Cook (1992). For analysis of wartime personal documents, see Ohnuki-Tierney (2002), Yamashita (2005; 2016), and Moore (2013). Japanese scholarship on the social history of the war is, as one would expect, vast. Yoshimi's monograph was preceded by his 1987 article and contemporaneous with the equally important Takahashi (1988). Many other scholars subsequently made important contributions, including Tomiyama (1995), Fujii (1985; 2000), and Katō (2009).

2. Recent studies in Chinese history emphasize the importance of popular support in the resistance against Japan, even if mobilization there was less effective by comparison; see, in particular, van de Ven (2003), Lary (2010), and Mitter (2013).

3. This is central to Yoshimi's view of the 1937–45 war, especially when analyzing the experiences of individual soldiers. As just one example, see Nitō Seikichi's account at the beginning of chapter 3, wherein Yoshimi demonstrates how the behavior in China was transported to the Pacific; it is also essential to read chapter 1, part 3 very closely, to fully grasp how, by 1941, "Japan had become a totally different country." Our artificial separation of these battlefields is partly an artifact of postwar trials; see Kushner (2015).

4. See the critical analysis of American war in Bodnar (2010).

5. For an analysis of Britain and Germany, see Süss (2014), and in

particular, pp. 171–238. I will compare Britain and Japan in my forthcoming book *Bombing the City: Civilian Narratives of the Air War in Britain and Japan, 1939–1945*.

6. See the discussion in Gerteis (2009).

■ **WORKS CITED**

Bodnar, John. 2010. *The "Good War" in American Memory*. Baltimore: Johns Hopkins University Press.

Calder, Angus. (1969) 2008. *The People's War: Britain 1939–1945*. London: Pimlico.

Cook, Theodore, and Haruko Taya Cook. 1992. *Japan at War: An Oral History*. New York: New Press.

De Grazia, Victoria. 1993. *How Fascism Ruled Women: Italy, 1922–1945*. Berkeley: University of California Press.

Fujii Tadatoshi. 1985. *Kokubō fujinkai*. Tokyo: Iwanami shoten.

———. 2000. *Heitachi no sensō: tegami, nikki, taikenki wo yomitoku*. Tokyo: Asahi shinbunsha.

Gerteis, Christopher. 2009. *Gender Struggles: Wage-Earning Women and Male-Dominated Unions in Postwar Japan*. Cambridge: Harvard East Asian Monographs.

Katō Yōko. 2009. *Sore de mo, Nihonjin ha "sensō" wo eranda*. Tokyo: Asahi shuppansha.

Kucherenko, Olga. 2011. *Little Soldiers: How Soviet Children Went to War, 1941–1945*. Oxford: Oxford University Press.

Kushner, Barak. 2015. *Men to Devils, Devils to Men: Japanese War Crimes and Chinese Justice*. Cambridge, Mass.: Harvard University Press.

Lary, Diana. 2010. *The Chinese People at War: Human Suffering and Social Transformation, 1937–1945*. Cambridge: Cambridge University Press.

Mitter, Rana. 2013. *China's War with Japan, 1937–1945: The Struggle for Survival*. London: Allen Lane.

Moore, Aaron William. 2013. *Writing War: Soldiers Record the Japanese Empire*. Cambridge, Mass.: Harvard University Press.

Ohnuki-Tierney, Emiko. 2002. *Kamikaze, Cherry Blossoms, and Nationalisms: The Militarization of Aesthetics in Japanese History*. Chicago: University of Chicago Press.

Orbaugh, Sharalyn. 2015. *Propaganda Performed: Kamishibai in Japan's Fifteen-Year War*. Leiden, Netherlands: Brill.

Schrijvers, Peter. 2002. *The GI War against Japan: American Soldiers in Asia and the Pacific*. London: Palgrave Macmillan.

Stargardt, Nicholas. 2007. *Witnesses of War: Children's Lives under the Nazis*. London: Vintage.

Summerfield, Penny. 1989. *Women Workers in the Second World War: Production and Patriarchy in Conflict.* London: Routledge.

Süss, Dietmar. 2014. *Death from the Skies: How the British and Germans Survived Bombing in World War II.* Oxford: Oxford University Press.

Takahashi Saburō. 1988. *Senkimono wo yomu: Sensō taiken to sengō Nihon shakai.* Kyoto: Akademia shuppan.

Thurston, Robert W., and Bernd Bonwetsch. 2000. *The People's War: Responses to World War II in the Soviet Union.* Urbana: University of Illinois Press.

Tomiyama Ichirō. 1995. *Senjō no kioku.* Tokyo: Nihon keizai hyōronsha.

Van de Ven, Hans. 2003. *War and Nationalism in China: 1925–1945.* London: Routledge.

Yamashita, Samuel Hideo. 2005. *Leaves from an Autumn of Emergencies: Selections from the Wartime Diaries of Ordinary Japanese.* Honolulu: University of Hawai'i Press.

———. 2016. *Daily Life in Wartime Japan, 1940–1945.* Lawrence: University of Kansas Press.

Yoshimi Yoshiaki. 1987. "Nicchū sensō to kokumin dōin." *Rekishi hyōron* 447: 9–17.

Young, Louise. 1999. *Japan's Total Empire: Manchuria and the Culture of Wartime Imperialism.* Berkeley: University of California Press.

"Total War" or "Fascism"? Reflections on *Grassroots Fascism: The War Experience of the Japanese People*

SHELDON GARON

Ethan Mark's translation of Yoshimi Yoshiaki's *Kusa no ne no fashizumu (Grassroots Fascism)* is indeed welcome. Originally published in 1987, the book stands as a pioneering work. It was one of the first scholarly efforts to investigate the experiences and attitudes of ordinary Japanese in the China and Pacific wars (1937–45). Beginning in the late 1980s, many Japanese scholars set about investigating "war responsibility" on the part of nongovernmental groups and individuals. *Grassroots Fascism* goes further than any of these other books, examining popular thought and behavior on both the battlefield and the home front.

Yoshimi resists the temptation to reduce the Japanese people's experiences to any one behavior—whether "resistance" to the regime or support for the war effort. Instead, we see a variety of experiences and attitudes. This, I believe, is the only persuasive way to assess home front and battlefield narratives. In my current research on home fronts in Japan, Germany, and Britain, I have been struck by the diversity of popular responses. In the face of aerial bombardment, many Japanese civilians dutifully stayed with their neighborhood associations to fight fires, yet millions fled the cities in panic. In Britain, too, notwithstanding myths of "Keep Calm and Carry On," terrified families in Hull, for example, defied government instructions and "trekked" into the countryside each night to evade German bombing, sleeping in open fields and farmyards (Garon, forthcoming-a).

Still, Yoshimi is not content to leave us with a set of diffuse anecdotes. He incisively draws on his cases to present important generalizations about the Japanese people and war. We may posit a continuum of popular responses, ranging from active support and acquiescence to nonconformist behavior, refusal, protest, and outright resistance (see the categories of "dissident behavior" explicated by Peukert 1987, 83). Rarely in *Grassroots Fascism* do we see popular resistance to the war effort and the regime or even open refusal. Instead, Yoshimi relates many episodes involving civilians who privately grumbled about *some* aspects of wartime mobilization while expressing overall support for the war. We also learn of erstwhile left-wing individuals who nonetheless as soldiers carried out cold-blooded murder in China.

At the same time, *Grassroots Fascism* provokes us to consider several issues that remain unresolved in the historiography of wartime Japan. The first concerns the conflation of fascism with the Japanese war effort. Although the book repeatedly uses the term *fascism* to describe both the state's policies and popular actions, it avoids specifying what makes either fascist. It is noteworthy that the concept of fascism has recently made a comeback in American scholarship on Japan (Tansman 2009a; 2009b). The new work likewise does not adequately contextualize the development of Japanese fascism, echoing Basil Fawlty's "don't mention the war." In these accounts, the fighting in Asia and the Pacific scarcely figures into Japan's authoritarian transformation, which appears driven in large part by changes in global capitalism. However, the authoritarian reconstitution of Japanese society that most resembled Nazism and Italian Fascism occurred not in the wake of the Great Depression during the early 1930s but considerably later in the context of *mobilization* for an increasingly "total war" with China (from 1937), and particularly in preparation for war with the Western powers (from 1940). Notable among these developments were the top-down mobilization of communities into block associations *(chōnaikai)* and neighborhood associations *(tonarigumi)*; the compulsory cartelization of small businesses; draconian food rationing;

mandatory air raid defense exercises; and the dissolution and absorption of labor unions, political parties, and other independent groups into the state-run Imperial Rule Assistance Association. Unlike current American scholars of Japanese fascism, Yoshimi *does* mention the war, prominently and vividly. Yet, in nearly every instance when he discusses "fascism," he actually refers to post-1937 wartime measures like food rationing or labor conscription. This book might be more productively titled *Total War at the Grass Roots*.

Accordingly, we might build on this richly documented book to insert wartime Japan into a more comparative and transnational framework of total war. Yoshimi's depictions of everyday life in 1937–45 remind us of practices found on most home fronts in World War II—not only among the fascist belligerents but also in Soviet Russia and democratic Britain (Garon, forthcoming-b). Despite enormous political differences, the warring states all ran savings and austerity campaigns, established grassroots mobilization organizations like neighborhood associations and air raid defense units, imposed stringent food-rationing programs, and generally regimented daily life as never before. These similarities were no coincidence. In the run-up to World War II, the would-be belligerents—Japan included—had vigorously investigated other nations' home front programs aimed at mobilizing civilians in the coming "total war." *Grassroots Fascism* is hardly to be faulted for limiting its focus to Japan, but a "transnational turn" in future research would surely result in more rigorous judgments about the particularities of wartime Japan.

Yoshimi's findings also compel us to ask whether the Japanese home front held or collapsed as the war wore on. On the basis of reports of popular discontent by the Special Higher Police, John Dower suggests that the Japanese people not only became demoralized and defeatist but also expressed "growing contempt for existing authority extending even to the emperor himself." The state, he concludes, "had become discredited and sorely wounded well before Japan surrendered" (Dower 1983, 103, 123). *Grassroots Fascism* provides a more nuanced account. Despite police reports of war weariness and workers' absenteeism due to food shortages, the people's pervasive grumbling did not result in outright resistance. Popular support for the war, notes Yoshimi, did not crumble until the devastating firebombing of the big cities and nearly sixty provincial cities in the last five months of the war. Even then, the people did not turn to mass protest or revolution, as elites had feared. Rather, the Japanese home front collapsed as millions of terrified, hungry civilians fled the cities.

Finally, although Yoshimi illuminates grassroots "fascism" on the home front and battlefield, we must ask whether the Japanese people were merely "complicit" with the wartime regime or whether they bore actual "war responsibility"? Did they simply carry out state dictates in neighborhood associations, or did local people proactively use and exacerbate authoritarian rule to advance their own interests and control others? Yoshimi has gone further than perhaps any other scholar to assess the degree of agency exercised by the Japanese people in war, but clearly there is much more to be done.

Sheldon Garon is Nissan Professor of History and East Asian Studies at Princeton University. Publications include *Beyond Our Means: Why America Spends While the World Saves* (2012), *Molding Japanese Minds: The State in Everyday Life* (1997), and *The State and Labor in Modern Japan* (1987).

▪ WORKS CITED

Dower, John W. 1983. "Sensational Rumors, Seditious Graffiti, and the Nightmares of the Thought Police." In *Japan in War and Peace: Selected Essays,* 101–54. New York: New Press.

Garon, Sheldon. Forthcoming-a. "Defending Civilians against Aerial Bombardment: A Transnational History of Japanese, German, and British Home Fronts, 1918–1945." In *Online Encyclopedia of Mass Violence.* Paris: Sciences Po. http://www.sciencespo.fr/mass-violence-war-massacre-resistance/.

———. Forthcoming-b. 2017. "The Home Front and Food Insecurity in Wartime Japan: A Transnational Perspective." In *The Consumer on the Home Front: Second World War Civilian Consumption in Comparative Perspective,* edited by Hartmut Berghoff, Jan Logemann, and Felix Römer. Oxford: Oxford University Press.

Peukert, Detlev J. K. 1987. *Inside Nazi Germany: Conformity, Opposition, and Racism in Everyday Life.* Translated by Richard Deveson. New Haven, Conn.: Yale University Press.

Tansman, Alan. 2009a. *The Aesthetics of Japanese Fascism.* Berkeley: University of California Press.

———, ed. 2009b. *The Culture of Japanese Fascism.* Durham, N.C.: Duke University Press.

Fascism between Empire and Emperor

RETO HOFMANN

It was probably not Yoshimi Yoshiaki's intention to write a book that would break new ground twice. And yet, at a distance of almost three decades, *Grassroots Fascism: The War Experience of the Japanese People* has had a dual impact on the scholarship of wartime Japan. When he published the book in Japanese in 1987, Yoshimi challenged narratives that recounted suffering and loss by ordinary Japanese at the expense of forgetting the killing and maiming they had inflicted on other Asians. Highlighting the wartime experience of the "people" (by which Yoshimi meant nonelites), he undermined the Japanese discourse of self-victimization by depicting how ordinary Japanese actively participated in aggression and violence throughout Japan's wartime empire. Japanese memory of the war, he argued, should integrate that history. The book's 2015 English translation by Ethan Mark, however, has lent *Grassroots Fascism* an unexpected afterlife. If in the 1980s the book contributed to the debates on wartime "responsibility," now, as Mark has noted, it helps historians to understand the relationship between imperialism and fascism. This shift has much to do with the wider imperial turn since the 1990s and the revival of the question of fascism in Japan. *Grassroots Fascism,* we are realizing, already addressed these concerns, perhaps in embryo, linking them to what its author calls the Japanese people's "imperial consciousness."

Until the 1990s, historians studied fascism and imperialism as relatively distinct problems. "Fascism" referred to a transformation in Japanese domestic politics. More precisely, the term was used to denote the outcome of a shift from the "liberal" 1920s to the politics of the 1930s, characterized by government repression, the rise of the military clique, the proliferation of right-wing movements and thought, and the ideological function of the "emperor system" *(tennōsei).* The debate diverged on the origins of this shift. Marxists blamed the emperor system's need to resort to oppression in order to serve bourgeois class interests; modernists associated with Maruyama Masao (1969) preferred to speak of "ultranationalism," a kind of collective Japanese psychology that, according to Maruyama, resulted from Japan's failure to modernize along (Western) liberal lines. The historiography on imperialism, by contrast, focused on the reasons for Japan's grab for colonies as a matter of the country's quest for great power status—whether it was Tokyo's desire to be regarded on a civilizational par with the West or to gain access to overseas markets and raw materials. Thus domestic change rarely informed studies of imperialism (or vice versa). To be sure, the narrative of "militarism" stressed that the armada of generals in Tokyo or officers in the Kwantung Army edged the country toward aggression in Asia. But there was often an implicit distinction between the "expansionism" of the 1930s and the "imperialism" that had characterized the territories conquered by Japan until 1931.

Two scholarly developments, however, have enriched our understanding of the relationship between imperialism and fascism. First, the imperial turn has shed light on the centrality of the empire in the political, cultural, and social developments in the metropole. The main thrust of this historiography has been to move away from causal, center–periphery models, emphasizing instead the complex processes between empire and metropole that produced "colonial modernity"—things ranging from medicine to gender identities and prison systems. In the case of Japan, a side effect of this new work has been the rediscovery of fascism. Louise Young (1999) and Ken Ruoff (2010) have employed the term *fascism* when discussing the popular mobilization for empire and war; Kim Brandt (2007) has identified fascist traits in the aesthetics of folk art, a field of knowledge developed in the context of Japanese imperialism; Aaron Skabelund (2011) has found fascist values of loyalty associated with dogs (many of which accompanied Japanese armies in their imperial conquest); Janis Mimura (2011) and Aaron S. Moore (2013) have exposed how the empire provided the opportunities for Japanese economists, corporate executives, and military officers to experiment with fascistic technocratic regimes. In the juncture between empire building in Asia and radicalization at home, scholars stumbled across the specter of fascism.

Second, a number of cultural histories have also reopened the question of fascism in Japan. In the 1980s, political historians had declared fascism an ill-suited concept for Japan because the country did not develop the features present in Nazi Germany or Fascist Italy, such as a one-party state or a charismatic leader. However, the somewhat belated arrival of cultural histories of Japanese fascism has cautioned against taking the German or Italian experience as normative. Through close analysis of discourse, symbolism, and cultural exchanges, these studies have shown that fascism was widespread in interwar politics and ideology, even if often coded in a language that was distinct from that of Western fascism. Alan Tansman (2009a; 2009b), in his study of prewar Japanese literature, has identified an aesthetics of wholeness that, through myths, tropes, and sentiments, spurred readers into fascist violence, communal bonding, and sacrifice—acts that were frequently carried out in Japan's empire. Notions of Japanese cultural authenticity and uniqueness, embodied in the figure of the emperor, also served to legitimize what ideologues and politicians defined as Japan's New Order in Asia. Harry Harootunian (2000) and Naoki Sakai (2008) have shown that intellectuals disavowed wartime conquest as imperialism by brandishing the notion that the "Japanese spirit," unlike Western proclivities to subdue, tended toward harmony. The Japanese presence in Manchuria, China, and Southeast Asia, the argument ran, denoted not imperialism but the construction of a new communitarian, Asian space capable of overcoming the pitfalls of capitalist modernity.

Thus the new imperial history and cultural history jointly point to the need to reassess *Grassroots Fascism* in a new key. The English translation is likely to produce debate on the suturing of imperialism and fascism, entangled as they were in the subjectivity of ordinary Japanese. The several biographical sketches that Yoshimi presents give a picture of individuals at the intersection of often precarious conditions at home and the prospects offered by and in the empire, highlighting how, in this encounter between social reality and imperial imaginary, fascism was at work both as agent and as outcome. It is striking, for example, that many young men viewed the army, conquest, and empire as vehicles for improvement, both for themselves and the nation as a whole (Yoshimi [1987] 2015, 115). Several peasants joined the army hoping that it would open new prospects, not least material benefit (from Glico candy to looting). Villagers, though often reluctant to accede to the draft, reasoned that the efforts would pay off once the war was over, with at least one tenant farmer contemplating turning himself into the "master of some island in the South Pacific."

Realistic aspirations or sheer fantasies, these concerns did not grow out of the war itself, even though Yoshimi's periodization might give this impression. These were anxieties that reflected the longer social and economic conflicts of the post–World War I period in which fascism gained so much traction. Fascist movements and regimes made a broad, interclass appeal, coaxing broad popular support through promises of social advancement and status. We hear echoes of this rhetoric in the voices quoted. In these stories, the army appears as more than a military institution. By assuring the "people" that they would "get ahead" while also underscoring the need to harmonize the national community, the army played a similar social role to the fascist parties in Europe, even as it deflected social advancement onto military and civilian careers intimately bound up with imperial conquest.

The war overshadows Yoshimi's narrative, both chronologically and in terms of what many Japanese were doing: fighting and killing. As Sheldon Garon points out, this was a total war. The book displays vividly how ordinary Japanese participated, often eagerly, in the state's growing attempt to redirect all kinds of resources to win the conflict on the continent and in the Pacific. As illustrated in two recent studies of technocratic elites, the planning for total war harkened back to World War I, and the Japanese bureaucracy spent the interwar period gearing up for the likelihood of a similar conflict. Japan was not alone. Garon is right to argue that austerity campaigns, food rationing, and propaganda were patterns visible also in other national contexts.

Of interest in this book, however, is less how the modern state mobilized the industrial and human resources for war and more how individuals mobilized motifs, symbols, and myths to explain their acts and thoughts. The self-understanding of ordinary Japanese during 1937–45 suggests that what they thought they were doing was more than fighting a war, even a total war. In his comparative study of wartime diaries, Aaron J. Moore finds similarities in the way Japanese, Chinese, and Americans "self-disciplined" themselves, often resorting to a "rhetoric of nationalism." Not all nationalisms, however, were the same. The Japanese one was articulated in a language that evoked a range of values and practices that we can associate with fascism in Japan and beyond. Invoking the officially sanctioned ideology centered on the divine emperor, some soldiers evoked the "holy war" (not the "war"). Others reproduced clichés about the world historical significance of their sacrifice. A draftee deployed to China pondered the momentousness of the present, feeling "enthusiasm surg[ing] anew from within me" (Yoshimi [1987] 2015, 80). High levels of violence, coupled with male bonding, were also a constant. One man felt "pleasure" in meting out revenge for a fallen comrade. Racist pronouncements abounded, praising the superiority of the Japanese race over "natives" and "animals" (Chinese).

Taken in the context of the domestic politics and the emperor system, it seems to me that Japanese articulations of patriotism had a different valence to those pronounced by their American or British counterparts. All wars require some self-disciplining, but whereas in Britain and the United States, it served a defensive function, in Japan, Nazi Germany, and Fascist Italy, it was used for offensive purposes. Conquest and imperialism required a different level of self-discipline, and fascism helped to provide it. Dying for "king and country," for example, did not mean quite the same as sacrificing oneself for the emperor: both statements signified patriotism, but the former gestured toward democracy, albeit a conservative one, whereas the latter symbolized a regime bent on fascist transformation of state and society. Indeed, the fascist kind of self-disciplining we observe in places like Japan, Italy, and Germany promoted a new social imaginary to make people change their understanding of themselves. In sum, the processes might be similar, but the ideological content was different.

At a subjective level, the ideological work of fascism was to disavow imperialism—fascism and imperialism blotted each other out, leaving an ill-defined "imperial" discursive space. What is striking in the testimonies presented by Yoshimi are the silences about imperialism. There is little evidence that Japanese considered themselves colonizers, much in line with the official, and fascist, rhetoric of Asian liberation. When the "people" express their thoughts about Japan's work in Asia, it is often by reference to their country's (or the emperor's) benevolent, even anti-imperialist, aim to eject Westerners from Asia. Not imperialism, then, but Greater East Asia Co-Prosperity Sphere, as Ethan Mark also found in his research on the Japanese occupation of Indochina.

In the fine-grained testimonies of ordinary Japanese, we see fascism as cultural and social practice, latched, on one side, to the ideology of the emperor system and worked out, on the other side, in the act of empire building. Does this mean that, analytically, imperialism and fascism also collapse into each other? I don't think so. The point is to recognize an overlap between the fascist and imperialist goals, as is also emerging in the literature on Nazi Germany's aims on the eastern front (Baranowski 2011; Gerwarth and Malinowski 2009; Mazower 2008). Through human exploitation, both fascism and imperialism sought to forge new communities, whether through comradeship and emotional (male) bonding, national togetherness, or neo-imperial links between the peoples of Asia. As the reviewers recognized, the Japanese experience was variegated, with the "people" retaining existing identities as peasants, daughters, or youth. Even opposition was possible. And yet the empire had a socializing, even conforming, effect. Ordinary Japanese began to relate to one another in novel ways, using a language of fascism that emphasized national community in the emperor, though like their German counterparts, they did not share every tenet of a neatly packaged ideology or set of policies (such a thing did not even exist). *Grassroots Fascism,* much as studies on popular attitudes in Nazi Germany since the 1990s and, more recently, in Fascist Italy, emphasizes greater and perhaps more diffuse convergence with the regime (Föllmer 2013; Duggan 2013).

The amalgamation of fascism and imperialism in the 1930s and 1940s suggests that it may no longer be very fruitful to pose the ontological question whether Japan was fascist based on a tight comparison with Fascist Italy or Nazi Germany. *Grassroots Fascism* reminds us that fascism develops in a contingent way. In Japan, this meant following a nonlinear way, not an unfolding of the predetermined model scripted by postwar social scientists and historians. There was no trajectory from movement to regime and, last, to empire, as was the case in Italy and Germany. This does not entail, however, reverting to the argument that Japanese fascism was sui generis. To the contrary, the imperialism–fascism link opens up the possibility for new comparisons and connections between these regimes by focusing, for example, on the question of the radicalization of violence, racial politics, or resettlement policies.

Despite the rapidly (and objectively) deteriorating course of the war, Japanese in the empire and on the home front fought on, displaying a determination that matched and, perhaps, surpassed that of their Axis counterparts. The welding of (total) war, empire, and fascism in the consciousness of ordinary Japanese goes some way toward explaining this tenacity. Moreover, the fascist-powered zeal that becomes apparent in so many sources presented by Yoshimi will need to be taken into consideration when debating issues of war responsibility. In light of the evidence presented by Yoshimi, it becomes more difficult to blame the militarists, propaganda, and brainwashing for the acts and thoughts of ordinary Japanese. As individuals, they appear as much agents as recipients of "imperial consciousness." Thus *Grassroots Fascism* points to the need to incorporate fascism into the debates on wartime memory by remembering Japan's place among the most violent and murderous regimes of the twentieth century. *Grassroots Fascism* urges us to insert Japan into the global history of fascism but also fascism into the history of imperialism in Asia.

Reto Hofmann is lecturer in history at Monash University, Australia. His first monograph, *The Fascist Effect: Japan and Italy, 1915–1952,* was published in 2015.

■ WORKS CITED

Baranowski, Shelley. 2011. *Nazi Empire: German Colonialism and Imperialism from Bismarck to Hitler.* New York: Cambridge University Press.

Brandt, Kim. 2007. *Kingdom of Beauty: Mingei and the Politics of Folk Art in Imperial Japan.* Durham, N.C.: Duke University Press.

Duggan, Christopher. 2013. *Fascist Voices: An Intimate History of Mussolini's Italy.* New York: Oxford University Press.

Föllmer, Moritz. 2013. "Historiographical Review: The Subjective Dimension of Nazism." *The Historical Journal* 56, no. 4: 1107–32.

Gerwarth, Robert, and Stephan Malinowski. 2009. "Hannah Arendt's Ghosts: Reflections on the Disputable Path from Windhoek to Auschwitz." *Central European History* 42, no. 2: 279–300.

Harootunian, Harry. 2000. *Overcome by Modernity: History, Culture, and Community in Interwar Japan*. Princeton, N.J.: Princeton University Press.

Maruyama Masao. 1969. "Theory and Psychology of Ultra-Nationalism." In *Thought and Behaviour in Modern Japanese Politics*, edited by by Ivan Morris, 1–24. Oxford: Oxford University Press.

Mazower, Mark. 2008. *Hitler's Empire: How the Nazis Ruled Europe*. New York: Penguin.

Mimura, Janis. 2011. *Planning for Empire: Reform Bureaucrats and the Japanese Wartime State*. Ithaca, N.Y.: Cornell University Press.

Moore, Aaron Stephen. 2013. *Constructing East Asia: Technology, Ideology, and Empire in Japan's Wartime Era, 1931–1945*. Stanford, Calif.: Stanford University Press.

Ruoff, Kenneth J. 2010. *Imperial Japan at Its Zenith: The Wartime Celebration of the Empire's 2,600th Anniversary*. Ithaca, N.Y.: Cornell University Press.

Sakai, Naoki. 2008. "Imperial Nationalism and the Comparative Perspective." *Positions* 17, no. 1: 159–205.

Skabelund, Aaron Herald. 2011. *Empire of Dogs: Canines, Japan, and the Making of the Modern Imperial World*. Studies of the Weatherhead East Asian Institute, Columbia University. Ithaca, N.Y.: Cornell University Press.

Tansman, Alan. 2009a. *The Aesthetics of Japanese Fascism*. Berkeley: University of California Press.

———. 2009b. *The Culture of Japanese Fascism*. Durham, N.C.: Duke University Press.

Yoshimi Yoshiaki. (1987) 2015. *Grassroots Fascism: The War Experience of the Japanese People*. Translated by Ethan Mark. New York: Columbia University Press.

Young, Louise. 1999. *Japan's Total Empire: Manchuria and the Culture of Wartime Imperialism*. Berkeley: University of California Press.

Portfolio

CURATED BY **CHARLOTTE EUBANKS**

Playing at Empire: The Ludic Fantasy of *Sugoroku* in Early-Twentieth-Century Japan

THOSE OF US WHO CAME OF AGE in the 1960s, 1970s, and 1980s may remember the board game Risk as a Cold War phenomenon. Debuting in France in 1957 under the name La Conquête du Monde (World conquest), it was purchased by Parker Brothers and released to the U.S. market in 1959 under its new name. While the rules of play are quite involved, and have evolved over time, the general description posted on current-owner Hasbro's site gives a fair approximation: "Lead your troops. Take a risk. Rule the world! Rally your armies to march across continents. Carefully craft your strategy—you'll face your opponents on the field of battle and they'll give the fight everything they've got. Keep advancing until you've defeated all your foes and taken over the world!" (Hasbro 2015).

In 1979 my parents gave me Risk for Christmas. I remember playing the game with my brother later that month, while my parents watched the evening news coverage of the Soviet invasion of Afghanistan. Watching my parents watching the news made the game seem all the more real, and on returning to school the next week, I talked with friends about mujahideen and Soviet aircraft. In the months to come, I tried to figure out the best way to fortify North America from attack, and I found my natal allegiances challenged as I came to prefer Australia for its ease of defense.

Ludic (playful, game-based) fantasy often develops in tandem with geopolitical events, and children often play at grown-up games. That was the case in my own childhood, when my friends and I engaged in the board-game Cold War, and it was the case some decades earlier in Japan, when many children rolled the dice of Japanese imperialism in Asia. In recent decades, sociologists have begun to plumb the ways in which children's toys and games, like many other forms of media, work at "representing and reinforcing dominant conceptions of 'appropriate' social identities," both through the visual packaging of game materials and via the narrative and kinetic structures of gameplay (Glasberg et al. 1988 , 130). Though playing a game does not equate automatically into acceptance of the game's culture (witness my preference for Australia), the play experience is necessarily shaped by the sorts of strategy (principles of cooperation or competition) one must use to win, the identitarian norms (of class, race, gender, job, age) suggested by visual elements, and the extraludic worlds (political, religious, geographic, and economic) to which the game refers. *Sugoroku* games from the early twentieth century provide clear evidence of the "imperial jingoism" that came to dominate the mass media during Japan's colonial era, and their visual culture suggests some of the ways in which "the process of mobilization left . . . an imprint" of empire on "the domestic landscape," primarily on the minds of children who learned to imagine themselves as military heroes, colonial elite, and the winners of the global race for empire (Young 1998, 416).

Sugoroku (literally "double sixes") refers to two very different games in Japan. The first, and older, type (*ban sugoroku, "dais sugoroku"*), related to the Western game of backgammon, is played on a large wooden board, and its fortunes do favor those who roll the coveted double sixes, enabling the player to advance her board pieces toward the final goal. The other type of *sugoroku* (*e sugoroku,* "pictorial *sugoroku*"), which I will be discussing here, is quite different. A snakes-and-ladders-style game, it is played on a flat sheet of paper; players roll a die and follow the narrative directions for the (often illustrated) square on which they land. This type of *sugoroku* also has a long history in Japan, becoming very popular during the publishing booms of the Edo period (1600–1868), when artists developed a multitude of subgenres (stage stars, exotic animals, health, monsters, leisure travel, and so on). In the seventeenth century, *sugoroku* came to be sold around the start of the New Year by door-to-door salesmen who peddled them alongside other seasonal goods, and they were also a common prize in New Year's luck-of-the-draw contests. Scholars typically argue that early modern *sugoroku* were a mass phenomenon, marketed to commoners and reflecting a shared communal consciousness (Yamamoto 1986; Yoshida 1981).

Moving to the modern era, Iwashiro Noriko (1994) has argued that, from the first years of the Meiji period (the 1870s), at the same time that a rigid class system was being dismantled and personal ambitions to worldly success were receiving unprecedented boosts, a national struggle was developing around the preservation of Japanese sovereignty in the face of unequal treaties and laws of extradition, and the definition of

Japan's place in the world of colonial powers was an open and hotly debated issue. During the 1910s and 1920s, this struggle irrupted into an aggressive mercantile and political imperialism, the headlines of which were rapidly repackaged and heavily marketed in the form of serialized novels, travelogues, manga, and popular games like *sugoroku*.

If the paradigmatic genre of early Meiji-era *sugoroku* was the "personal success" game *(shusse),* which capitalized on people's individualist fantasies of rags-to-riches transformation, *sugoroku* board games from the transwar period (1910s–1940s) focus the playing experience on new subgenres concerned with modern military glory *(sakusen)* and the development *(kensetsu)* of Japan's colonial, imperial, and aspirational territories in greater East Asia (Silverberg 1991). The transwar genres of imperial militarist advance and colonial settlement coopt the earlier game structure of personal success, leveraging the momentum of ludic fantasies of individual advancement toward the increasing speed of national mobilization. This essay traces the cooption of personal success narratives for imperial and colonial ends.

The *sugoroku* board games I discuss in this *Portfolio* combine the narrative ambitions of Risk with the game mechanics of Chutes and Ladders. There are basically two types of illustrated *sugoroku* board games: *meguri* ("turning," "circling") and *tobi* ("jumping," "leaping"). In both variants of the game, all players have a game piece *(koma),* and all players begin with their koma at a square labeled "Start" *(furidashi).* If squares have no numbers written on them (as is the case with most *meguri sugoroku*) and are laid out in a spiral pattern, then each player rolls a die and moves his game piece ahead that many spaces, always progressing toward the Goal *(agari)* square. The first to arrive—by spiraling inward or twisting upward—wins. In the other iteration of the game *(tobi sugoroku),* squares typically have numbers written on them and are connected in more complex or chaotic ways. Each player rolls the die. If there are no directions for the number rolled, the player just stays put for that turn. If there are directions, the player reads them and moves her piece to the indicated square, which may be closer to or farther away from the Goal. As with the other form of the game, the first to arrive at the final square—by jumping forward and falling back—wins.

Understanding *sugoroku*'s game mechanics—"the underlying rules, structures, elements and processes that make [the game] work"—and the atmosphere of play provides a sketch of the basic relationships that players have with each other and the game (Lerner 2014, 50). In terms of its conflict type, *sugoroku* makes use of a "footrace" style of individual-versus-individual competition, in which conflict between players is minimized and one wins not by defeating or destroying another player but merely by crossing the finish line first. The game has no feedback loops, whether reinforcing (whereby strategic moves are rewarded and unwise moves punished) or balancing (whereby play gets harder for successful players and easier for struggling ones). It is purely a game of chance. The goal of the game is not to best one's score or even, really, to beat other players; rather, the point of the game is more oriented toward indulging in a group fantasy, using the board game to support imagination.

Most commonly, games were included as freebies along with special New Year's editions of popular magazines. During this national work and school holiday, most people will have traveled to their natal homes to gather with extended family in a multiday period of snacking, sitting around the *kotatsu* (heated table covered with a quilt), and passing time by playing table games. Over the weeklong holiday, players can engage in repeated attempts to envision, and to play out, various paths to the Goal, determining those paths they find most desirable, whether because heroic or comic, disastrous or laudatory. Most *sugoroku* from the early twentieth century depend on "evoked narrative" (Lerner 2014, 79), drawing on current-event media coverage of war, colonial expansion, and military glory that children may see as being important to teachers, parents, and other grown-ups in their world. The games, then, provide a place for children to try on adult identities and fates and to imagine how they might navigate the news stories of their day, show up in the headlines of mature newspapers, or elicit the pride and appreciation of peers and elders.

Boards are typically oriented in one of two ways. Either the text all faces the same direction, in which case there may be a specifically pedagogical angle, as with the 1939 Japan–Manchukuo–China Sightseeing *sugoroku* published by the Manchukuo Branch Office of the Japan Travel Bureau, which includes the note, "When New Year's vacation is over, hang this board game on your wall, and you have an excellent map to study!" (see Figure 4). Alternatively, the game board may be divided into quadrants and the text for each quadrant arranged perpendicularly to the text adjacent. The layout of these games is all about enjoyment: the directional alignment of text is such that family members, seated in a circle around a *kotatsu,* for instance, can each enjoy one-fourth of the illustrations and read one-fourth of the text, as players move around the board.

So, imagine yourself on New Year's Day. You are sitting around the *kotatsu* with your siblings and cousins, maybe an aunt or a grandfather with you. A pile of tangerines and savory snacks lies within easy reach. The cold wind rattles the paper windows, and your parents are napping in the corner. You open the special issue of your favorite magazine, which just arrived in the morning mail, and spread out the *sugoroku* board on the table. After taking a few minutes to examine the richly colored illustrations, you place your game pieces and let the youngest cousin roll first. Where might the rolls of the die lead?

If the year is 1904, you may be enjoying Minegishi Rinbei's Invasion of Russia, Navy board game (Figure 1), which follows a *tobi* (jumping)-style layout. The game was published on November 14, right in the midst of the brief but revolutionary Russo-Japanese War, waged from February 8, 1904—when Commander Heihachirō Tōgō (1847–1934) opened the war (not yet formally declared) with a surprise torpedo attack on Russian ships at Port Arthur—until May 28, 1905, when the Japanese Combined Fleet virtually annihilated the Russian fleet at the Battle of Tsushima. The Japanese army and navy then occupied Sakhalin Island, forcing the Russians to sue for peace, which was mediated by U.S. President Theodore Roosevelt at Portsmouth, New Hampshire, and concluded on September 5, 1905.

The Invasion board game was riding the crest of current events: as the game was released to the public, for enjoyment on their New Year's vacation, Japanese forces surrounded Port Arthur, having been victorious at sea and now attempting to win on land against the entrenched Russians, the goal being to topple the city before Russian naval reinforcements could arrive from the Baltic in early spring. Each player begins as a cadet, receiving his commission from Commander Tōgō. Players move about the board, variously reliving the past (by landing on squares relating to the already-historical events of sea mining and blockade) and imagining the future (attempting to rout the entrenched Russian land forces, capture the city of Port Arthur, and thus reach the Victory Ceremony).

There is a clear strategic division between the top half of the board, from which positions a player may reach the Victory Ceremony directly, and the bottom half, from which victory is, at best, two steps away. The shortest route to victory takes but two turns: from Start, one must roll a 1, thus advancing to the "God of War" Commander Hirose square, from which spot a 2 results in winning the game. Initially assigned to torpedo duty on the battleship *Asahi,* Hirose Takeo (1868–1904) volunteered to command an old cargo vessel, the *Fukui maru,* in what was essentially a suicide mission to blockade the entrance to Port Arthur. The ship was struck and Hirose was fatally wounded, going down with the ship on March 27, 1904, while trying to save other survivors. He was posthumously promoted to the rank of commander and deified, at a Shintō shrine constructed in his honor, as a military deity, the very model of a "go-fast" imperialist (Dower 1979, 85). There are, of course, many more circuitous

Figure 1. Minegishi Rinbei, Sei-Ro kaigun *sugoroku* (Invasion of Russia, Navy board game) (Tokyo: Minegishi Rinbei, (Meiji 37) 1904). Ink on paper, 48 × 48 cm. Cotsen Children's Library, Department of Rare Books and Special Collections, Princeton University Library.

routes to the Goal, which may involve semaphore duty, manning the cannons, sinking an enemy ship, and laying sea mines.

In keeping with the times, and as suggested by the emblematic figure of Hirose, the Victory Ceremony is accessible from all ranks—most prominently via troop review before the two Imperial Princes whose squares sit at the top corners of the game board, but also from the squares of Lieutenant Commander Shiraishi, Admiral Kamimura, "God of War" Commander Hirose, and the squares of the unranked sailors Hamazaki Heisō and Hayashi Monpei. Additionally, one may reach the ceremony via the Sea Mine square, presumably losing one's life in the process and passing, in spirit, before one or the other of the Imperial Princes and so onward, to victory.

Reaching victory is thus predicated upon the completion of one or more acts of extraordinary, iconic, individual bravery—or upon achieving death in such an attempt. Hayashi, for instance, was a second class warrant officer who sent in an application, signed in blood, asking to be part of the suicide squad blockading the mouth of Port Arthur. Kamimura, after an early disgrace, redeemed himself with his acts in command of the Imperial Japanese Navy Second Fleet at the Battle of Ulsan (August 14, 1904) and, in the game's future, again at the Battle of Tsushima (on May 27, 1905). And Shiraishi, while in command of the *Sakura maru*, exploded a sea mine and sank in an attempt to block the port to Russian maneuvers. The game incorporates some "mini-deaths" as well: players can "lose a turn" on the Sea Mine, Suicide Squad, "Take That!" hand-to-hand combat, and Imperial Review squares. Notably, none of these positions is irrecoverable insofar as a player is never ejected from the game. Victory will come, sooner or later, and individual death is but a brief pause along the route.

Themes of military glory received treatment each time the Japanese navy or army engaged in battle. One updated version of the invasion theme, by the prolific pair of illustrators Itō Kikuzō and Iizuka Reiji, is set in China, shortly after the onset of the Second Sino-Japanese War (July 7, 1937, to September 9, 1945). The Courageous Japanese Army board game (Figure 2) was printed and submitted for approval on December 5, 1937, hard on the heels of the twin captures of Shanghai and Nanjing, and it was published on January 1, 1938, again to coincide with the New Year's holiday. While families enjoyed imagining strafing Chinese aeronautical factories, capturing enemy positions, and participating in cavalry raids, soldiers of the Imperial Japanese Army committed horrific, extended mass atrocities at what came to be known as the Rape of Nanking, which lasted from December 13, 1937, through mid-January 1938.

A *meguri sugoroku* with an almost strictly linear plot, the game features a start square showing a train full of young soldiers being seen off by flag-waving family members as they head for the front. Bookending the narrative, the final square depicts a column of young soldiers marching behind a mounted commander, all triumphantly entering a fallen Chinese city whose inhabitants, in an echo of the send-off scene, are all waving Japanese flags. In marked contrast to the Invasion of Russia game, from start to finish, the Courageous Army board shows very little narrative flexibility. Players landing on square 8 (Standing Night Guard) lose a turn, while players landing on square 16 (Sending Out Messenger Pigeons) fall back to square 12 (Strategy Meeting at Headquarters). And players must roll the exact number needed to reach the final square: if a player only needs a 2 but rolls a 6, he boomerangs back four spaces and so is further

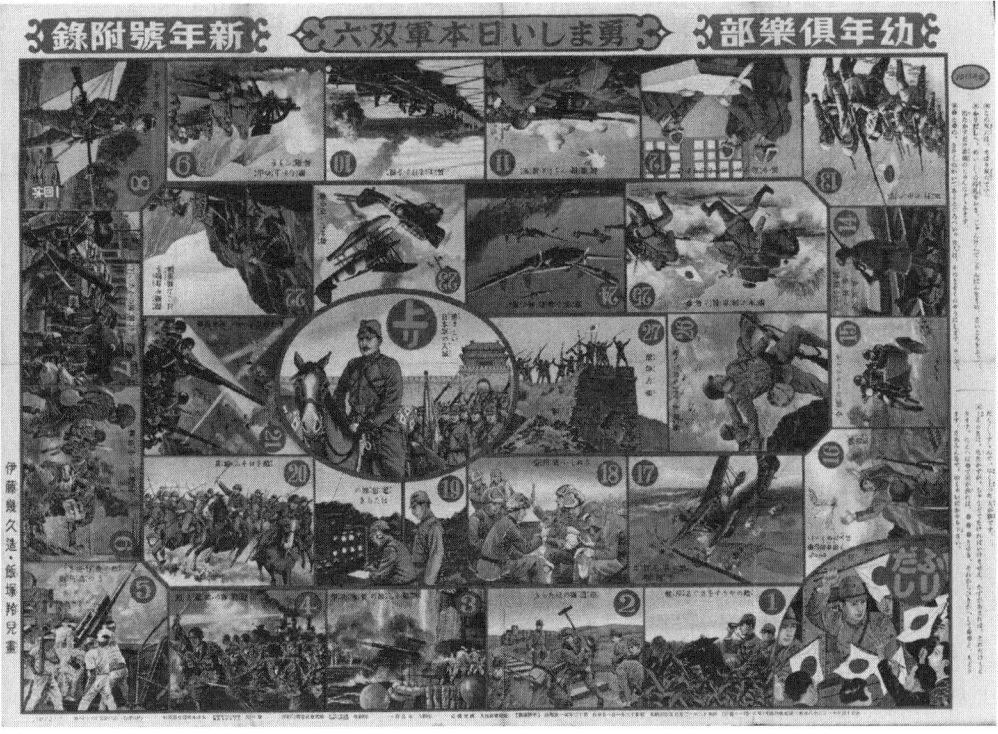

Figure 2. Itō Kikuzō and Iizuki Reiji, illustrators, Isamashii Nippongun *sugoroku* (The Courageous Japanese Army board game), special New Year's supplement to *Yōnen Kurabu* (Children's club) 13, no. 1 (Tokyo: Dai Nihon Yubenkai Kōdansha, 1938). Ink on paper, 55 × 77 cm. Cotsen Children's Library, Department of Rare Books and Special Collections, Princeton University Library.

from the Goal than before, so that the game mechanics mimic the siege processes enacted at Shanghai and Nanjing.

In all of the steps between Start and the penultimate square, we never see a single enemy soldier or civilian, nor do we ever see an injured Japanese soldier or even a dirty or torn uniform. All the machines are well oiled, all the soldiers look clean and well fed, and, with the exception of the final square and possibly the strategy session, we only see the rank and file. This is a remarkably flat war, much less visually and narratively dramatic than the Invasion of Russia game and affording very little in terms of ludic possibility. The color palette is limited, and the soldiers are all look-alikes: no more stand-out performances, none of the individual heroism of a Hayashi or a Hirose. Instead, we see (or, we are told in the titular framing) that heroism is a group quality. Although advancement is more orderly, without the sudden reversals of fortune seen in the earlier game, and though victory is more certain, in a sort of lockstep fashion, the game is simply not as exciting. Perhaps there is a sense, here, of acknowledging the slower pace of war on the continent, where Japanese and Chinese air forces were engaged in a battle of attrition, cities held up stubbornly under siege, and an unprecedented number of Japanese troops were committed to the ground effort.

Military engagement, however, was not the only available template for imagining visual access to and ludic fantasy on the continent in the late 1930s. One year after the release of Courageous Army, Itō Kikuzō provided the concept and illustrations for a very different vision of Japan's role, not only in China but in East Asia more broadly, this time as a special New Year's supplement to the *Tōnichi shōgakusei shinbun,* a monthly magazine marketed to elementary school students.

Released on January 1, 1939, the New East Asia development game (Shin Tōa kensetsu *sugoroku*) (Figure 3) revisits many of the same scenes from Itō's 1938 game but widens the angle ever so slightly to include, following the military actions of young men, a few glimpses of women and children. As before, we begin with a column of young soldiers "departing for the holy war" to the cheers of a flag-waving crowd of children. These soldiers go on to land at a beachhead under enemy fire (square 1) and participate in tank advances, the training of military dogs, and the grueling labor of maneuvering supply carts and horses through deep mud. We see them participating in war reportage, receiving care packets from home (in square 6), and steaming upriver. Some are part of naval landing parties or air squadrons (squares 8 and 9), whereas others conquer rough terrain to capture the enemy's position. Wounded soldiers are tended to by "angels in white," while members of the "pacification unit" hand out rice rations to Chinese civilians. Having achieved their objectives, Japanese soldiers enjoy a military band's rendition of "The Continental March" (Tairiku kōshin kyoku), theme song for the 1938 Nikkatsu film of the same title, written and directed by Taguchi Tetsu and starring Todoroki Yukiko and Kosugi Isamu. In square 14, four children and one soldier share "elation at the development of a New East Asia": a Japanese boy and a Chinese boy shake hands, while a Japanese soldier, a Japanese girl, and a Chinese girl look on, the children waving Japanese Hinomaru and Chinese Five-Colored flags. This, at least, is the linear narrative the panels present when viewed in numerical order.

The game design does show, however, just a bit more creativity than Itō's 1938 effort, in that each square features a possible "snake" or "ladder." Any player on the first square (landing at a beachhead) who rolls a 2, for instance, is informed, "You are a special correspondent for the Tōnichi

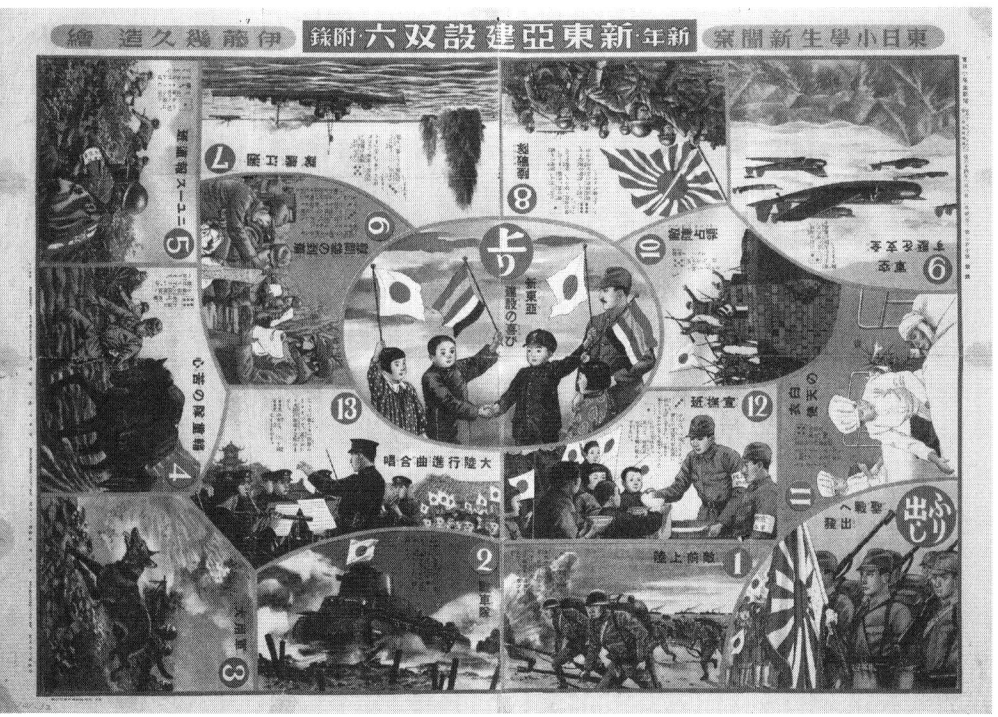

Figure 3. Itō Kikuzō, illustrator, Shin Tōa kensetsu *sugoroku* (New East Asia development board game), monthly magazine supplement to *Tōnichi shōgakusei shinbun* (Eastern Japan primary school news) 710, New Year's issue (Tokyo: Tokyo Nichinichi Shinbunsha, 1939). Ink on paper, 55 × 79 cm. Cotsen Children's Library, Department of Rare Books and Special Collections, Princeton University Library.

Elementary School Student Newspaper. Get the news of our troops' successful landing to the press corps as soon as possible! Advance to square 5" (war reportage). From square 5, one's reportage work can continue: any player rolling a 1 is told to "jump ahead to square 12. You've got to get photos of the pacification corps!" Less felicitously, any player on square 4 (supply train) rolling a 6 is notified that his supplies are needed back at the beachhead: "Return to square 1."

The game's instructions also require players to participate in the extra-ludic culture of war, whether by bowing in the direction of Yasukuni Shrine, where the war dead are enshrined (on square 8); by offering a song or dance to regale one's coplayers' sense of heroism (on square 6); or (on square 12) by "offering something of your own to your new friends in China. A piece of your candy, a tangerine, or a pencil will do." The game also admits the possibility that one or more of its players will die. One-sixth of players who land in the hospital (square 11) will find out, on rolling a 4 (四 *shi*, homophonous with 死, "death," also *shi*), "Unfortunately, you have suffered irreparable internal injuries. Return to Start and begin again." Even death is not final. The fantastic wars of imperialism can be played again and again.

Not all visions of East Asian "development" were so grim. In fact, more upbeat visions abounded, as, for instance, in the Japan–Manchukuo–China Sightseeing game (Nichi–Man–Shi kankō *sugoroku*) (Figure 4), issued by the Manchukuo Branch of the Japan Travel Bureau for enjoyment during this same holiday season. This game, printed and submitted for inspection on December 25, 1938, and then published on January 1, 1939, to coincide with the New Year's holiday, is a creative mix of the *tobi* (jump forward and fall back) and *meguri* (spiral upward or inward) styles.

Every player begins in Tokyo, with the goal of getting to Beijing, but must do so by way of Shinkyō (in Chinese, Xinjing), capital of the Japanese puppet state of Manchukuo and crown jewel of colonial development of urban infrastructure, with more than ten thousand new buildings erected during just the "first phase of construction [ending] in 1937" (Young 1998, 244). Beyond that stipulation, however, the game involves an unprecedented amount of ludic flexibility, enabling players to choose routes through Korea, the Shandong Peninsula, or northern ports like Dalian, and allowing players to tour a large swath of the globe, from the mountainous heights of Tibet to the open grasslands of Manchukuo, from the steppes of Mongolia to the southern tip of Korea. Some of these routes are dead ends from which players must boomerang back toward the central routes, whereas others (marked in thicker red lines) lead quickly toward Beijing.

Each player begins with a game piece shaped like either a Manchurian flag or a vehicle (a locomotive, airplane, or passenger ferry) and may switch out pieces over the course of the game. One's first roll determines the initial direction of travel. Players rolling a 1 or 4 take a steamship to the northern Japanese port of Niigata or Tsuruga, respectively, and move onward to northern Korea; rolls of 2 and 3 result in airplane rides to the western Japanese cities of Osaka or Fukuoka; a 5 earns a slow locomotive ride to Osaka, whereas a 6 affords the most luxurious route, a steamship from the Japanese port at Kobe to the Chinese coastal city of Dalian. The instructions note that, after this original throw, players are "free to choose their own courses to Beijing by way of Shinkyō, moving in any direction the number of squares shown on the die when thrown and following the instructions relevant to their vehicle." In another bid for flexibility, players may change their modes of transport as appropriate,

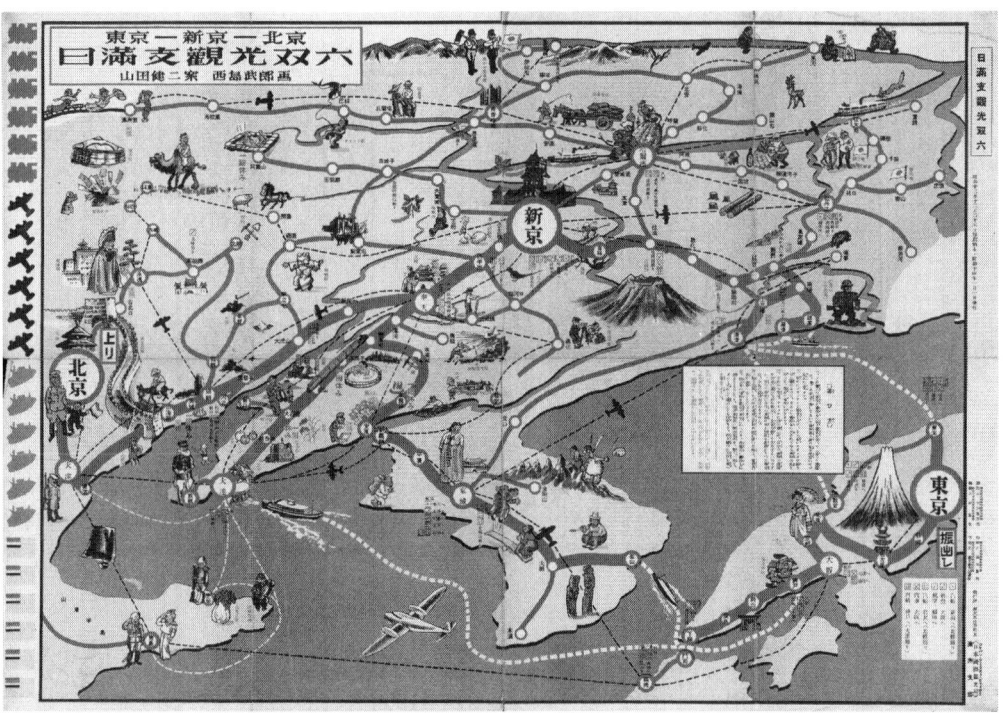

Figure 4. Yamada Kenji, concept, Nishijima Takerō, illustrator, Nichi–Man–Shi kankō *sugoroku* (Japan–Manchukuo–China Sightseeing board game) (Hoten-shi, Manchukuo: Nihon kokusai kankōkyoku Manshū shibu (Japan Travel Bureau Manchukuo Branch), 1939). Ink on paper, 54 × 78 cm. Cotsen Children's Library, Department of Rare Books and Special Collections, Princeton University Library.

switching, for example, from steamship to locomotive after arriving on the continent. The instructions also offer other, more expansive ways to play the game. A round-trip version, ending back in Tokyo, is one option mentioned, as are variations involving group play, vehicle relays, and so on.

The game opens various vistas of armchair travel and imaginative adventure, with nary a bomb or battle to be seen. Moving around the continent, Japanese boys and girls can imagine themselves and their families fishing, riding a camel, skiing, panning for gold, watching ethnic performances, visiting archeological sites, and soaking in any number of hot springs. Everyone on the map is smiling, many couples carry babes in arms or push strollers, the land is fecund, the locals are hardworking, and Japanese soldiers and civilians are (peacefully) everywhere: a "modernist utopia" that rested, as Louise Young (1998, 250) has noted, "on the foundation of the absolute power of the colonial state."

But as the red ink at the end of the instructions reminds us, play is merely a respite from work: "When New Year's vacation is over, hang this game sheet on your wall to use as a map. It will provide a fantastic bird's-eye view and, in addition to learning about tourist destinations in Northern China and Manchukuo, you can familiarize yourself with topographical features, regional produce, and potential vehicular routes." Indeed, the game does visually summarize a great deal of information, including place-names and their pronunciations and the locations of major Japanese settlements, ethnic groups, and natural resources, and the game's entertainment value translates easily into educational value for Japan's up-and-coming generation of colonial officers and imperial soldiers, many of whom were, indeed, headed for Manchuria, which was soon to become home to the largest concentration of overseas Japanese.

Two years later, in 1941, the ever-productive Itō tried his hand at the colonial development genre with his Nihonjin kaigai hatten *sugoroku* (Japanese overseas expansion game) (Figure 5). As one might by now expect, Itō's visual presentation and narrative conception of the game remain comparatively militaristic in nature. One of the modes of transportation in the travel bureau's 1939 Japan–Manchukuo–China Sightseeing board game was a passenger steamship, and a similar vessel occupies the central space of Itō's 1941 game. The vessel is, indeed, the players' final destination. But Itō's featured steamship is not just any vessel; it is the *Yawata maru*.

Originally constructed as the second of three flagship passenger vessels for the shipping company NYK, the *Yawata maru* was launched on October 31, 1939, for service between Japan and Seattle, later with service to San Francisco. On June 15, 1940, it was taken over for use by the Imperial Japanese Navy. Its naval debut came in July 1942, when it served as an aircraft carrier escort along the shipping lanes past Saipan to the Ulithi Atoll, at which point it was renamed *Un'yō* and commissioned as a Taiyō-class escort carrier. It continued to serve in the South Seas, primarily around Truk, until it was torpedoed by the USS *Haddock* on January 19, 1944. The injured ship made Saipan, was repaired, and returned to duty until it was sunk by the USS *Barb* on September 17, 1944.

Issued in 1941, the game features the *Yawata maru* in its glory, as a fully decked-out ship that has proven seaworthy as a civilian vessel and has just been claimed and outfitted for military service by the Imperial Navy. The ship, the arrival at which signals a player's win, rides at the cusp of a civilian-to-military transition, a transition that at least some of the many fifth-grade boys and girls to whom the game was marketed must have anticipated themselves making in the not-too-distant future.

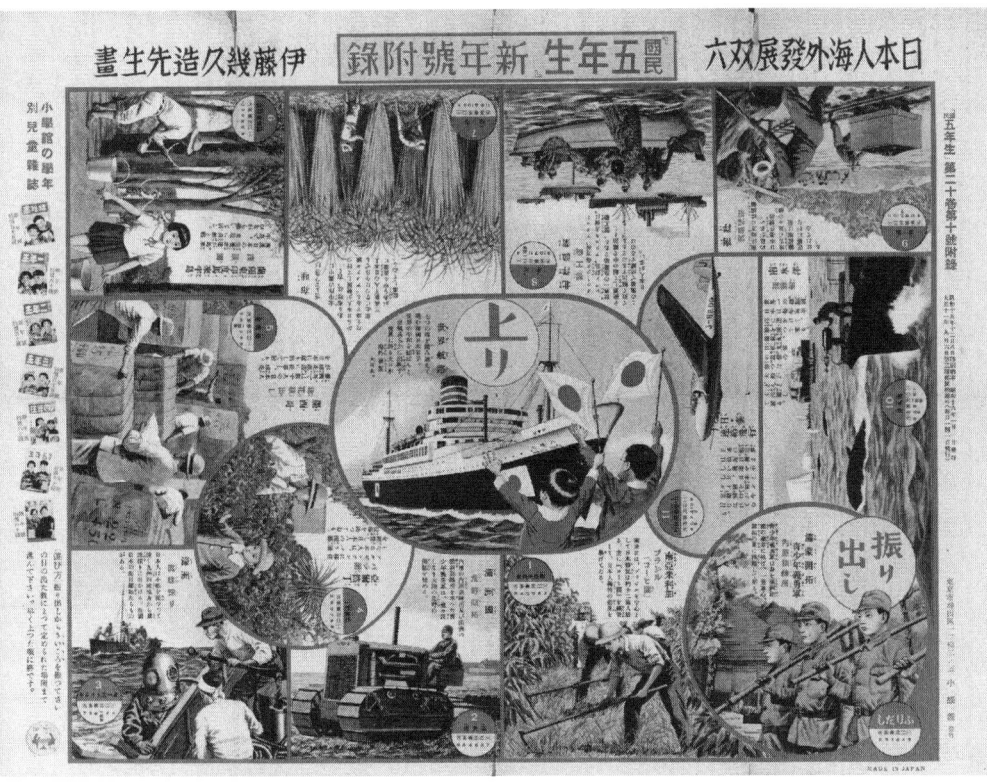

Figure 5. Itō Kikuzō, illustrator, Nihonjin kaigai hatten *sugoroku* (Japanese overseas expansion board game), supplement to *Kokumin gonensei* (Fifth grade countrymen) 20, no. 10 (Tokyo: Shogakkan, 1941). Ink on paper, 47 × 63 cm. Cotsen Children's Library, Department of Rare Books and Special Collections, Princeton University Library.

The repurposing of cruise ships for military purposes was one of the many stories of the increasingly overt militarization of what had long been sugarcoated as the benign visitation of an enlightened rule. To give another example of the transition, the Overseas expansion game takes as its start one of the more remote lull waters of the Sightseeing game, namely, the outpost of the Manchurian and Mongolian Youth Development Corps, which had been marginalized, literally, at the top edge of the Sightseeing game board. If the Sightseeing game imagines youths moving from the metropole to the imperial margins, the Overseas expansion game turns that orientation inside out, launching its players on an around-the-world trip beginning with the "holy duty" of land cultivation in Manchukuo and ending with a seaborne arrival in Japan.

Along the way, we see communities of ethnic Japanese harvesting coffee in Brazil, diving for pearls off the coast of Australia, tending rose gardens in Argentina, packing cotton in Mexico, and tapping rubber trees in the Dutch East Indies. In Hawai'i, where "Japan's people have been involved in development since ages past," "tens of thousands continue to persevere" in cutting sugarcane "even under the current US rule." Off the coast of the Aleutians, Japanese people fish, in the South Seas Mandate they work phosphate mines, and they whale in the Antarctic Ocean. Most wonderfully, however, Japanese ingenuity has resulted (in the penultimate square) in a "booming aeronautical industry" with Japan and Thailand "now linked with regular service!" and finally (at the Goal) Japan has a hold on "world shipping lanes: the boys of Naval Country Japan cross the Seven Seas. They set sail with high hopes of securing world peace. Greater Japan shall be vaunted throughout the world! Greater Japan develops the lands across the seas!" As was common with illustrated maps of the time (Figure 6), particularly those aimed at a juvenile or popular audience, each locale is associated with a specific product or resource: arable land on the continent, sugar in Hawai'i, rubber in the Dutch East Indies, and—by extended association—crops of eager young Japanese boys and girls in the home islands.

Though laid out in the *tobi* style, where sudden reversals of fortune are the ludic norm, the game contains a definite tiered structure. There are only three squares from which a player can reach the Goal: the Japan–Thailand Airline square (square 11, where rolling either a 3 or a 5 results in a win), the South Seas square (square 9, where a 3 does the job), and the Antarctic Ocean square (square 10, where a 5 wins you the game but a 3 loses you a turn). Aside from the Goal itself, these three squares—all featuring naval and aeronautical supremacy—represent the most coveted spots on the board. The next most important spots are those that afford advancement to squares 9, 10, or 11 and that thus are, at best, two moves away from the win. From the North Seas square (number 8) and Hawai'i (number 7), a player has a 50 percent chance of advancing to the Japan–Thailand Airlines, South Seas, or Antarctic Ocean squares. From the Dutch East Indies, one has a 33 percent chance, and from Mexico, Australia, or Argentina, a one-in-six chance.

What these odds do is to encourage positive ludic associations with certain geographical locations. Notice, for instance, that the geopolitical gaze of the game favors advancement largely south and east, across the ocean and toward the Americas or Southeast Asia. By contrast, though all players begin in Manchukuo and Mongolia, movement through the continent is downplayed, and the one further square located there (number 2,

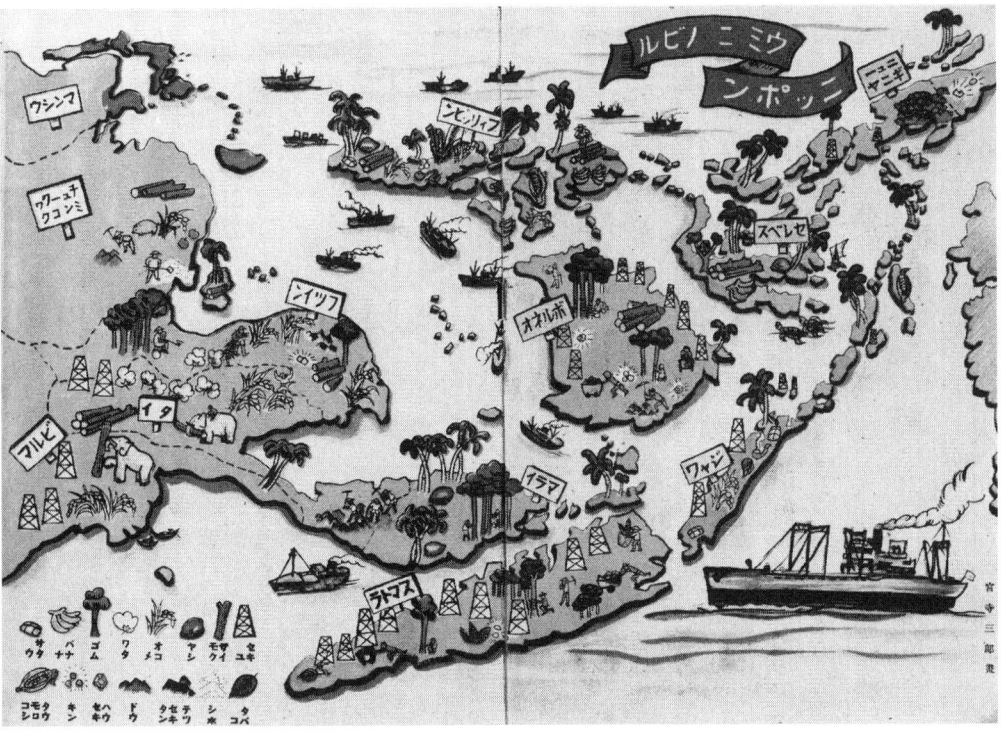

Figure 6. Miyadera Saburō, illustrator, "Umi ni nobiru Nippon" (Japan spreads across the seas), *Nihon no kodomo* 8, no. 7 (Tokyo: Kokumin Tosho Kankōkai, 1944). This colorful map is featured on the inside back cover of a popular children's magazine aimed at younger elementary school students. The magazine cost thirty-five sen, was published on June 28, 1944, and belonged to a boy named Umaba Nobuto, who wrote his name on the back. Cotsen Children's Library, Department of Rare Books and Special Collections, Princeton University Library.

Manchukuo) does not afford the same rapidity of advancement, a fact that cannot have been lost on a Japanese populace already accustomed to news about Japanese troops mired down in China.

Travels in the South: Long Live the Greater East Asia Coprosperity Sphere (Figure 7), printed on November 1 and published on November 11, 1942, seizes on these positive associations with Japanese advances into Southeast Asia. This game was not included as a give-away supplement to the New Year's issue of a magazine but was available for separate purchase at an affordable twenty sen and was released in time to be stocked on store shelves before the holiday season. The cover envelope shows three children riding on an elephant: a Japanese boy in a white pith helmet; a Japanese girl with the typical bobbed hair of the time holding on to his

Figure 7. Watanabe Shigekuni, illustrator, Nanpō meguri *sugoroku*: Dai Tōa kyōeiken banzai (Travels in the South: Long Live the Greater East Asia Coprosperity Sphere board game) (Tokyo: Fujiya ganguten, 1942). Ink on paper, 55 × 78 cm. Cotsen Children's Library, Department of Rare Books and Special Collections, Princeton University Library.

waist; and a slightly older, turbaned Malay boy serving as mahout. The children smile gently against a backdrop of lush, tropical foliage.

The game layout is *meguri* style, with players winding clockwise from the bottom right-hand corner (labeled "Thailand") and spiraling inward to the final goal, labeled "Long Live the Greater East Asia Coprosperity Sphere!" and showing a Japanese colonial officer, complete with pith helmet, holding two South Pacific islander children aloft in his arms while a young Japanese boy, also in pith helmet, and girl look on in admiration, against a backdrop of palm trees and high-peaked architectural structures known as *bai*. Each square is numbered, 1 through 19, and each includes a note instructing players where to move their game pieces according to what number they roll. There is no underlying logic to players' movements (no structure of sense making for lost turns) and no narrative linkage between squares (why should rolling a 2 or 5 on Bananas send a player to encounter a tapir or rolling a 4 or 6 on Leopard send one to the festival?).

There is, however, a basic organizational scheme to the game board when viewed in its entirety. The ordering of the squares by number, though not encountered in this orderly way during play, follows in a very straightforward fashion Japan's imperial advance to the south. We take as our point of beginning Thailand, which was invaded by Japan on December 8, 1941, and surrendered within a matter of hours, concluding a formal alliance with Japan on December 21. Malaya (square 2) and the southern Philippines (represented by Moros separatists on square 4) were also invaded on December 8, resulting in access to rubber (square 3) and food supplies (bananas on square 5 and water buffalo for cultivation on square 6). Japan invaded Borneo (square 7) on December 16, seizing important oil fields as well as, presumably, some tapir (square 8) and the tree-top houses (square 9) of some native populations. Moving forward, Japan attacked New Guinea, then under an Australian Mandate, on January 23, 1942 (square 10), and invaded the Andaman Islands, a part of India (square 11), on January 23, 1942, before marching on Sumatra (square 17) from February 14 to March 28, 1942, and the Celebes (square 19) on February 8, 1942. French Indochina (square 18) upsets this temporal scheme a bit, having been invaded in September 1940, but it fits with the general southerly and westerly cartographic movement.

The military take-over of Southeast Asia, however, is at best implied. Rather than platoons of uniformed soldiers shooting at largely invisible enemy combatants, Travels in the South shows native men and children at work and play and smiling Japanese colonial officers, in crisp white shirts and pith helmets, interacting happily with native women and family groups. Japanese children—a girl in iconic bob and a boy in mini-pith helmet—look on in admiration. The Malay square (2) shows a Japanese boy and a Javanese one with their arms around each other's shoulders, watching a mahout work with timber-harvesting elephants. The only potential interruption of this smooth, ludic flow is the mounted Indian policeman (square 11, the least fortunate locale on the board), who sends fully half of those who land on his square toward a lost turn. Many *sugoroku* aimed at younger audiences (lower elementary school and below) feature animals, and so perhaps this mash-up of imperial advance and exotic fauna was the result of a savvy marketing decision, aimed at making the product appealing to a broad spectrum of potential consumers, a New Year's game of imperial advance that even the youngest of children could be expected to enjoy.

If Travels in the South is pitched toward a younger age group, Sawai Ichisaburō's 1944 game Trip around the Greater East Asia Coprosperity

Sphere (Figure 8) has a more sophisticated edge to it. Published as a supplement to the New Year's edition of *Ie no hikari* (Light of the household), a general-interest family magazine produced by the Japan Agricultural Cooperative and targeted primarily at people living in smaller farming villages, Trip around the Greater East Asia Coprosperity Sphere is visually rich, cartographically expansive, and journalistically informative. Featured as insets laid over a map of the Coprosperity Sphere, we find headshots of several men who were presidents and political leaders of Imperial Japan's puppet states: Wang Jingwei representing China, Ba Maw for Burma, Subhas Chandra Bose for India, and José Laurel for the Philippines, each set against an iconic landscape from his home country.

A Japanese boy, outfitted in a blue hat and knee-length trousers, gaiters, and a white shirt, and carrying a rucksack, functions as the players' stand-in and appears in each of the main scenes across the board. He begins in Japan in front of the impressively modern brick facade of Tokyo Station, observes farmers harvesting wheat in the fields of Manchukuo, watches Chinese civilians bowing before Sun Yat-sen's mausoleum, and enjoys the shade at a park in Hanoi. In Thailand, he visits the impressive temple complex at Wat Phra Kaew and a memorial to seventeenth-century adventurer Yamada Nagamasa, who founded a Japanese settlement in the Ayuttha Kingdom; in Burma, he joins monks before the reclining Buddha statue at Manuha Temple outside Bagan. With increasing imperial zeal, he cheers a parade of Indian National Army troops allied with Japan in a bid to overthrow British rule, and in Shōnan (modern-day Singapore), he visits Shōnan Jinja, a grand imperial symbol modeled after Japan's Ise Jingu, where Amaterasu (the sun goddess) is enshrined, and meant to be the ritual center of Japan's southerly colonial holdings. The shrine opened on February 15, 1943, on the first anniversary of the fall of Singapore. Constructed by POWs, and planned to include a thousand-acre park, the building honored the Japanese war dead. In Java, the boy joins a Japanese man amid a gathering of flag-waving locals, and we reach a crescendo in the form of a mass street celebration before the central cathedral in Manila before steaming back to Japan and anchoring just off the coast, with Mount Fuji in our sights.

Again stressing the importance of the aeronautical industry, players may travel between each major cartouche by one of two routes. A lucky roll wins one a nonstop airplane ride, while other numbers result in a lost turn or in slower land and sea routes, where one may be beset, and turned back to the last major stop, by forces as varied as storms at sea, towering mountains, impassable deserts, and an encounter with an orangutan.

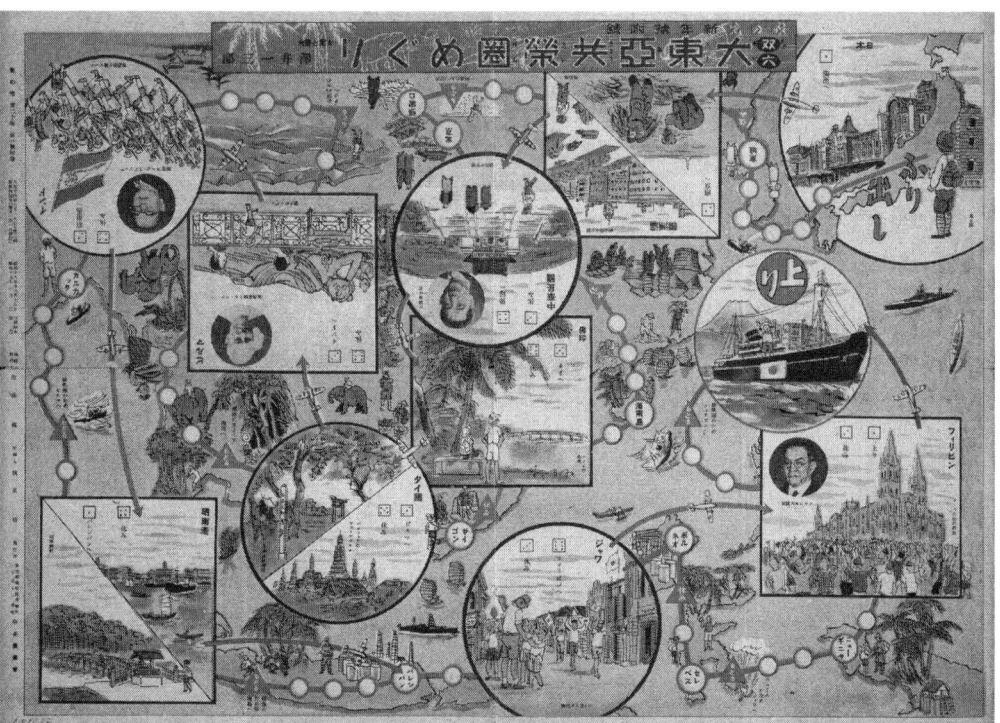

Figure 8. Sawai Ichisaburō, *Dai Tōa Kyōeiken meguri* (Trip around the Greater East Asia Coprosperity Sphere), New Year's supplement to *Ie no hikari* (Light of the home) 20, no. 1 (Tokyo: Chūō Nōgyōkai, 1944). Ink on paper, 38 × 54 cm. Cotsen Children's Library, Department of Rare Books and Special Collections, Princeton University Library.

Watanabe submitted a print of his game for governmental approval on December 18, 1943, and it was accepted and published on January 1, 1944. The game thus celebrates the Greater East Asia Coprosperity Sphere at its largest extent: the New Year's issue of *Ie no hikari* would have arrived in the mail on the morning of January 1, and eager readers may have unfolded the board game and begun playing less than twenty-four hours after Subhas Chandra Bose and the Azad Hind, who were allied with the Japanese, raised the flag of Indian independence on the Andaman Islands on December 30. By stretching to include the eastern edge of an independent India, the game design draws a veil over the Pacific Ocean, where Japan had lost important battles to the United States in the Gilbert Islands in late November 1943, enabling U.S. forces to advance on the Marshall Islands in late January 1944: the beginning of the end of the Greater East Asia Coprosperity Sphere and the conclusion of Japan's half-century-long ludic fantasy of military dominance, colonial expansion, and imperial superiority.

The artwork we see in these imperialist board games lies firmly within the purview of the government-sponsored "culture for little countrymen" (*shōkokumin bunka*) concept. The idea arose from early-twentieth-century debates about the pedagogical and moral uses of juvenile literature and illustration, both on the part of proletarian authors (who wished to move children's culture away from fantastical and temporally remote folkloric settings to a focus on contemporary conditions and sketches of daily experience) and on the part of language theorists (who saw children's culture as a place to solidify affective bonds with a national tongue). As many Japanese scholars have noted, the move from using children's culture to enforce socially engaged morals and communitarian language practices to using children's culture to enforce nationalist and militarist aims was less a marked leap than a smooth evolution (Ōfuji 1986).

We can trace part of that smooth evolution in the visual culture and ludic norms of transwar *sugoroku,* a game of group fantasy in which players envision themselves and their peers variously enjoying the fruits of colonialism, finding success in life, and making a contribution to the military glory of the nation. Players are not ferocious or cutthroat with one another. Indeed, the losers, insofar as the game posits any, are those places and environments relegated to the flat surface of the game board: the people on whose bodies, and the nations atop whose imagined soil, the players engage in their ludic fantasies of imperial conquest.

Indeed, the visual and ludic culture of these games evinces the vital importance of imperial, colonial propaganda for the Japanese war effort and suggests the degree to which media was turned toward full-on cultural mobilization. Though the games accept the possibility of death, at least as a temporary setback, their artwork is remarkably "sanitized," with a marked tendency to "spiritualize rather than visualize the imperial landscape" (Winther-Tamaki 2011, 125, 127). With its preferences for bird's-eye viewpoints and a focus on the beauty of lands and peoples, colonial *sugoroku* invite their players to perform a version of the ancient imperial prerogative of *kunimi* (surveying the realm) from the comfort of the metropolitan center. Furthermore, the games suggest that, on the whole, Japanese occupation (whether of Manchuria, China, Korea, Taiwan, the Pacific Islands, or Southeast Asia) is a progressive, productive, civilizing influence resulting in cooperative coprosperity. Though no doubt effective as recruiting tools, the games did little to prepare young people for the realities of colonization and imperial war.

Charlotte Eubanks is associate professor of comparative literature, Japanese, and Asian studies at Penn State University. She is the author of *Buddhist Textual Culture: Miracles of Book and Body in Medieval Japan* (2011).

■ **NOTE**

The author would like to thank the staff of the Cotsen Children's Library for making the materials discussed here accessible and for making my research time in Princeton enjoyable and fruitful. Andrea Immel, Minjie Chen, Annalee Pauls, Gabriel Swift, Linda Olivera, Ian Dooley, and Charles Green have all been eminently helpful. Research for this project was conducted with support from the Friends of the Princeton Library and the North-East Asia Council.

■ **WORKS CITED**

Dower, John. 1979. *Empire and Aftermath: Yoshida Shigeru and the Japanese Experience, 1878–1954*. Cambridge, Mass.: Council on East Asian Studies, Harvard University.

Glasberg, Davita Stilfen, Barbara Nangle, Florence Maatita, and Tracy Schauer. 1988. "Games Children Play: An Exercise Illustrating Agents of Socialization." *Teaching Sociology* 26, no. 2: 130–39.

Hasbro. 2015. "Product Description for *Risk: The Game of Global Domination*." http://www.hasbrogames.com/en-us/product/risk-game.

Iwashiro Noriko. 1994. "Shusse sugoroku no henka: bakumatsu kara Meiji e." *Fūzoku: Nihon fūzokushi gakkai kaishi* 32, no. 3: 62–87.

Lerner, Josh. 2014. *Making Democracy Fun: How Game Design Can Empower and Transform Politics*. Boston: MIT Press.

Ōfuji Mikio. 1986. "Senchūki no jidōbungaku hyōron: seikatsu dōa kara shōkoumin bungaku e no nagare o otte." *Gakudai kokubun* 29: 153–69.

Silverberg, Miriam. 1991. "Constructing a New Cultural History of Prewar Japan." *boundary 2* 18, no. 3: 61–89.

Winther-Tamaki, Bert. 2011. "From Resplendent Signs to Heavy Hands: Japanese Painting in War and Defeat, 1937–1952." In *Since Meiji: Perspectives on the Japanese Visual Arts, 1868–2000*, 124–43. Honolulu: University of Hawai'i Press.

Yamamoto Masakatsu. 1986. "Sugoroku yūkō 2: sugoroku." *Nihon bijutsu kogei* 569: 12–14, 54–57.

Yoshida Michiko. 1981. "Sugoroku no ikarigawari." *Nihon kosho tsūshin* 46, no. 1: 3–5.

Young, Louise. 1998. *Japan's Total Empire: Manchuria and the Culture of Wartime Imperialism*. Berkeley: University of California Press.

HILDE DE WEERDT, CHU MING-KIN, AND HO HOU-IEONG

Chinese Empires in Comparative Perspective: A Digital Approach

WE EMBARKED ON A COLLABORATIVE PROJECT, titled "Communication and Empire: Chinese Empires in Comparative Perspective," to examine how political communication and, in particular, elite communication networks impacted the formation, maintenance, or fragmentation of empires and other kinds of polities.[1] We proposed to do this through the quantitative and qualitative analysis of textual corpora, including notebooks and correspondence, that best convey individuals' engagement with politics but that have never been examined in the aggregate and for their relevance to Chinese political culture. Here we briefly introduce the historiographical background and goals of the project and the digital methods we developed and used.[2] We end with two case studies illustrating how digital methods can facilitate research on communication networks on the micro- and the macroscale. We hereby also aim to suggest that the combination of digital text analysis, biographical databases, historical geographic information systems (GIS), and social network analysis (SNA) can also be applied to a wide range of other questions in the historical study of empires and other kinds of polities.

Chronologically, the project focuses on a crisis moment (the twelfth and thirteenth centuries) in Chinese political history. In 1126–27, the Jurchen army occupied the Song Dynasty (960–1279) capital of Kaifeng, one of the largest cities in the medieval world; took the reigning emperor captive; and set out to occupy the northern half of the Song Empire. The Song court retreated to the south and settled for a peace treaty that effectively divided rule over the Chinese territories between two competing states for the next 150 years: the Jurchen Jin Dynasty (1115–1234) in the north and the Song Dynasty in the south. Many literati experienced this period as a territorial crisis. Because the geopolitical crisis of 1127 marked the last time that the Chinese heartland became an object of lasting contention among multiple states, it provides an ideal case study for the broader examination of the factors that were critical in the revival and maintenance of empire. The project originated from a long-term interest to test and elaborate the hypothesis that the political institutions and political culture of provincial elites that developed during this period played a crucial role in consolidating elite preferences for unified imperial rule.

Within the comparative literature on pre-twentieth-century empires, ideological factors in the form of public legitimacy, an imperial mission, or "cultural programmes" have long been considered fundamental in the formation and consolidation of pre-twentieth-century empires (Doyle 1986; Münkler 2007; Eisenstadt 1963). In this literature, ideological or cultural factors are reduced to broad transhistorical cultural orientations. In his seminal macrosociological study, *The Political Systems of Empires,* Shmuel N. Eisenstadt (1963) identifies the cultural visions of imperial elites as the primary reason for successive Chinese regimes' ability to accommodate change within preestablished political frameworks. Herfried Münkler (2007) has argued that the formation of an imperial mission and its embedding in elite self-conceptions were decisive factors in the history of lasting premodern empires. Key questions that are left unanswered in this work are how and to what extent provincial elites had access to political information concerning the larger polity and how the structure of elite sociopolitical networks affected the history of polities and politics.

Chinese historians have previously shown that the viability of empire in the last centuries BCE and again later in the sixth century depended on the inscription of empire as an imaginary realm in a classical canon and historical, administrative, philosophical, literary, and encyclopedic texts (Lewis 1999; McMullen 1988). This work shifted attention from the detection of the formal characteristics of empire (the military conquest of wide territories and many peoples; the exploitation of the conquered through taxation, tribute, or conscription; imperial projects; imperial symbols and institutions; imperial elites and collaborating classes) to the historically and culturally specific conceptualization of empire as a crucial factor in its formation. Besides the ethical orientation and universal and legitimating rhetoric highlighted in the earlier mentioned comparative work, Chinese historians have also pointed to the administrative and geographic dimensions of imagined empire. Even though many of the classical, literary, and historical texts that expressed and shaped earlier political imaginaries became canonical and thus continued to exert influence over the imaginations of Chinese elites, by the beginning of the second millennium, different kinds of information contributed to the conceptualization of empire. The imperial vision of the cultural elite was no longer solely informed by the coherent and durable knowledge of the classical canon and the large administrative, historical, literary, or medical compendia sponsored by successive dynasties' founding emperors; it was continually reinforced by current information about the polity in the form of court gazettes, compilations of state documents, military and geographic maps, and so on, all of which had for the first time become available to provincial elites across the empire from the late eleventh century onward. In this project, we are investigating how individuals shared and commented on current affairs and how political networks and social boundaries were constructed through the sharing of political information.

We found that such questions can be best answered by a combination of traditional philological and historical research methods with the use of digital text analysis, biographical databases, historical GIS, and SNA. In the first instance, we manually tagged content of interest (authors, oral informants, letter recipients, document titles, topics and events discussed, time references) in a select number of Song Dynasty notebooks. By interlinking our own data with existing databases such as China Biographical Database (CBDB) or China Historical GIS (CHGIS), we were able to examine the structure, geographical distribution, and social makeup of the social networks embedded in these records (Bol et al. 2004; Bol et al. 2001). Hilde De Weerdt found, for example, that the networks embedded in twelfth- and thirteenth-century notebooks were cross-regional in scope and tended to include a large number of mostly contemporaries who increasingly shared a lower literati background (without office or examination degree) (De Weerdt 2015b). After a dedicated programmer, Brent/Hou-Ieong Ho, joined the project, we translated this methodology into an open access semiautomated tagging platform named MARKUS (Figure 1), allowing any researcher to automatically detect and manually correct personal names, place-names, time references, official titles, and other kinds of user-supplied named entities and to export the results with links to geographic and biographical databases for further analysis (Ho and De Weerdt 2014).[3]

Tagging content is useful in a variety of ways. First, by tagging names, all references to a particular person are standardized. This implies that when searching for persons either individually (by clicking on it in any module) or collectively (in the filter passage module), all relevant passages will appear regardless of the particular way in which the person is referred to. Tagging is therefore usually preferable over natural keyword searching.

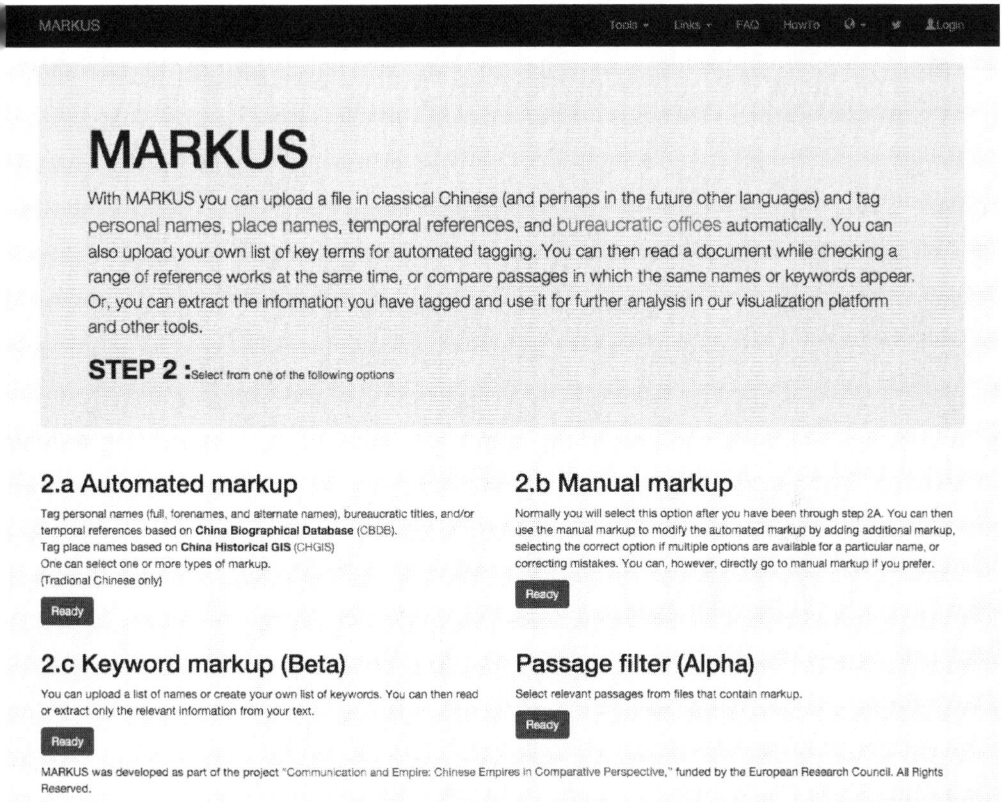

MARKUS

With MARKUS you can upload a file in classical Chinese (and perhaps in the future other languages) and tag personal names, place names, temporal references, and bureaucratic offices automatically. You can also upload your own list of key terms for automated tagging. You can then read a document while checking a range of reference works at the same time, or compare passages in which the same names or keywords appear. Or, you can extract the information you have tagged and use it for further analysis in our visualization platform and other tools.

STEP 2 : Select from one of the following options

2.a Automated markup

Tag personal names (full, forenames, and alternate names), bureaucratic titles, and/or temporal references based on **China Biographical Database** (CBDB). Tag place names based on **China Historical GIS** (CHGIS) One can select one or more types of markup. (Traditional Chinese only)

Ready

2.b Manual markup

Normally you will select this option after you have been through step 2A. You can then use the manual markup to modify the automated markup by adding additional markup, selecting the correct option if multiple options are available for a particular name, or correcting mistakes. You can, however, directly go to manual markup if you prefer.

Ready

2.c Keyword markup (Beta)

You can upload a list of names or create your own list of keywords. You can then read or extract only the relevant information from your text.

Ready

Passage filter (Alpha)

Select relevant passages from files that contain markup.

Ready

MARKUS was developed as part of the project "Communication and Empire: Chinese Empires in Comparative Perspective," funded by the European Research Council. All Rights Reserved.

Figure 1. Overview of markup options in MARKUS.

Second, when tagging names, MARKUS automatically supplies the unique ID attached to it in the default databases. Through this means, users can also link the data obtained from the analyzed texts to any data of interest in CBDB or CHGIS. These resources can be accessed in real time by clicking on tagged content, which will call up all relevant information about the term in the reference section on the right of the screen. When exporting tagged content in MARKUS to one of the supplied formats (CSV, Excel, or XML), a user will have access to the following information for further analysis: the tagged term, the location of the occurrence (paragraph), the entity ID, and the entity type. The ID will allow a user to import data from CBDB and CHGIS, including dates, family relations, offices held, places of origin and residence, other kinds of social relationships, works authored, geographic coordinates for places mentioned, and so on.

In the following, we provide two examples of how this kind of tagging can be used to analyze both smaller and larger textual corpora. These examples relate to the focus on correspondence networks and political networking in the Communication and Empire project. The methodology can, however, be applied in research on all sorts of questions in social, economic, medical, religious, literary, or intellectual history. One researcher has, for example, used the platform to map the spread of knowledge about medicinal plants by tagging places, time references, and plants based on an externally obtained list of thousands of plants. Similarly, socioeconomic terms can be combined with places, persons, or time references to discover, organize, and analyze appropriate content from the extensive digital archives that already exist for most periods of Chinese history.

■ LETTER COLLECTIONS AND COURT POLITICS

In less than half a century, the Mongols established an empire across Eurasia. How did they administer the empire's vast territories? Historians have attributed the success of the Mongols in maintaining the empire to their effective mobilization of resources and flexible adoption of various indigenous traditions of governing in different conquered territories (Morgan 1986; Allsen 1987; Biran 2004). In what is now north China, the Mongol ruling elites, with the help of Han literati, adopted the so-called Han ruling methods to govern (Rossabi 1987; Franke 1994). On the basis of a digital analysis of a rare collection of letters, Chu Ming-kin has revisited the following questions: How did the Mongols recruit Han literati? How did the latter manage to assume influential positions in the Mongol administration and persuade the Mongol rulers to adopt Han measures to govern? To what extent can an analysis of Han literati networks help solve these questions?[4]

We reconstructed the epistolary network of Han literati who resided in the northern territories during the Jin-Yuan transition in the thirteenth century on the basis of two hundred letters collected in *Zhongzhou qizha* (Epistolary writings of the Central Plain) (Wu 1988). After manually transcribing the corpus of two hundred letters into digital format, we imported it into MARKUS and tagged the names of the authors and recipients of all letters, all place-names, and official titles.

Using both the data in CBDB and the letters themselves, we mapped the native place and trajectories of all letter writers and recipients. The geographical distribution of the native place of the authors and recipients shows that the epistolary network was not confined to a single region but spread across different regions in what is now north China. This network was also dynamic as the authors and recipients of the letters frequently traveled and seldom stayed in their native places. The movements of Han literati were due in part to their pursuit of a career in the civil service. Because many of them lacked the opportunity to assume senior positions in the Mongol administration prior to 1260, they also went in search of clerical positions that scholar-officials traditionally despised.

A comparison of the official titles mentioned in the letters written before and after 1260 shows a 30 percent increase in senior positions in central and regional administration after 1260. This phenomenon owes much to the ascendance of Han literati after Qubilai's (1215–94, r. 1260–94) accession in 1260. Among the twenty-seven authors and recipients whose careers before and after 1260 can be traced, seventeen had only held junior official and subbureaucratic positions before 1260 and became senior officials in central and regional administration after 1260.

How did those mentioned in the letters establish ties between the Mongol rulers and Han literati and subsequently facilitate the latters' rise in officialdom? An analysis of those mentioned in the letters sheds light on the relationship between Han literati and the Mongols as well as between Han and Central Asians *(semu ren)*. After excluding all authors and recipients, nearly three hundred names (including full name, partial name, and abbreviated name) appear in the main text of the two hundred letters, referring to approximately two hundred people. Almost all of these referred to Han people. Those mentioned most frequently were Zhou Hui 周惠 (?–circa 1261) (eight times), Lian Xixian 廉希憲 (1231–80) (four times), and Kuokuo 闊闊 (1223–62) (three times); the latter two were Central Asian and Mongol, respectively. A closer examination of the lives of Lian Xixian and Kuokuo reveals that they were familiar with Han cultural traditions despite their non-Han ethnic background (Su 1996; Song 1976). Serving as a bridge between the Han literati and the Mongol ruling elites, they facilitated the initial recruitment and subsequent promotion of Han literati under Qubilai.

We can further examine how the Mongols recruited Han literati by analyzing the epistolary network in *Zhongzhou qizha*. In Figure 2, we show the relationships between authors and receivers. We identify the core agents as those who sent and/or received the highest numbers of letters. Despite the lack of direct correspondence between them, the six core agents who sent and/or received fifteen or more letters were connected to each other through three intermediary brokers. Most Han literati in the epistolary network joined Qubilai because of their direct or indirect ties to these brokers. When these Han literati assumed key positions in the Mongol government after Qubilai's accession, they were transformed into an indigenous network of political elites. These political elites managed to persuade the Mongol rulers to adopt Han measures to govern

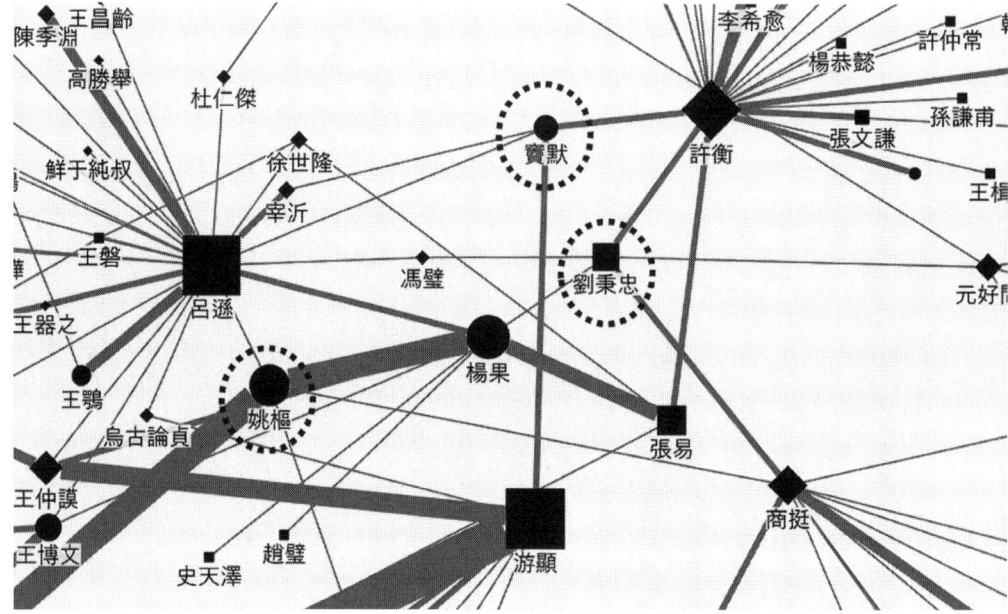

Figure 2. Epistolary network of Han literati during the Jin-Yuan transition. Diamond nodes represent authors, square nodes are receivers, and circle nodes are those who acted as both authors and receivers. The size of the nodes and the thickness of the edges represent the number of letters sent and/or received. Brokers are circled by dotted lines.

and, in turn, contributed to Mongol governance and administration in the northern territories.

■ REEXAMINING COLLECTIVE ACTION AND FACTIONALISM

As shown in the preceding cases of the communication networks of Song provincial scholars or of Han advisors at the Yuan (1271–1368) court, tagging and linking data can help us gain new insight into the sociopolitical networks that sustained polities and into the sources we use to reconstruct the politics of empires at a microlevel. We can also use these same methods to explore the structure and dynamics of empires at a macroscale. Our recent work on the history of parties or factionalism provides a good example of how digital methods can be employed to formulate and tackle new questions across large corpora of texts.[5]

A seventeenth-century historian, Wang Fuzhi 王夫之 (1619–92), pointed out that factionalism was not an exceptional thing in Chinese history; he noted that from the Song Dynasty onward, it became part of being a literatus (Wang 1985, 10.201). Networking was intertwined with the career of literati at various stages. It was essential when preparing and sitting examinations, when seeking appointment and reappointment, or when obtaining patronage for other types of employment. Networking involved literati in political coalitions. If it is the case that networking of this kind was necessary for careers and therefore pervasive, it follows that historians need to understand how factional politics worked not only at the top but also in the provinces. Our inquiry builds on earlier work that stresses the continuity of factional politics in imperial politics past the 1104 debacle that in the eyes of many brought down the Northern Song government but also asks how factional alliances were transformed in the context of the broader social and cultural changes of the twelfth century.

How do we get a grip on the question of how factional politics operated in the vast collections of private writings? One could opt for a case study approach focusing on known individuals, but we believe that the larger question of how far factional politics filtered through to the provinces can be better answered by devising methods to explore the entirety of the existing record. With a group of postdoctoral and doctoral students, we have begun to analyze how the names of the men who appeared on factional lists can be used to explore such questions: When and how did their names begin to cluster in the record? Did the lists reflect real political coalitions in the sense that they were reflected in textual exchanges between those listed or in the perception of contemporaries, were these random listings by paranoid leaders, or were they the invention of later historians (Hartman 2000)? Around what issues did coalitions form?

In a preliminary experiment, we ran the names (including alternate names) of all those mentioned on the Yuanyou list (1100s), those persecuted by Councilor Qin Gui 秦檜 (1090–1155) (1140s), and those on the Qingyuan roster (1190s) through three collections of texts.[6] Each collection consisted of all prose texts gathered in the collected writings of authors who were active during the time the lists were compiled. We included the collected writings of all Song authors whose CBDB index year (normally sixty years of year of death) fell within a sixty-year range (–30 to +30) of the date established as the publication date of the list of names: 1104, 1142, and 1196. The 1104 corpus consisted of 56,969 documents in 23,701,759 characters by 2,231 authors; the 1142 corpus of 47,040 documents in 18,780,575 characters by 1,139 authors; and the 1196 corpus of 52,593 documents in 23,446,605 characters by 2,598 authors. Given the limitations of automated detection at this point, the data need to be curated carefully before we can formally present our findings, work that will not be completed until December 2015. The preliminary test runs of the clustering of names suggest, however, that the structure of the presumed twelfth-century factions varied considerably, with the Yuanyou list forming loosely connected subgroups and the Qingyuan list a tightly connected core, whereas no clear connections appear in the record for those persecuted by Qin Gui—demonstrating that historical network analysis can also be used to demonstrate the absence of relationships and network effects. We are currently also advancing current practice in historical network analysis and taking advantage of the large-scale prosopographical and textual databases for Chinese history by developing sampling methods, comparing the networks resulting from cooccurrence and other types of relationship data to those of random samples of contemporaries.

■ IN CONCLUSION

The formation and maintenance of empires have depended on the collaboration of provincial elites of different kinds. We designed the Communication and Empire project to inquire into the channels through which those in the core and those in the periphery communicated and to map the development of communication networks among provincial elites. Research of this kind is conceivable now due to the existence of large digital corpora in classical Chinese and prosopographical and geographic databases, which facilitate both markup and data analysis (this is far less the case for other places and languages). The project demonstrates that historians are not reliant on these databases to conduct research; they can explore and analyze their preferred text collections in new ways by linking them to the rich data gathered from many reference sources in biographical and geospatial databases, modifying the latter if need be. In designing MARKUS, we learned that historians in all fields stand to gain much by critically engaging and participating in the design of digital methods and tools for historical research.

Hilde De Weerdt is professor of Chinese history at Leiden University. She is the author of *Competition over Content: Negotiating Standards for the Civil Service Examinations in Imperial China (1127–1276)* (2007) and *Information, Territory, and Networks: The Crisis and Maintenance of Empire in Song China* (2015).

Chu Ming-kin is a research associate in the project "Communication and Empire: Chinese Empires in Comparative Perspective" at Leiden University.

Ho Hou-Ieong is a research associate in the ERC project "Communication and Empire: Chinese Empires in Comparative Perspective" at Leiden University. He conducted his doctoral research at the Department of Computer Science of Information Science, National Taiwan University, with a focus on digital humanities and digital libraries.

■ **NOTES**

1. This project is funded by the European Research Council (project 283525).

2. We will not discuss the comparative aspect of the project here. For more information about individual and collective contributions and plans in this respect, see the workshop, seminar, and bibliography section of the project site (De Weerdt et al. 2012).

3. For short video introductions on functionality and limitations, see De Weerdt, Ho, and Feng (2014). For a longer introduction in Chinese, see De Weerdt (2015a). The further improvement of MARKUS has been funded by the Arts and Humanities Research Council and the National Endowment for the Humanities. See Bol, De Weerdt, and Ho (2014–16). For a critical reflection on the reception of digital history, see De Weerdt (2014a, 2014b).

4. The following discussion is based on Chu (2014).

5. The following text is largely based on De Weerdt (2014d).

6. The lists are based on the following titles: Li (1995, 2.5a–7a), Yong Rong (1983, 61.3b–4a), Cangzhou qiaosou (1984, 1a–7b). I acknowledge the help of Chu Mingkin in compiling the lists. For an overview of the preliminary results, see De Weerdt (2014c).

■ **WORKS CITED**

Allsen, Thomas T. 1987. *Mongol Imperialism: The Policies of the Grand Qan Möngke in China, Russia, and the Islamic Lands, 1251–1259.* Berkeley: University of California Press.

Biran, Michal. 2004. "The Mongol Transformation: From the Steppe to Eurasian Empire." *Medieval Encounters* 10: 339–61.

Bol, Peter K., Merrick Lex Berman et al. 2001. "China Historical GIS." http://www.fas.harvard.edu/~chgis/.

Bol, Peter K., Hilde De Weerdt, and Brent Ho. 2014–16. "Automating Data Extraction from Chinese Texts." http://did-acte.org/.

Bol, Peter K., Robert M. Hartwell, Michael A. Fuller et al. 2004. "China Biographical Database Project (CBDB)." http://isites.harvard.edu /icb/icb.do?keyword=k16229&pageid=icb.page129708.

Cangzhou qiaosou 滄州樵叟. 1984. *Qingyuan dangjin* [慶元黨禁], Siku quanshu ed. Reprinted in *Yingyin Wenyuange Siku quanshu* [景印文淵閣四庫全書], vol. 451. Taibei: Taiwan Shangwu yinshuguan.

Chu, Ming-kin. 2014. "Indigenous Elite Networks and Mongol Governance in 13th-Century North China." Presentation delivered at the International Medieval Congress, Leeds, U.K.

De Weerdt, Hilde. 2014a. "Digital Interpretations." http://chinese-empires .eu/blog/digital-interpretations/.

———. 2014b. "Isn't the Siku quanshu Enough? Reflections on the Impact of New Digital Tools for Classical Chinese." http://chinese-empires .eu/blog/isnt-the-siku-quanshu-enough-reflections-on-the-impact -of-new-digital-tools-for-classical-chinese/.

———. 2014c. "MARKUS and the New History of Collective Action." Paper presented at the International Conference on Digital Archives and Digital Humanities, Academia Sinica, Taipei. https://www.academia .edu/12428169/2014_by_invitation_MARKUS_and_the_New_His tory_of_Collective_Action.

———. 2014d. "Reinventing Chinese Political History." Inaugural lecture, Leiden University. http://media.leidenuniv.nl/legacy/oratie -de-weerdt-nl.pdf, http://media.leidenuniv.nl/legacy/oratie-de -weerdt-eng.pdf, https://www.academia.edu/9212965/Reinventing _Chinese_Political_History._Inaugural_lecture._Leiden_University _2014.

———. 2015a. "文本標記與歷史研究" [Textual markup and historical research]. Academia Sinica, Institute of History and Philology, Taipei. https://www.youtube.com/watch?v=NltG3EjC9_A.

———. 2015b. *Information, Territory, and Networks: The Crisis and Maintenance of Empire in Song China.* Cambridge, Mass.: Harvard University Asia Center.

De Weerdt, Hilde, Brent Ho, Ming-kin Chu, and Julius Morche. 2012. "Communication and Empire." http://chinese-empires.eu/.

De Weerdt, Hilde, Brent Ho, and Y. Feng. 2014. "How To." http://dh.chinese-empires.eu/beta/video.html.

Doyle, Michael W. 1986. *Empires*. Ithaca, N.Y.: Cornell University Press.

Eisenstadt, S. N. 1963. *The Political Systems of Empires: The Rise and Fall of the Historical Bureaucratic Societies*. London: Free Press of Glencoe.

Franke, Herbert. 1994. "From Tribal Chieftain to Universal Emperor and God: The Legitimation of the Yuan Dynasty." In *China under Mongol Rule*, IV.3–85. Aldershot, U.K.: Variorum.

Hartman, Charles. 2000. "The Stele-Register of Partisans from the Era of Primal Bounty." Presentation delivered at the Association for Asian Studies Annual Meeting, San Diego, Calif.

Ho, Brent, and Hilde De Weerdt. 2014. "MARKUS: A Markup, Reading, and Visualization Platform for Classical Chinese Texts." http://dh.chinese-empires.eu/beta/.

Lewis, Mark Edward. 1999. *Writing and Authority in Early China*. Albany: SUNY Press.

Li Xinchuan 李心傳. 1995. *Daominglu* [道命錄], Qing manuscript ed. Reprinted in *Xu xiu Siku quanshu* [續修四庫全書], vol. 517. Shanghai: Shanghai guji chubanshe.

McMullen, David. 1988. *State and Scholars in T'ang China*. Cambridge: Cambridge University Press.

Morgan, David. 1986. *The Mongols*. Oxford: Blackwell.

Münkler, Herfried. 2007. *Empires: The Logic of World Domination from Ancient Rome to the United States*. Cambridge: Polity Press.

Rossabi, Morris. 1987. *Khubilai Khan: His Life and Times*. Berkeley: University of California Press.

Song Lian 宋濂. 1976. *Yuan shi* [元史]. Beijing: Zhonghua shuju.

Su Tianjue 蘇天爵. 1996. *Yuanchao mingchen shilüe* [元朝名臣事略]. Beijing: Zhonghua shuju.

Wang Fuzhi 王夫之. 1985. *Song lun* [宋論]. Taibei: Liren shuju.

Wu Hongdao 吳弘道. 1988. *Zhongzhou qizha* [中州啓劄], Qing manuscript ed. Reprinted in *Beijing tushuguan guji zhenben congkan* [北京圖書館古籍珍本叢刊], vol. 116. Beijing: Shu mu wen xian chu ban she.

Yong Rong 永瑢 et al. 1983. *Qinding Siku quanshu zongmu* [欽定四庫全書總目], Siku quanshu ed. Reprinted in *Yingyin Wenyuange Siku quanshu* [景印文淵閣四庫全書], vol. 1–5. Taibei: Taiwan Shangwu yinshuguan.

PETER K. BOL

Mapping China's History

THIS ESSAY INTRODUCES several issues relating to the conceptualization and representation of historical geographic space. I have based these comments on our experience with the China Historical Geographic Information System (CHGIS) project, currently a collaboration of the Harvard University Center for Geographic Analysis and the Fudan University Center for Chinese Historical Geography.[1] The purpose of CHGIS is to make possible the spatial analysis of historical data by providing them with the locations of the historical and administrative hierarchies of which they were part between 221 BCE and 1911 CE. In essence, spatial analysis refers to discovering both the spatial distribution in a particular set of data and the relationships between different kinds of spatialized data.

■ **THE GEOGRAPHIC AND THE HISTORICAL IN**
A GEOGRAPHIC INFORMATION SYSTEM
Historical events happen somewhere—as we say, they "take place"—and we assume they can be mapped. To state this more exactly, we assume that the visual representation of relations across space is possible. There are rivers and mountains, roads and bridges, administrative and non-administrative populated places, religious sites and monuments. In general, all these places have names. Figure 1, the map of a township *(xiang)* in Yiwu 義烏 county from the 1590s, is an example of such mapping. The map is a heuristic; it depicts features as coexisting in a shared moment in time. Yet river courses change, buildings burn, bridges are washed out, and towns are pillaged. Later editions of the local gazetteer from which Figure 1 has been taken gave up on mapping the townships at this level of specificity, precisely because too much had changed. Mapping is good for representing spatial relationships but not at representing change over

Figure 1. Map of Zhizhe *xiang* from the *Yiwu Gazetteer* (1596) is a rare example of a detailed township map. More commonly, gazetteers provide county-level maps and lists of named human and natural landscape features.

time. Conversely, a historical narrative can represent change over time, but it is not much use for narrating all the changes taking place across the landscape. Here I will leave aside the question of scale—something that holds when representing either space or time—and instead note that historical GIS solves the problem of combining spatial and temporal change not by drawing a series of maps but by creating a relational database from which maps for different moments in time can be generated. A GIS database actually combines two things: a set of spatial features (points, lines, and polygons) that have x, y coordinates, where x and y represent longitude and latitude, and a table of attributes of those features. Taking CHGIS as an example, the attributes of a spatial feature include the type of feature (town, county seat, prefectural seat, prefectural polygon, etc.), the names of the feature, the times at which this name at this location is valid, the exactitude of the begin and end dates of the temporal span, and the administrative unit to which it was subordinate. Moreover, a table with the sources attesting to these attributes can be linked to the feature table. The CHGIS online gazetteer provides much of this information at once.[2]

■ WHAT TO REPRESENT: STATES AND EMPIRES

The first question to be asked in creating a historical GIS is simply, what is it that we want to represent? We answered that question by asking what research and teaching purposes a historical GIS of China could serve. Our starting point was simple: the historical record includes various kinds of geographies, and historical documents are replete with references to places. An intellectual historian might have a list of places with private academies or of places whence teachers and their students came, a social historian data on the burial locations of a person's kin, an economist records of county tax quotas, a demographer population data, and so on. If they wanted to locate their data in space and relate them to other kinds of data with spatial attributes (e.g., degree holders relative to tax quotas), they would need to know the location of the places named in the documents. Thus the conclusion: spatially enabled historiography requires knowledge of the locations of places named in the texts.

We did not begin from an interest in representing China's past international borders and changes in dynastic territory. A map series devoted to that issue has been created for teaching purposes and is open to the public.[3] However, representations of international borders are problematic, and not only because they change. Any formal collaboration with institutions in China requires compliance with two rules, one public and the other less so. First, at the time of writing, maps of better than 1:500,000 scale are legally state secrets (CHGIS is 1:1,000,000), which ensures that the representation of borders is inexact. Second, depictions of all international borders from the Yuan period into the present published in China must agree with the borders recognized by the Ministry of Foreign Affairs (this rule applies to visualizations, not historical research). Nevertheless no one denies the magnitude of territorial change (e.g., from mid-Tang to late Tang, from early Ming to late Ming). Although the complete international borders in CHGIS time slice layers for 1820 and 1911 include the official international borders, the locations of administrative places are based on historical records rather than modern mandates and provincial maps from the end of the Qing Dynasty.

CHGIS began with the best-attested place-names in the historical record—administrative places, beginning with the unification of the several states by the Qin in 221 BCE and ending with the fall of the Qing in 1911 CE—and the hierarchy of the field administration, recording all changes in names, locations, and hierarchical relationships.

This has a consequence that bears on this volume of essays on digital humanities for "Asian Empires and Imperialism." CHGIS serves the digital humanities, but it may not be a good resource for empires and imperialism. I propose that we distinguish states from empires in a manner suggested by Li Jifu in his 813 preface to the administrative geography of the Yuanhe reign period. Li distinguishes between those places that were administered by the centralized civil bureaucratic system, thus his use of "commanderies and counties" 郡縣 in his title, from those regions in the west over which the Tang court exercised a certain military dominion, which he excluded. He thus defines the "Great State of Tang" 大唐國 and delineates the territories that constitute it (Li 1983). By his definition, Tang is a state. It is centrally administered, it has a unified system of government, and it has local officials chosen according to well-defined standards who are sent from and represent the central policy-making bodies. Here I shall reserve the term *empire* for those areas, mainly in the far west in the Tang case, over which Tang tried to exercise dominion without integrating them into the Tang state system. Thus we can say that the Tang state created an empire and that the Tang state was an imperial power while recognizing that the vast majority of its population lived within the territory of the Tang state and did not belong to the empire.

Distinguishing between state and empire allows us to accommodate the terms in which historical actors thought about themselves. What we call "dynasties" were what those who lived in them called *guo,* states, that had clear beginning and ending points in time but with spatial extents that were always in some degree of flux. It helps us understand what they saw as being inside, outside, and in between. The state of Song insisted unsuccessfully that the sixteen prefectures around present-day Beijing occupied by Liao were rightfully part of its field administration, but it did not claim the rest of Liao territory. It lived in a world composed of many states that were not under Song dominion, as Yue Shi's early Song geography recognized (Yue 1983). Song invested in defending and sometimes in extending its frontiers, but when it did so, it struggled with the question of whether the peoples on the frontiers were to govern themselves or should be brought under the civil administration (Mostern 2011). This also helps us distinguish between the Song and Ming, states that did not establish empires, and the Jurchens, Mongols, and Manchus, who did and who arguably saw themselves as allowing the natives to follow their traditional mode of administration (and even have a named state).

The result, however, is that with the exception of the Northern and Southern dynasties period, the historical record gives us reasonably good information on the administrative geography of most territory in the dynastic states that was administered through the civil bureaucratic system. With few exceptions, we lack information on the territories of the larger empires they were part of or on the imperial dominions the Han and Tang created that were outside the centralized civil bureaucratic system. That is not, however, the only problem.

■ POPULATED PLACES VERSUS BOUNDED SPACE, OR POINTS VERSUS POLYGONS

Since the introduction of Ramsden's theodolite in the 1790s, the world has gradually been mapped with mathematical precision. This makes it possible to create maps showing administrative units as areas with clearly defined borders and leads us to think of them in the first place as bounded space. Having such maps made it possible for the Great Britain Historical GIS to track changes in administrative boundaries and thus map nineteenth- and twentieth-century demographic data relative to population at the local level.[4] Without such surveying tools, however, the challenges of defining the Chinese field administration as a collection of bounded spaces would have been insurmountable, and indeed, we have no historical maps before the very late Qing that suggest that such an effort was made. Clearly the idea of bounded space was not foreign to China—the "fish scale map registers" 魚鱗圖冊 of the Ming (originating in Southern Song) may be crude, but they make the point that for tax purposes, arable land is to be construed as a series of parcels. We find similar crudely bounded spaces being used to represent province-level circuits in the world's earliest printed historical atlas, as in Figure 2.[5]

Given the page size, it is understandable that prefectural boundaries were not included, but in fact we have no maps showing prefectural, much less county, boundaries. The famous *Traces of Yu Map* 禹跡圖 from 1136 CE (Figure 3), the world's earliest extant grid map, locates prefectures on the grid by name rather than area, although it had ample room to do both. The *Traces of Yu Map* is particularly interesting because it shows the prefectural seats claimed by Song but does not rely on boundaries to depict states, for which it had the room. This and the near-total absence of gazetteer maps showing boundaries suggest that the alternative to thinking of administrative units as spatial territories was to conceive of them as nested hierarchies of places. This fits a tax system in which a quota was assigned to the prefectural government, which divided it among the county governments, which parceled it out through its subordinate units down to the household, at the same time that a register was kept of who owned which parcels around a village. This makes eminent sense. An administration needed to know which villages it could collect taxes from, but it could only collect taxes from households in its hierarchy, making absentee landlordism a continuous problem once land distribution shifted from government assignment to the private market during

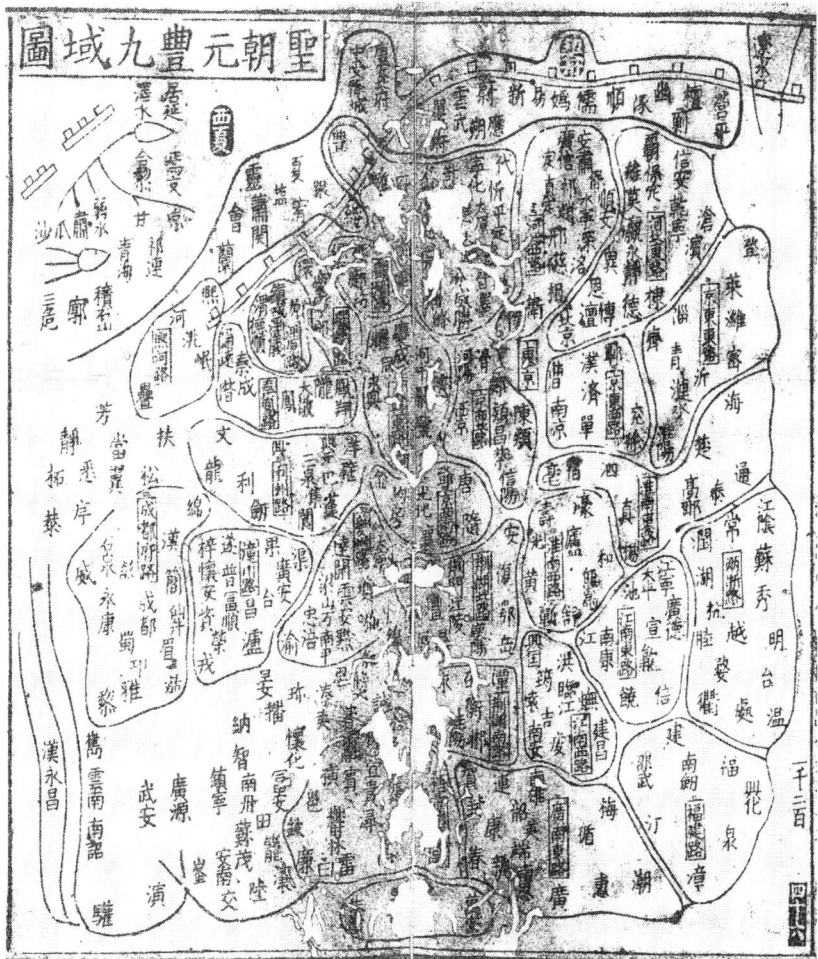

Figure 2. Map of the circuits *(lu)* based on the Yuanfeng (1078–75 BCE) administrative geography. Circuits are named in the cartouches, and the names of prefectures are given in their correct spatial relationships. From the twelfth-century atlas *Lidai dili zhizhang tu,* held in the Tōyō Bunko.

the Tang–Song transition. This argument for networks of points in administrative hierarchies rather than polygons changes the way we see the world. Consider the two renditions of administrative change in Figure 4.

Nevertheless, the Tang–Song transition did see a shift from an earlier view of administrative geography in which distances between administrative seats were recorded to a new view in which information about spatial boundaries was seen as worthy of note. We find this in the Yuanfeng administrative geography of the 1080s CE, which records the distance

Figure 3. *Traces of Yu Map* 禹跡圖, 1136 CE, now in Suzhou. The purpose of the map was to relate contemporary places to the landscape of the "Tributes of Yu" chapter of the *Book of Documents*. From a rubbing in the Harvard University Library.

from the prefectural boundary to the border to the next prefectural seat; Figure 5 is an example. However, the discrepancies in distances in Figure 5 illustrate the larger point that boundary precision was not of such importance that it was necessary for the authoritative national geography to reconcile differences.

Thus, although local governments had a concept of boundaries, and knew where they were on roads between administrative seats and, more roughly, which landscape features, such as rivers and mountain ranges, divided counties from each other, there was no need to be exact about boundaries if the taxpaying villages were identified.

CHGIS provides county boundaries for 1911 and prefectural boundar-

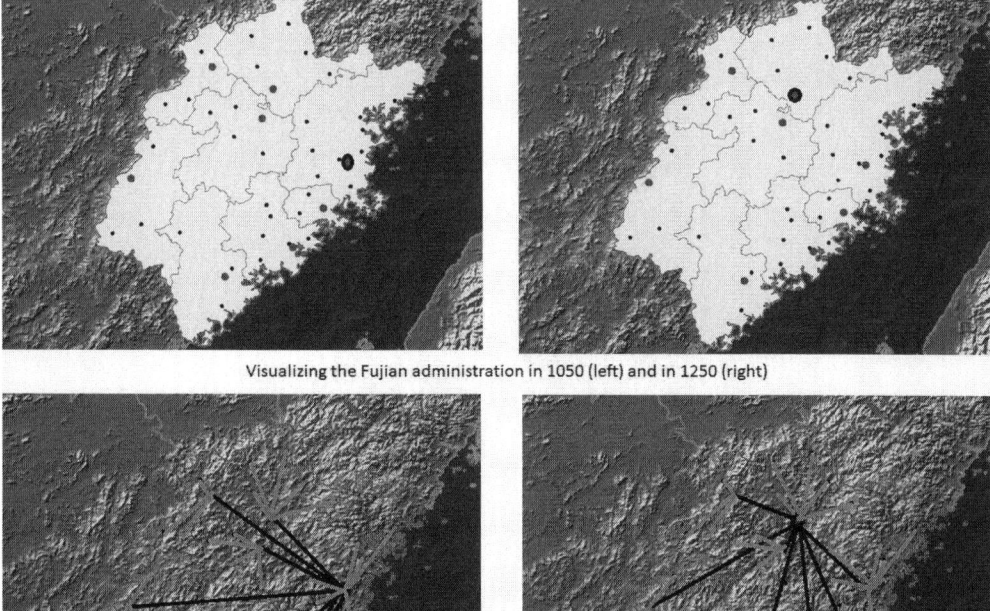

Visualizing the Fujian administration in 1050 (left) and in 1250 (right)

Figure 4. Contrasting a representation of bounded space with the hierarchical administrative network. Maps by Merrick Lex Berman. Data from CHGIS 2.0.

ies for all periods. It accomplishes this by working backward from 1911, assuming that unless the historical record records a change, those boundaries have at least heuristic value. Nevertheless, the most reliable data are not the polygons that depict bounded administrative space but the points that identify administrative seats and, for later periods, towns.

■ STATE AND EMPIRE

If we want to gain an accurate picture of the relations between China's historical state systems and their surrounding territories, we need to discriminate between different kinds of administrative seats and their respective administrative hierarchies. Figure 6, showing different kinds of administrative units in the southwest in 1900, illustrates this. One can clearly see the difference between the centralized bureaucratic administration that predominates in Sichuan, Hubei, eastern Hunan, and

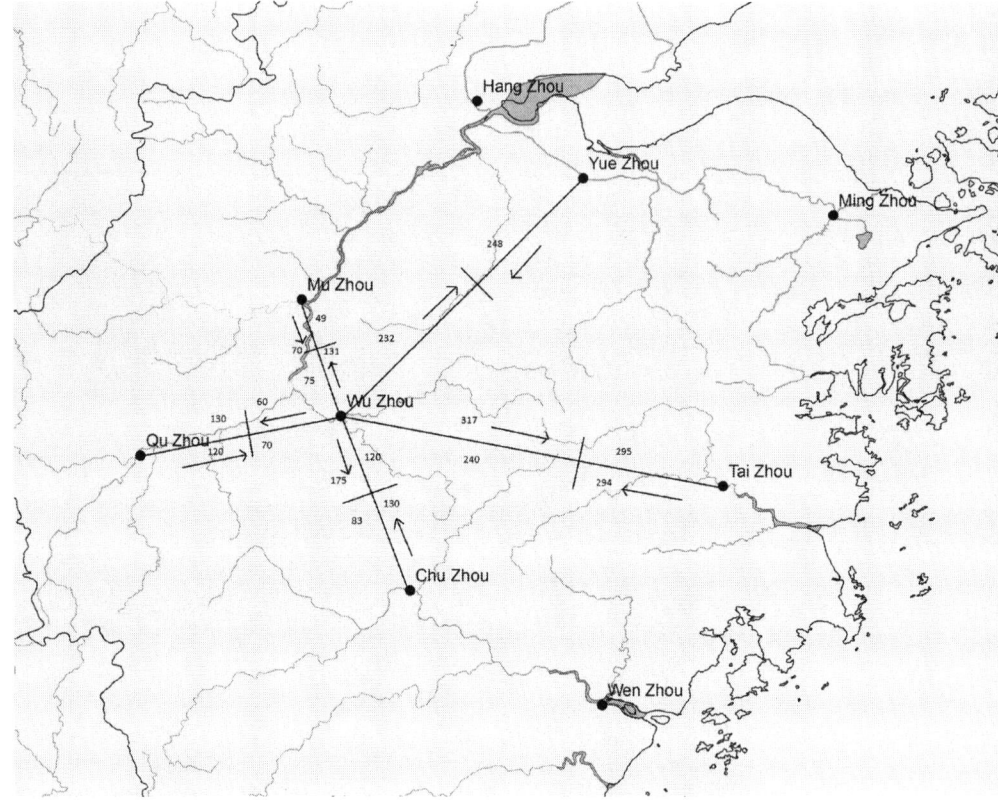

Figure 5. Distances from southeastern prefectural seats to the border of the next seat as recorded in the Yuanfeng administrative geography. Arrows identify the prefectural entry that is the source of the distance. Map based on data from CHGIS 4.0.

Guangdong and the mixed administrative systems in Yunnan, Guizhou, and Guangxi. The interdigitation of administrative types, especially in Guizhou, Guangxi, and western Hunan, is also evident.

CHGIS unfortunately does not cover the administrative system outside of the eighteen core provinces. Nevertheless, Figure 6 adequately illustrates the transition from the state system to the frontier. If we shift our gaze from the units created for "minority peoples" to the civil bureaucratic state system, we can see the penetration of the state system into the frontier. From that perspective, the state system appears as a colonial power, encroaching into foreign territory but creating a separate administrative order for the frontier peoples and erasing their own conceptions of governance.

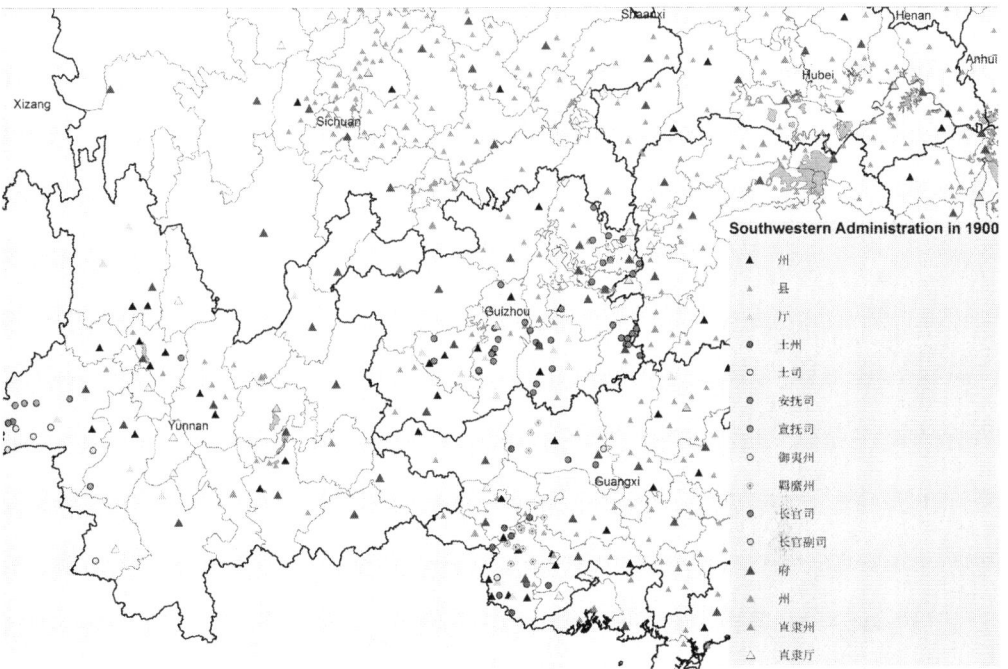

Figure 6. Different kinds of administrative units in the southwest in 1900. Triangles represent levels of the normal civil administration; circles represent various kinds of administrative units used for (semi-)autonomous frontier peoples. Data are from CHGIS 5.0. The full-color version of this map is available in the JSTOR electronic edition.

The reverse happened as well. The imperial powers who conquered areas administered through the bureaucratic state system inserted their own administrative units into the conquered territory alongside the bureaucratic state administration. Examples include the Jurchens' Meng'an 猛安 and Mouke 謀克 in the Jin Dynasty, the appanages of Jurchen and Mongol aristocrats in the Yuan and Jin, and the Eight Banners of the Qing Dynasty. In contrast to the units of the civil bureaucratic system, none of these formations survived, perhaps because they were colonial outposts that depended on continued military force to be sustained.

■ CONCLUSION

In developing an historical GIS for China, we have identified administrative seats and, for more recent centuries, nonadministrative towns and related them to one another in hierarchical networks. Although our sources for the administrative geography of areas beyond the centralized civil bureaucratic administration are limited, there is enough to see that the state systems in China's history are readily distinguishable from the imperial dominions on the frontiers, be they internal or external. We can at least imagine the diversity that a historical GIS that included all the territories claimed by a Tang or a Yuan might have looked like.

Not all dynastic states can be called empires, but the kind of map that shows a Han or Tang, a Yuan or Qing, extending over vast areas in the north and west obscures the great differences in the governance of those territories. If, instead of drawing boundaries and treating all the land within them as a single empire, we could identify populated places and the networks they belonged to and, at the same time, track the changes that took place as armies advanced and retreated and rebellions rose and spread, we would have a more dynamic map. Scale applies to chronology as well as to cartography, and the granularity of a year limits our ability to capture the rapidity of change. This applies not only to the frontiers and imperial dominions but also to the extension of bureaucratic governance into the southern half of what is sometimes called China proper.

This brings us back to where this essay started. The goal of CHGIS is to support critical, spatially enabled historiography rather than to visualize a series of dynastic states and empires as cartographies with shifting boundaries. Instead, we begin with the establishment of known points, where things took place, based on the best possible evidence, with an understanding of the uncertainties that result from any temporal and geographical scale. Given the limitations of sources, we are sometimes dealing with approximations when it comes to precise dating of administrative changes, for which CHGIS notes the degree of approximation. These points are the basis for identifying the itineraries, trade routes, marketing systems, and relationships of jurisdiction, taxation, field administration, and other spatial data that are referred to in historical documents. The one network that is consistently part of all CHGIS data sets is the hierarchy of the field administration; others depend on the particular interests of researchers. Such networks allow us to ignore notions of empires as large and encompassing spaces within which a single political reality dominated all and instead create a framework for the study of human interaction and the differentiated forms of administrative or military reach. The internal structure of the *tianxia,* of "all under heaven," as imagined by dynastic courts, can only be reconstructed historically out of the overlapping claims and varieties of governance structures of various peoples that inhabited continental East Asia.

Peter K. Bol is the Charles H. Carswell Professor of East Asian Languages and Civilizations and vice provost for advances in learning at Harvard University, where he founded the Harvard Center for Geographic Analysis.

■ NOTES

My thanks to Merrick Lex Berman for his comments; the conclusion adopts his comments in part.

1. The initial historical GIS data set was created by the late Robert Hartwell and bequeathed to the Harvard Yenching Institute. Although the Hartwell data sets are available for download from the CHGIS website (http://www.fas.harvard.edu/~chgis/), they were created through a method that inevitably resulted in considerable inaccuracy. The CHGIS data sets are new work, not based on the Harvard legacy. With the exception of the CHGIS 1820 "time slice," which is indebted to the maps in volume 8 of the *Historical Atlas of China* (Tan 1982), all CHGIS data sets are original work. CHGIS was originally funded by the Henry Luce Foundation, the Harvard University Asia Center, and the National Endowment for the Humanities. The general editors of CHGIS are Peter K. Bol and Ge Jianxiong 葛劍雄; the executive editors are Merrick Lex Berman and Man Zhimin 滿志敏. For the history of the CHGIS project, see the website and articles by Berman (2005) and Bol (2007).

2. For the earlier mentioned Yiwu county, see http://maps.cga.harvard.edu/tgaz/placename/hvd_40720.

3. These maps, created principally by Wen Yu, with the assistance of Jeffrey Blossom, Fei Meng, Timothy Baker, and Peter Bol, can be viewed on and downloaded from ChinaXmap on the open access http://worldmap.harvard.edu/ platform.

4. For the Great Britain Historical GIS project, led by Humphrey Southall, see http://www.port.ac.uk/research/gbhgis/.

5. Shui Anli 稅安禮, *Lidai dili zhizhang tu* [歷代地理指掌圖] Shanghai: Shanghai guji chubanshe, 1989). This work is discussed by De Weerdt (2011) and others.

■ WORKS CITED

Berman, Merrick Lex. 2005. "Boundaries or Networks in Historical GIS: Concepts of Measuring Space and Administrative Geography in Chinese History." *Historical Geography* 33: 118–33.

Bol, Peter K. 2007. "Creating a GIS for the History of China." In *Placing History: How Maps, Spatial Data, and GIS Are Changing Historical Scholarship,* edited by Anne Kelly Knowles and Amy Hillier, 25–57. Redlands, Calif.: ESRI Press.

De Weerdt, Hilde. 2011. "The Cultural Logics of Map Reading: Text, Time, and Space in Printed Maps of the Song Empire." In *Knowledge and Text Production in an Age of Print: China, 900–1400*, edited by Hilde Godelieve Dominique De Weerdt and Lucille Chia, 239–72. Boston: Brill.

Li Jifu 李吉甫. 1983. *Yuanhe Junxian Tu Zhi* [元和郡縣圖志]. Zhongguo Gudai Dili Zongzhi Congkan. Beijing: Zhonghua shu ju.

Mostern, Ruth. 2011. *"Dividing the Realm in Order to Govern": The Spatial Organization of the Song State (960–1276 CE)*. Harvard-Yenching Institute Monograph Series. Cambridge, Mass.: Harvard University Asia Center.

Tan Qixiang 譚其驤. 1982. *Zhongguo Li Shi Di Tu Ji* [中國歷史地圖集]. Shanghai: Di tu chu ban she.

Yue Shi 樂史. 1983. *Taiping Huan Yu Ji* [太平寰宇記]. Ying Yin Wen Yuan Ge Si Ku Quan Shu. [Taipei]: Taiwan shang wu yin shu guan.

Essays

PAMELA KYLE CROSSLEY

The Imaginal Bond of "Empire" and "Civilization" in Eurasian History

WE HAVE BECOME ACCUSTOMED to a paradigm of "civilization" and "empire" as mutually reinforcing. Empires distribute the fundamentals of civilization, and after the demise of empire, civilization endures. In such reasoning, the "West" was the legacy of the Roman Empire; the Islamic world was the legacy of the Umayyad and Abbasid caliphates; and the "Confucian world," as Huntington and a few others had it, was the legacy of the Han Empire. Today this is hard to find credible. There is an ecology of presence for empires before the early modern period that would appear to have precluded these empires from maintaining the consistent intimacy with their populations necessary to actually instill grand and transformative ideas or cultural practices. Except for military force, most aspects of what we call "empires" before the beginnings of mass education and mass media in the seventeenth century were porous and ephemeral. Language change we now understand as a complex issue of divergent uses at the elite and popular levels and not as imposed by imperial demands (Winford 2003). Low literacy rates and the persistence of folk religion, among other factors, must have mitigated persistently against cultural change imposed from an imperial center (Scheidel 2013). The coherence claimed by any ancient or medieval empire was largely generated by local and regional elites—in their own time or later—using emblems of imperial affiliation to secure their own status and enhance local stability; after their own times, the conceit of vast, centrally emanating power was retrospectively conjured by new elites seeking to legitimate themselves.

In this essay, I use the handy (too handy) terms *classical* empires— primarily Rome and Han, because they were regarded afterward as typical of the large civilization-imposing empire; *confessional* empires (and this will be used very loosely), prevailing between about 300 and 1400 CE; and *monarchical* empires—some of which I will call "neo-confessional," as in the case of the Ottomans and Timurids—becoming prominent after about 1400. I draw these crude and intrusive lines knowing that cultural historians increasingly see continuities over the centuries that invalidate them. Nevertheless, for specific purposes of this essay, these clumsy tags help to delineate the layers of a progressively imbricated myth of the links of civilization with empire. Many readers will also find that they are embedded in an argument that because of limitations of space may stray here and there into overstatement; I am serious about the argument, which does not mean that every simplification will be immune to variant readings or challenge.

■ EMPIRES, CIVILIZATION, AND PROGRESS

Edward Gibbon (1737–94)[1] did not use the word "civilization" often. In the case of Rome, Gibbon understood "civilized" to denote the results of the process by which imperial tutelage brought the provinces more into conformity with the culture of the Italian peninsula: "Their partial distinctions were obliterated and they insensibly coalesced into one great nation, united by language, manners and civil institutions, and equal to the weight of a powerful empire" (Gibbon 1782). A rising empire was cultural dissemination by its nature. But a stable empire was a moribund one. Third-century Roman civic ethics gave way to corruption, cowardice, sloth, and disloyalty, all of which could be remedied best by an influx of vigorous peoples from the north, still seeking the moral salubrities of civilization that, in their native condition, they lacked. Initiative ultimately returns to the localities (or at least to the cities), where iteration and elaboration of the imperial cultural legacy underwrites "progress"— toward rule of law, economic prosperity, and humane values. With other contrasts, Gibbon reinforced the association of empire and civilization: the Persians—who had been civilized in the past but sank into corruption, as would the Romans—and the Umayyad caliphate, which in its dramatic early military victories planted the ground from which the Islamic world sprouted, at least in part as an inevitable response to the vacuum of civilization caused by recession of the Roman and Sassanian empires (Roberts 2014).

Seeing widespread standardized culture as a production of the Roman Empire made Gibbon a bit different from his predecessor and professed inspiration Charles-Louis de Secondat, Montesquieu (1689–1755). In *Considérations sur les causes de la grandeur et de la décadence des Romains*, Montesquieu had approved of the Roman values of self-discipline, courage, and loyalty where he found them but had based his understanding of the sources of the empire's existence on the ability of the leaders, and particularly the emperors after the first century CE, to summon an image of a vast moral order that balanced the abstractions of legal justice, reverence for institutions, and respect of the preeminence of the aristocracy against the central government's accumulation of financial and military power (Secondat 1734). This was his *gouvernment ambigu* (Secondat 1734); the loss of this rhetorical finesse, this control over image, was as much a cause of the Roman decline as were reductions in revenue and losses of military capacity.[2]

Both Gibbon and Montesquieu wrote for audiences living under states on the threshold of large-scale overseas conquest, and both used the Romans as foils to advise the conquerors of their own time—sometimes to advise them against conquest.[3] Their approximate contemporary, Zhao Yi 趙翼 (1727–1814),[4] writing during the Qing Empire, was also offering himself as an unappointed advisor to the conquerors of his day, who were busy in Mongolia and Turkestan. When he mused upon the demises of empires based in China from Han (203 BCE–220 CE) to Ming (1368–1644), like most traditional scholars in China, he found moral issues fundamental because the ethical condition of the ruler determined the fate of the empire. But he departed from some earlier thinkers—notably Wang Fuzhi 王夫之 (1619–92),[5] who lived through the demise of the Ming and conquest by the Qing in the seventeenth century—who attributed the essence of empire to the ability to demarcate and expand a zone of "civilization" (*wenhua* 文化). In contrast, for Zhao (and this was a necessity, because he wrote under the rule of ostensibly "foreign" and politically sensitive Manchus), imperial vitality was a matter of proper economic management and wise military ventures as much as a matter of the defining and defending civilization. He did not come very close to Montesquieu's suggestion that empire was largely a production of image, gesture, and ritual, but he was far removed from the positions of Gibbon and Wang that imperial vitality depended on cultural coherence and moral stability. In English-language writing on "empire" and in Chinese-language writing on something cognate to "empire" through at least the late twentieth century,[6] views such as those of Gibbon and Wang Fuzhi associating empire with cultural transformation and the trajectories of civilization prevailed over views such as those of Montesquieu and Zhao Yi that large-scale political orders are at base delicate managerial regimes integrating economic and military power, on one hand, with conjurings of heritage and morality, on the other.[7]

Studies of local deviation from imperial prescription and persistence of folk traditions, as well as the tensions between contemporary identity concepts and those imposed by future historians, are too rich to sustain the former simplifications (Keay and Terrenato 2001; Lewis 2009; Pitts and Versluys 2014; Shelach-Lavi 2015). Nevertheless, the assumption that empires have something to do with inculcating culture still controls our discourse. To the extent that we incorporate a role for illusion in these matters, we consider it—as did Montesquieu—as contemporaneously generated by the rulers or the state that answered to them. This essay is not a consideration of the mirages emanating from imperial performance and representation, shaping public perception of authority, dominion, and identity in its own time; these were suggested by Montesquieu and are a fundamental part of our modern studies of "empire" (e.g., Cherniavsky 1969; Necipoglu 1991; Kafadar 1995; Wortman 2000; Crossley 1999; Kołodziejczyk 2012). The question here is the importance of retrospective attribution of cultural and moral transformations to past empires on the basis of conditions in their own time, but in response to the ideological and strategic requirements of later regimes.

■ LOOKING FOR THE MATRICAL "EMPIRES"

As a rhetorical matter, we make Julius and his adopted heir, Augustus Caesar, the emblems of the transition to empire, remembering that in later centuries *caesar* in various forms *(kaisar, kayser, czar/tsar, geser)* would equate with what we might otherwise call an emperor (Crossley 1999, 221–44; Bang and Kolodziejczyk 2012, 1–41). Yet, in his lifetime, Julius Caesar was not an emperor or anything like it, and when he attempted to seize powers that we would now call imperial, he was murdered through a conspiracy of senators. He was one moment in the long history of social tension, ambitions for wealth, factional infighting, and regional competition that wore the republic away from the inside, while a succession of ambitious men tried various kinds of oligarchy, dictatorship, and military coups to concentrate more and more power in the hands of, ultimately, a single man. By 27 BCE, Augustus (then Octavian) rose above a threshold in that process and became emperor *(imperator)* in name, but until the third century, the rulership was still meandering toward our understanding of "emperor"—increasingly elevated in ritual and rhetoric, increasingly overt in the assertion of personal power over aristocrats, soldiers, senators, and commoners. Forceful suppression of large-scale conflict, what the Romans as well as we now refer to as "Pax Romana," was sustained in the empire for roughly two centuries. But ultimately the regime's authority weakened in its provinces, and its borders were violated and obliterated by formerly subject or at least subdued peoples, all of them assimilated to some Roman institutions, all of them eager to seize the imperial mantle of *caesar* for themselves.

The Roman transition to empire does not very well fulfill the criteria of our modern construction of conscious, overt, strongly ideological state transformation—something along the lines of Tony Judt's (2015, 247) comment that "for an empire to be born, a republic must die"—but the transition from Zhou to Qin, completed in China in 221 BCE, very nearly does. It featured the concentration of power in the hands of a single ruler, building his regime by systematically undermining the power of the regional aristocrats who, for two millennia at the least, had ruled their distinct regions of what is now northern China. Moreover, the process was accompanied by the widening influence of the Legalist school of political thought, which overtly legitimated the destruction of the traditional elites and the imposition of an ostensibly impartial and inflexible legal code to assure uniform administration, dispute resolution, and punishment. The new ruler was the *huangdi* 皇帝, not the king (*wang* 王) of earlier times. The Han dynasts who seized power from Qin in 203 BCE retained the basic institutions and territory, though they adapted them to achieve greater stability by accommodating the interests of the extended imperial family (with princes enfeoffed on their own lands) and participation of regional elites. Eventually, their own regime saw an increase in the interlocking developments of internal fracture and foreign invasion—after which its authority weakened in its provinces, and its borders were violated or obliterated by formerly subject or at least subdued peoples, all of them assimilated to some Han institutions, all of them eager to seize the imperial mantle of *huangdi* for themselves.

We often assume the coincidence of the refinement of the authority of an emperor with a well-defined territory under his authority. But it may have been sufficient for the emperor to be recognized by the ruling classes near the capital or in irregular clusters farther away, and for them to radiate some symbolic representation of that refracted authority to their inferiors. In the Roman case, it is this idea of refracted authority that is implicit in the term *imperium*. It meant discretion to act as an agent of the state by mobilizing troops or meting out death to misbehavers and was usually part of the description of a government office. One might assume that in the Chinese case, Legalist prescriptions for elimination of aristocratic authority would mean imposition of direct imperial rule, at least at the level of the early administrative districts. The institutions designed to do this in Qin—county magistrates; standardization of law, weights, measures, roads; centralization of tax collection, military management, and projects such as expanding the Great Wall, as examples—are very well known. In the subsequent Han period, magistrates had something corresponding to *imperium,* which was their delegated authority to direct troops and to judge crimes, sentence the convicted to death, and oversee execution of the sentence. In both the Roman and Han cases, the central government used the right of appeal as a means of monitoring local judicial activity and spotting abuses that were otherwise obscured in the hazy area between stipulations and real practice. The geographical extent of each empire could be understood as the limits to which this refracted authority could in theory be extended—not the reach of an ascribed imperial culture. Each of these regimes subscribed to the fiction of uninterrupted spatial designation and dominion, sometimes drawing an edge of that dominion by erecting a stela implying not only a point of customs duty but a solid rim of sovereignty on one side of the monument. But the degree to which power was exercised by the state within these spaces is not determined by any legal code or imperial edict. It was determined by the ecology of presence.

This was partly a matter of the relative magnitudes of state on one side and society on the other. I am not providing here a definition of the state, but I would point out that I am not suggesting that a state consists of nothing but power negotiation between classes, even if I am suggesting that as the proximate origination point of the illusion of ancient imperial cultural hegemony (an issue very distinct from the "state" in my view). That is, I am not intending to contribute here to issues associated with Michael Mann (who has consciously eschewed Eurasia) or James Scott (e.g., Mann 2010; Scott 2010). There seems good reason to describe both Rome and Han as more specific than their predecessor regimes had been in designating government officials as distinct from society. We see this manifestly when looking down the tube of historical documentation—regulations, edicts, salary schedules, the occasional surviving list of taxpayers or statement of actual expenditures—but regardless of the degree of detail we can bring to a description of any ancient office, our ability to actually place these actors on the ground in any specific numbers is weak or missing (Niaz 2014). We can use the similarities of Rome and Han to estimate rough relative magnitudes of state presence. Likely because of their temperate-zone placement and their roots in Eurasia's Iron Age, they were comparable in size, population, state income and expenditure, and military power.[8] Han reached its greatest expansion in the early first century BCE and Rome in the first century CE, with Han claiming about 6 million square kilometers and Rome about 5 million. At the point of greatest expansion, by present convention, we heuristically attribute a population of about 60 million people to each empire. Each had a capital city with a population assumed to have been more than a million people. Their estimated daily caloric intake was about the same (2,100–2,200 calories), their revenue was about the same, and their estimated expenditures were about the same (Scheidel 2015, 150–80). Given the material similarities in the claimed space and population under the control of Rome and Han, the commonly accepted estimates of their civil state sizes are in bizarre contrast. In Roman studies, Keith Hopkins offered the famous estimate of one civil official per 350,000–400,000 people. That suggests about 150 civil officials for the entire empire. The Roman system was notoriously top heavy in compensation and documentation, leaving a question of how many undocumented lowly officials were involved in administration; the amounts spent each year by Rome on its officials could hardly have been absorbed by only a few hundred officials. There is something wrong with this figure, which Hopkins himself noted (Hopkins 1980; 2002). First, the total population of the empire cannot be confidently fixed. In Hopkins's view, it could have been 30 million or it could have been 120 million, which means that even on the "four hundred thousand" axiom, civil officials could have totaled seventy-five or three hundred. But a comparison to the accepted figures for Han suggests another problem.

There is every reason to regard Han as the largest and most well-defined civil government of its era; for centuries after, in China itself, there was probably not another government to equal it in this regard. Specialists have found certain kinds of documentary justification for estimates of 120,000–150,000 officials in annual service, of which we might consider the following examples: a passage in the imperial history (*Hou Han shu* 後漢書) for the year 5 BCE that states that from the prime minister down to the lowly "transcribers," there were 120,285 men; Michael Loewe's magnification of numbers from a set of documents detailing the administration of Donghai Commandary in what is now Shandong province, suggesting a total of 150,000 civil officials (Loewe 1967; Bielenstein 1980);[9] or a reference, found in chapter (卷) 67, to "more than 30,000" students entering the imperial academy (太學) in a single year.[10] The obvious possibility of scribal error aside, there are problems of contextualization; there is no cumulative series of statistics on Han officials. The *Hou Han shu* total for 5 BCE is an orphan number, stuck into a passage detailing salary ranks; the source supplies no categorically similar figures from any other year for comparison. Loewe's numbers apply to one of the earliest and most densely populated of the Han commandaries; in a period in which the number of commandaries was falling and their configurations in size and population were tending toward irregularity, there is no obligation to regard the figures as representative. With regard to the imperial academy, other passages in the imperial history make clear that, except for the Wang Mang period, the academy normally hosted a few hundred to a few thousand men (Wang 1949, 152). The *Hou Han shu* suggests that this "more than 30,000" in the first century was an extraordinary occasion (the appointment of a new director, in fact) and uses the term "of various kinds" to describe the group, who are being "transferred"; there is nothing to indicate that all or most of the students were headed for the civil service or were not already serving.

The most obvious explanation for the discrepancy of state size estimates between Rome and Han is also the most significant. My standard here of full-time civil officials selected and paid by the central government as a way of limning state against society is heuristic; there is not a great deal in Han or Roman documentation that allows an estimate of this kind to be made, and I presume that is because such a description does not apply well to the actual conditions of Han or Roman civil officialdom. Han may have recorded every part-time or even expectant appointee as an official, whereas Rome may have left undocumented a very large number of occasionally employed local literate men. The practices, I would suggest, were so widely variant because in each empire, there was a hazy, patchily attested reserve of qualified local men who could be drawn on as needed, whether for routine tasks such as moving the mail or collecting customs duties or for special road, river, or irrigation projects; for popular relief in the event of famine or flood; or for recording the number of taxpayers (which in writing about Chinese history is sometimes referred to as a "census").[11] These large and to us only awkwardly classifiable semi-professional regional populations constituted a littoral state, embedded in local elites, and invocable for service by a successful empire.

The resources sustaining this littoral state (and supporting the small successor states of these empires) were local and private and predated the imposition of imperial control; the localities were not dependent on the empire, but the illusion of imperial cultural sponsorship was dependent on the localities. There was tribute to be paid, but before the empires, local magnates had demanded tribute anyway; diversion of some portion of the proceeds to the capital could not have been of great interest to those supplying the products and cash at the point of collection. When we look back at these empires, we see, saliently, documents on the institutions of emperorship, law, the military, regulating offices such as the Roman Senate or the Han censors (Qin and earlier Han *yushi* 御史), and local administration through sorts of governorships and magistracies. These documents constitute the refracting lens through which the images of past "empires" is, in our reading, generated. On the ground, Rome and

Han as cultural or moral entities were, in all likelihood, notional outside of the capital or the cities that were the base of provincial government.[12] As a matter of numbers, I would guess that one in a couple of thousand people in the Roman or Han empire had a chance of encountering a civil official—a much, much greater chance for those living in the capital and a vastly smaller chance for those living any distance from it.

It is certainly credible that Han may have had a full-time professional civil bureaucracy two or even ten (not hundreds or thousands of) times the size of Rome's. By the later Han period, the number of commandaries had fallen to thirteen for the domestic territories and a few more planted in Korea, Vietnam, and the transitions to Central Asia. Below the level of the commandaries were a few more than eighteen hundred counties of several varieties, each of which had a civil magistrate and a military intendant. There were also numerous inspectors traveling between the commandaries, the counties, and the capital, but overall, it is difficult to come up with a total of civil officials outside the capital that would have come anywhere close to fifteen thousand. I assume that both in the Roman and Han cases, there were many more officials within the capital than without, and if we assume twice as many in the capital as in the provinces, we would have a total of thirty thousand to forty-five thousand active full-time officials selected and paid by the central government. That has the virtue of being within range of comparison to later empires based in China, particularly the Ming (1368–1644) and Qing (1636–1912), which made do with about twenty thousand to forty thousand active full-time civil officials,[13] despite being much larger and much more populous than Han.

Whatever dissimilarities Rome and Han had in the size and shape of their civil bureaucracies, their military infrastructures were overwhelmingly the vaster portion of their expenditure. In both empires, full-time soldiers and part-time auxiliaries could be activated for specific campaigns. Roman- and Han-period histories report armies larger than two hundred thousand soldiers—in the Han case, sometimes several times larger—for particular battles, which does not obligate any historian to believe that all or most of the soldiers involved were part of a permanent standing force. Based on its legions and their support troops, in the time of Octavian, Rome's standing armies could have reached a size of somewhere between eight hundred thousand and 1 million men. This is virtually the same as estimates of the standing Han forces a century or so later. In both cases their distribution was, not surprisingly, relative to population and generally inverse to distribution of the civil officials (who were heavily concentrated in the capital). We can make a crude guess that at a minimum, one in sixty (or to make it simple, let us say one in a hundred) persons in the empire experienced the military either as a physical establishment or through enrollment of an associate or family member. The evident reason that the military magnitudes and structures of Rome and Han were so tightly aligned to their territories and populations—and so divorced from the sizes and structures of their civil governments—was that the military presence was in fact the essence of empire. It responded to the overriding strategic necessity for continued intake of resources, and its spatial configuration was governed by the requirements of population. It built and maintained the physical edifices and road systems that suggested imperial power. Its uniforms symbolized the imperial presence, and its weapons inflicted upon the population the punishments that ostensibly followed violation of imperial law. Local populations not being subjected to conquest or coercion had only an abstract awareness of the regime's claim to dominion, and perhaps none. But they knew the meaning of an army, its uniforms, and its weapons. In comparison to the tiny candle of civil and cultural presence of these empires, their military presence is a blazing sun.

Even schoolchildren today will readily acknowledge that Rome and Han were mighty military powers, so this may seem a meaningless observation. But those same schoolchildren will also add that in each case, military force was combined with a transformative civilizing presence, bringing writing, the rule of law, and the ideals of justice to peoples who had not previously enjoyed them. Yet neither of these regimes had sufficient presence in most of the communities it claimed to dominate to have had much impact apart from the intermittent coercions made possible by the presence of a local garrison. Their legal codes, though looking rather uncompromising in our present understanding of them, are known to have been enforced or not enforced in response to a great variety of local circumstances—not least the ability to physically enforce an imperial or magisterial edict. What we call the Roman and Han empires were suspended on trade networks that in many cases predated them and punctuated by military installations vividly branded as imperial.[14] Rome and Han were, at root, corporations of conquest and commercial inducement.

The question of colonies is difficult to negotiate. Rome as a republic conquered the landed rim around the Mediterranean and as an empire maintained and extended its hold. Han expanded the pre-imperial Zhou territories to encompass the water rim comprising the network of rivers originating on the shoulders of the Tibetan Plateau. Both in Roman and in Han history, the sequence of military conquest of distinctly external territory followed by establishment of an occupying military government and subsequent settlement of farmers and merchants is clear. Rome undertook such ventures in central and western Europe, in Britain, in North Africa, and in Syria and Palestine. Han undertook similar ventures in what is now south China, northwest China, Hainan Island, and parts of what are now Korea and Vietnam. But colonization rapidly become dependent on the agenda of either existing elites in the new territories or the wishes of elites based in the imperial territories to expand their wealth or political leverage to the frontiers. In some cases, continued occupation was not viable because neither local nor migrating elites saw it in their interest to govern or develop the new territories. In others, the willingness of local elites to subscribe to the imperial framework created a foundation for indirect rule, federation or vassalage. In still others, imperial elites migrated to conquered territories as landowners and governors.[15] The longevity of any colony appears to have been determined by two factors: the willingness of the central government to expend its resources to support as much military force as needed at any particular time and the willingness of colonial elites (whether native or immigrated) to participate in the ostensibly imperial networks of wealth, information, and social exchange. This is a description of Rome and Han as ephemeral webs, only as stable as their ability to maintain and occasionally expand a military infrastructure and to cling to the affiliations of local elites. When the old networks of which they were composed were no longer sufficient to provide elites the information and wealth they could get from new networks, the empires were gone.

These early empires were generated and regenerated through the subscription of local elites to the legitimating cues transmitted by very scarce civilian officials and the occasional military spectacle. At the local level, communities were in turn based on preexisting lineage structures and possibly on cultic affiliations, and were linked to other communities by trade networks of long history (Bang 2011, 1–14, 239–89). These empires were regimes of affiliation, in which very widely spaced elites were knit together by rewards from the capital; by reasonably consistent conformity to an acknowledged set of rules or regulations; by effectiveness in gathering, accounting for, and transporting local tribute; by trade and tax policies advantageous to regional wealth; and by a willingness to inspire awe in the local population by the strategic application of terror. Symbols of empire were displayed and venerated by the local agents of empire for one primary reason: the strengthening of their own hand in dealing with the local communities. A written medium (sooner or later acknowledged as "classical"), a style of official dress, and infrequent public displays were the minor manifestations of imperial affiliation that elites affected as part of a program for enhancing and stabilizing their standing. At the root of the illusion of cultural presence and dominion was the ability of the elites—whether in the capital or in the provinces—to employ the imperial army and social hub of the capital for their own advantage; from this engine was emitted the vaporous shapes of cultural and political preeminence of the capital.

The care with which the emperors and their close affiliates cultivated a veneer of deference to elite and aristocratic institutions is striking. In the Roman case, this largely took the form of Octavian and his successors ostentatiously honoring the traditions of Senate governance, while struggling to disembowel the power structures that had once allowed the aristocratic Senate to actually govern Rome. In the Han case, this meant adapting a wide variety of Legalist institutions to the management of its territories, while using the morally charged rhetoric of the political school—in retrospect called "Confucian" in English—that had resisted for centuries the accumulation of power in the hands of a single ruler. In such early examples are seen an enduring characteristic of the phenomena we often lump under "empire": sufficient control over legal writ, public rhetoric, and historical narrative to coerce credulity in contemporary elites. We very often see this as a demand by the emperorship on unwilling elites. If we are limiting ourselves to discussion of relationships between the emperors and elites within a few miles of the capital, the coercive powers of the emperors could indeed have been considerable. But over the huge expanse of the territories claimed by Rome or Han, the coherence of the empire rested primarily on the interest of local elites in using imperial emblems to enhance their own local prestige and to keep themselves connected to networks of exchange that functioned under the protection of the imperial armies. It was these elites who generated cultural change in these empires, even to a degree of language change that we once imagined was catalyzed by imperial prestige or massive population movement. Hegemony of the emperors outside the capital was among the earliest illusions that we bundle under our modern notion of "empire." It was local landowners, aristocrats, shipowners, factory and mine owners, and dominant merchants (not always different people) who were masters of the empires' fates, not the emperors in their capitals.

■ **COLORING INSIDE THE LINES:**
THE AGE OF CONFESSIONAL EMPIRES

The trade and military presences of the empires were contact, and contact is leavening to a culture. Though I am arguing that attributing cultural change in the classical period to imperial control or initiative is unwise, there is no doubt that cultural change happened. The Romance languages of Europe really were produced by the influence of Latin, and the Chinese languages and writing system really did become rooted in the regions where Han dominion was asserted. Latin and Han-period standard Chinese were not, however, language killers; unlike modern global English, or *putonghua* 普通话 in China, they did not overwhelm local vernaculars but contributed to their production. If the impact of the empires on local cultures was as gauzy as I am claiming, the retrospective image of these empires as overwhelming civilizing systems must be explained. I would suggest that the means by which local elites generated a contemporary illusory imperial hegemony in their own time resembled the means by which hegemonic legacies for these empires were generated afterward. The Roman and Han reputations as civilizations may owe their beginnings to subsequent imperial dynasts, among them the Amal lineage of the Goths (circa 350–550) and the Merovingian lineage of the Franks (circa 450–700) in western Europe, the Sima lineage of the Eastern Jin (circa 260–320) and the Yuwen lineage of the Särbi founders of the Northern Wei (circa 390–540) in China. In each case, the aspiring rulers and the aristocrats around them invoked the previous empire not only as the source of their own legitimacy but as a universalizing mechanism for legitimacy across time and space (e.g., Holcombe 1994; Innes 1997; Graves-Brown, Jones, and Gamble 2013). It is probably not irrelevant that in both Europe and China, the new regimes were smallish and alien presences; the Visigoths in Rome and the Särbi in Luoyang had use for vivid and imposing myths of a literally classical empire from which they could claim inheritance (Kang 1995; Heather 2000; Christensen 2002).

These pretensions were occasionally represented through claimed connections to previous ruling dynasties, but much more often they were made by claiming continuity with the morals and institutions of the vanished empire. "Roman law" as venerated in the later Roman Empire of the Franks was an inheritance of a legal code not from Rome but from the civil codes of the fifth- and sixth-century emperors in Byzantium—Theodosius and Justinian—and echoed in the West by the so-called *Lex Visigothorum* (Stein 1999, 60–73). Its terms, processes, concepts of property, and basic notions of civil identities could well have been continuities of the laws of imperial Rome (this is suggested by their debts to the fourth-century Valerian code), but what matters here is the legitimation of the later code by reification of an imperial legacy. There was a cognate process relating to Han imperial law. The written code did not survive the fall of the empire in 220 CE (Wilbur 1943; Hulsewé 1955). But its terms, institutional delineations, principles of property and land rights, and prescriptions for obligations within families were believed to be reproduced in the legal codes of the small empires controlling parts of the former Han domain between about 200 and 600 CE and ultimately in the legal code (which survives) of the Tang Empire that ruled a unified China from circa 600 to 900. It is in these centuries that both the Roman and Han empires as civilizations began to take on solidity in the eyes of rulers and ambitious aristocrats—and of the councilors, secretaries, and historians who served them.

An interesting feature of this era is the establishing of a time dimension that has persisted in notions of legitimacy to the present. That is, a foundation era (I will call it classical) is not only given its own historical narrative but also allowed to survive in a parallel dimension, providing political and social legitimacy as well as moral and aesthetic education to a nominal "present." This was vividly represented in imperial ritual from the fourth century on (particularly as it related to imperial audience) but also in elite dress and language use, monumental arts, cartography, calendrical practices, monetary denominations, historiography, and general education (Mango 1980, 192–93, 219). What elites had read in the Roman or Han eras was classical in the present; the language they had used was universal; what they had worn was formal; what was believed to have been their law was authoritative. Their territories could be drawn in cartographic dimensions and claimed again by their self-appointed heirs. The military legacies of Rome and Han were distinct in some ways from their putative cultural traditions, because for subsequent rulers, the substance of "empire" still lay in the ability to intermittently apply overwhelming force against both soldiers and civilians. Roman military ranks became the basis of aristocratic designations in Europe and Britain. Some Han military ranks had a similar history among the Turkic and Tungusic peoples, who created their own regimes inside or on the periphery of former Han domains. For subsequent infantries, some Roman and Han terms have been perpetuated through their succeeding empires to the present day.

But in the succeeding era, there were new dimensions of universalizing moral missions for rulers and independent platforms for endorsement of the rulership. For convenience, I will call it the age of the confessional empires (a term I am using here in allusion to Hodgson 1974, 137–42), when not all empires were strictly confessional but all tended toward similar structures distinguishing the legitimacy of the ruler from the standing of his compromising peers—whether religious hierarchs, tribal leaders, aristocrats, or military elites. Rulers now sought justification for their conquests and tended to find it in the ostensible revival of fully fledged civilizations attributed to the vanished empires. The new Roman mission—enhanced by the alliance with Christianity—became part of the legitimation narrative of the empires of the Bulgars, the Muscovites, the Carolingians, and the Hapsburgs. The Han mission assumed particularly elaborate form, as the Tang, Song, Ming, and Qing all wrote the histories of their immediate predecessors and, in the introduction, usually invoked the heritage of Han and its championing of the teachings of Confucius as part of the legitimating narrative for themselves (e.g., Crossley 1987, 765).

Byzantium was central in a way earlier Rome had never been. In the East, the later Roman court encountered a model of confessional rulership that, starting from Hindu and Buddhist models and continuing through early Iran, had permeated central Eurasia. Intentionally or unintentionally,[16] Constantine (sometimes refracted in the narrative as his mother Helena) imitated this model by building huge structures of worship on the sites of Christian miracles, starting with the Church of the Holy Sepulchre in Jerusalem. He granted Christian clerics—many of them already deeply committed to Central Asian models of monasticism—the privilege of tax exemption that was consistent with the Central Eurasian tradition of *darkhan* for clerics, military heroes, and aristocrats. The great innovation of the empire in the East was to distribute the sacred mission of the ruler to the entire state. Now it was not the emperor who was *pontifex* but the leader of the Christian church and doctrines taking shape under imperial sponsorship. The church hierarchs, in turn, legitimated the emperor, in the way that Ašoka was claimed to have been legitimated by the Buddhist *saṅgha*. Iranian, Indian, Roman, and Greek practices—monarchical presentation, architecture, monasticism and scholasticism, dual court systems both secular and religious, and militarized aristocracy among them—produced a new imperial style of continental conquest in the service of a spiritual mission to convert humanity to the true religion.

The reasons for the explosion of dyarchic confessional regimes across Eurasia between the fourth and eleventh centuries are complex, but of interest here is the ability of these states to significantly change their ecology of presence. That the Sassanian (before Islam, a Zoroastrian confessional empire) and Byzantine empires escalated their official pieties in competition with each other is clear enough, and the model they set was rapidly adopted by the rising Islamic state. But it is worth considering a more fundamental logistical imperative: with rising populations, improved transportation, and increased urbanization across the continent, united domains the size of Rome and Han could have been managed only with improved state presence and greater state influence over local communities. None had the bureaucratic infrastructure, the literacy rates, or the revenue to significantly increase their civil presence, but clerics were a good substitute (so good that we now call civil functionaries by their name). In addition to garrison commanders, governors, and magistrates, Byzantine dominion was upheld by its priests and their cooptation of traditional religious practices that had helped bind communities together.

The Byzantine administrative model was the inspiration for the separate political order and its diverging Latin religious hierarchy at Rome after the mid-sixth century. It was also visible in the design of the Abbasid caliphate, which seized power from the Umayyads in 750. At Baghdad, the *khalifah* was the highest religious authority and the head of state in one, but secular power—*sulṭān,* which meant what *imperium* had meant in earlier Rome—was recognized as distinct in function and, ultimately, both in office and person; by the time of the emergence of the Seljuk regime in the late tenth century, *sultan* would be a term for the secular ruler legitimated by a caliph whether proximate or distant. Though the Islamic world of the time had no clerics as a class, its tendency to convert congregations *(millah)* into administrative units provided the Abbasids and their secessionist/successor regimes the same benefits as clerics in terms of government on the ground. Buddhism, Christianity, and Islam in all their sectarian richness still brought with them standardized written languages with pedagogical texts and schooling methods, communication networks among monastic or congregational centers, and—with the proselytizing mission—straight paths into the spiritual and cultic life of local communities, which earlier "empires" had left largely untouched by design.

Ideologically impelled regimes tending toward dyarchic legitimation/protection roles could be produced from the fundamental effects of logistical demands on a continent with rising populations and more elaborate systems of information exchange, but specific institutions could clearly also be spread by contact. An empire like the Tang in China, not a confessional regime in the Byzantine sense, was affected over time by the general influences producing dyarchic empires across the continent. Tang was in close contact with Tibet—an empire with a confessionalist and dyarchic orientation from the time of King Songtsen Gyompo (died not later than 649)—and knew also the Abbasid caliphate, which led an alliance that defeated Tang at the Talas River in 751. Like its predecessor Sui (581–618), Tang adopted the Chinese institution of emperorship but modified it to satisfy expectations of the Tang imperial lineage for influence, producing a mid- and late-Tang dyarchic relationship between throne and military aristocracy. This was interwoven with a political struggle in early Tang that largely revolved around the question of whether a strong emperorship based primarily on Chinese imperial tradition or a significant element of Central Asian corporate rule based on the interventions of the aristocracy would prevail. Temporary resolutions in favor of the Chinese emperorship were punctuated by dissent from elites among the aristocracy, the military, and, occasionally, landowners.

Moreover, Tang had its own ideological resources legitimating its rulers. From the earliest Tang period, the emperor had been a patron of *mahāyāna* Buddhist clergy, who legitimated him as an Ašoka-style conqueror (*čakvravartin*) bringing enlightenment to humanity.[17] In the mid-eighth century, not long after the Tang loss to the Abbasids, the court was challenged by Turkic and Sogdian elites at court and in the army; when the rebels were defeated, the process of ideological realignment began, culminating in dissolution of the Buddhist monasteries in the mid-ninth century. The result was not a robustly centralized rulership on the early Han model but a compromised rulership and effective control by regional elites. The court became a sponsor of archly self-conscious Confucianism (at the time, *daoxue* 道學) and began to style itself as the champion of Confucian rectitude in eastern Eurasia; its system of written examinations for selection of officials cemented the ideological mission to the bureaucracy and disseminated it to local communities, a parallel to the function of ideology and a clerical class on the western side of the continent.

In the Byzantine model particularly, the imaginal metamorphosis from the conquests of old Rome for wealth and territory to the new universal, divine mission to bring humanity under the rule of God was critical. What Rome could not establish in its own time it gained through the Byzantine and, later Frankish, incarnations of "Rome"—the empire existed not only for conquest but for the education and, ultimately, the salvation of humanity. It was not armies alone but written languages, churches, temples or mosques, schools, liturgies, vestments, histories, and doctrines that nurtured conquest. These devices not only permitted a less superficial—if not particularly deep—penetration of local life and a modest assault on local self-sufficiency but also created an additional facility for imperial manipulation of local elites. Aristocrats championing Mithraism in Anatolia or Bön in Tibet or Wodenism in Germany or Zoroastrianism in Iran could be marginalized and induced to submit to the imperially sponsored doctrine. Their wealth could be partly diverted into religious institutions as a show of their good faith. This model of universal, ideologically partnered empire—not merely emperorship—was compelling enough that competing regimes adopted it of necessity. The remaining Umayyads in Spain and North Africa needed a caliphate of their own to resist the universal authority of the Abbasids in Baghdad. The Khazars legitimated themselves with Judaism, the Bulgars after a struggle became warriors on behalf of Orthodox Christianity, and the Göktürk Empire attempted to raise its traditional shamanism to the level of an imperially coded legitimating ideology. And though the late-period Tang court had turned away from Buddhism to Confucianism, the courts of Korea, Tibet, Vietnam, and Japan continued to use Buddhist hierarchs to endorse their rulerships.

Though the advantages of these new tools to these empires seem obvious, military conquest and occupation remained their fundamental business. Eastern Rome, Sassanian Iran, and the Bulgar khaghanate struggled continually for territories at their mutual interfaces, while Abbasid, Göktürk, Tibet, and Tang traded hard-won expanses of Central Asia. And at the heart of the enterprises of conquest and occupation still stood the elites who constituted the empires and decided their fates. Militarized aristocracies were an ancient phenomenon all over Eurasia, but the rise of massive infantries in Rome and Han times had partly attenuated the aristocratic grip on military action. With the introduction of larger horses, better steel, and chain mail—all of which originated in Central Asia and spread outward to the better-populated temperate peripheries of Europe and East Asia—the aristocracy slightly enlarged its military participation. But as always, the investment of aristocrats, landowners, and large merchants in imperial militarism was premised on their ability to profitably supply the resources and claim a portion of the reward.

The huge scale of conquest attracted large numbers of mercenaries, often from geographically marginal territories. Normans, Varangians, and Turks were most prominent among the populations drawn into the struggles, and the importance of religious conversion in ratifying their roles in the conquest states intensified the association of divine mission with profitable military employment. By the twelfth century, the effects of the cultural battles fundamental to the internal centralization and external expansion of the confessional empires was evident. Religious agents were ubiquitous in the cities and countryside. Familiarity with liturgical languages in addition to local vernaculars was high in the religious networks, and very basic literacy was rising. Communities were often understood as religious congregations, and their hierarchies were either endorsed or partly controlled by provincial religious authorities. Travel and transportation systems mapped well over both religious and market centers. Late in the period, "crusades" tamed areas where popular religion or recalcitrant aristocrats challenged the extension of confessional authority.

When the confessional empires faded or broke apart in internecine struggle, their presences were often perceived as lingering in new codes of cultural affiliation. Now, war could be conducted in the name of faith, instead of exclusively in the name of the emperor, his dynasty, or his notional earthly domain. And like the mimetics of imperiality that followed the demise of Rome and Han, the fuel of the illusion was the interests of the landed gentry, new or old aristocracies, political elites, and merchants. In some places—most vividly in Song (970–1279) China—military expansion was accompanied by the emergence of a robust centrally controlled bureaucracy, strong enough to modestly contain the traditional role of the aristocracy and landowners in local administration yet as dependent on a civilizational justification for domestic expropriation and frontier wars as its contemporary regimes in Eurasia. For these rising orders, the constructed legacies of Rome, Han, and the Umayyad caliphate were the sources of neoclassical institutions of law, scholasticism, and the arts. But these institutional legacies were now bonded with the much later cargo of language, religion, and civic virtues supplied by the centuries of dyarchic mutual legitimation between hierarchical religion (or, in the case of Song China, moral philosophy) and military force.

■ MONARCHISM AND HERITAGE

Though there is much for which historians do not forgive the Mongols, the destruction of or fatal challenges to the confessional empires is the transgression most relevant to the present discussion. The Mongols were not in any way secularists, but most of the time they directed their interpretations of divinely derived legitimacy—the idea that Blue Heaven, or Tengri, consistently supported the Chinggisid lineage against its enemies, whether foreign or domestic—to the cultic elites associated with Chinggis-related sacrifices and in indirect forms to cooperative elites in subject territories. From Chinggis's time on, the Mongol rulers tended to deflect appeals from representatives of institutionalized religions hoping to gain the sponsorship of the Mongol rulers. When politically expedient, they may have adopted an indulgent stance toward regionally influential religious organizations, or they assumed the pose (in individual cases, it might have been more than that) of patron. But confessionalist dyarchism was dying as the Mongols rose, and where it lingered, it was killed off by individual Mongol regimes.[18]

This was demonstrated nowhere, perhaps, as well as in battles over Syria and Palestine. Though the Mongols of the Kipchak Horde were nominally Sunni Muslims and the Il-khans in Baghdad were by the late thirteenth century inclining, if without passion, toward Islam of one sect or another, their enmity toward each other split the Muslim world several different ways. The Il-khans bore the stain of having destroyed the Abbasid caliph as well as his caliphate. When, even after their defeat at 'Ayn Jalût in 1260, they continued for half a century their attempts to seize parts of Mamluk Syria, Muslim scholars—most famously Taqî ad-Dîn Aḥmad ibn Taymiyyah—declared that war against the Muslim regime in Baghdad was justified and in fact obligatory (Elverskog 2011, 143–44). The mere fact that the Il-khan rulers were Mongols was not sufficient to earn ibn Taymiyyah's condemnation; the Il-khans were indicted while the Mongols of the Golden Horde were not referred to in the *fatawa*. It was the religious pluralism of the Il-khans that ibn Taymiyyah rejected, their tendency to place their rulership above religious sanction and to tolerate Nestorian Christians, Jews, and all sects of Islam (except the Ismailis), while keeping their Mongol occupying force subject to the laws attributed to Chinggis. The Il-khans, like their close allies the Mongol Yuan rulers of China, were monarchists—not the dyarchists who had dominated medieval Eurasia. Their empires had no pretensions to do much more than enforce a regime of extraction. Those willing to surrender tribute and make no trouble for the occupiers were generally left in peace—including the peace to pursue the religion of their choice.

With the exception of the Kipchak Horde and a few minor regimes, the Mongol empires were gone by 1400, and the process of their repudiation by their successors had begun. But some Mongol conquest institutions persisted. This could take the form, as among the Timurids, of according preeminence to the Chinggisid lineage or association with it; or of retention and sponsorship of the mathematical, astronomical, and cartographic academies of the Mongol period, as in Iran, China, and, later, Uzbekistan and India; or of retention of the Mongol reconfiguration of political geography, as in China and Iran (and Russia, if the privileging of the Nevskii family is regarded as a feature of Mongol rule); or of retention of Mongol military terminology and practice, as in China, Iran, and Russia. But perhaps the most important legacy of the Mongol period was that the largest continental empires of the early modern period—Romanov Russia, Qing, Ottoman, and Mughal—continued to work on the Mongol principle of tiny governments and massive outsourcing of civil functions to aristocrats, large landowners, and, occasionally, very wealthy merchants (Skrynnikov 1986; Lincoln 2007; Dai 2009). In the case of the Ottomans, this was not a direct inheritance from the Mongols but more likely a parallel response to the exigencies of small conquering populations ruling over dense agricultural economies. One result was the tenuous position of the rulers in relation to their own lineage, to bureaucratic factions, and to military, landowning, and commercial elites. The monarchical rulerships of the early modern period were constantly challenged and constantly focused on centralizing administration, containing the privilege of compromising forces in the aristocracy or the clergy, and finding increasingly grand justifications for magnification of the ruler's power. In such an environment, for empires such as the Qing and Ottoman—and Romanov Russia in its own way—the need to incarnate classical or morally universal civilizations was stronger than ever (Hingley 1996; Tezscan 2011). These rulerships drew their mandates not from religious hierarchs in their own time but from the ascribed scope and character of their predecessor regimes, and over the centuries, they provided the greatest elaborations to the myth of civilizational dependence on empire. Among other overland empires, similar pressures—increased by rivalry—produced similar adherence to civilizational vectors of empire, while European imperialism in the domains of the old empires produced new myths of civilizational succession. As a result, apologists for the European and, later, American empires produced both the "civilizing mission" rhetoric that is well known and the curatorial ethos underlying modern anthropology and connoisseurship.

The early modern empires had tools that had never been available to the classical or confessional empires. The scholastic traditions of the confessional age became the foundation of imperial control over academic rhetoric and historical narrative. Historiographies retained their strong religious inflection, implying divine missions for conquerors and conquest empires, a style that required self-sanctification even in empires, such as the Qing, with no overtly theological orientation, or in neoconfessionalist emperorships (where the monarch claimed unilateral leadership of the rite and universal dominion over subjects outside the traditional confessional community), such as the Ottoman, Timurid, or Russian empires.[19] More important, printing and a concomitant rise in functional literacy disseminated imperial historical narrative in vernacular languages over a far vaster portion of the population than had been possible before. Consequently, all the empires consciously promoted printing (though in the Islamic world, there was some resistance to using it for religious texts),[20] and the pace of development was loosely correlated with the imperial demand for historical justification regarding their righteous struggles against rival empires. The growing size of infantries and development of military education provided another venue for inculcation of distinct cultural orientations and the importance of the imperial mission in protecting and advancing their particular civilizations. And it was not irrelevant that in the eighteenth and nineteenth centuries, diplomatic contacts, economic rivalries, and wars for expansion heightened the perceptions of identity and distinction among religious and linguistic groups, warping them around the military infrastructures and imperial rituals of the day. The early modern empires could employ representation technologies that allowed them to effect the most profound alterations in their ecologies of presence and the most vivid amalgamations of empire and civilization for both domestic and international audiences.

The continental empires of Russia, Ottoman, and Qing each put a high priority on the pluralistic representation of the monarchy, a style I have described elsewhere as "simultaneous" and distinguished from syncretic or cosmopolitan projects of rule (Cherniavsky 1969; Burke 1992; Kafadar 1995; Crossley 1999; Garthwaite 2006; Newman 2008; Kołodziejczyk 2012). As distinct cultural zones were absorbed in conquest, the local elites were bonded to the rulership through codification and incorporation of their histories—their orthographies would be prominently displayed, their emblems of rule would become part of imperial ritual, their religions would be invoked as divine resources of the emperors and their conquests, and their histories would be narrated under the sponsorship of the court. Effectiveness in binding the elites to the imperial lineage depended on sustaining discrete and recognizable personae within the rulership, not in blurring or creatively mixing elements familiar to one or another segment of the population. In ritual, imperial writ, and architecture, the emperors became incarnations of the ancient rulers of civilizations to which the identities of elites in the present could be cemented. The height of these simultaneous styles in the eighteenth century coincided with the climax of the struggles of these rulerships to neutralize the political standing of these same elites, apace with the glorification of their ascribed heritages.

The contemporary importance of symbolic solidarity with elites whose power the rulers intended to erode was illegible to—and useless to—later nationalists who saw the empires as having an entirely different meaning. From the early twentieth century, historians looked back to find that the Qing were considered "Confucian," and their Manchu, Mongolian, and various Buddhist personae were dismissed. The Romanovs became "Russian," their German, Cossack, Byzantine, and various Central Asian personae forgotten. The Ottomans became "Turks," overshadowing their claim to the Roman–Byzantine emperorship and universalist rule over Christians in Greece and the Balkans. For the nationalist, successor republics, the myth that the great empires had bequeathed to them defining (and monolithic) civilizational endorsement was an essential tool in their own internal and external representations.

Over the past two thousand years and a little more, ecologies of state presence have changed as radically as the natural environment. In the classical period, "empires" had minimal or no civil presence in most of the space they claimed outside their capitals. In the confessional era, they found a way to connect to local communities through management of a vast religious and small civil network but remained superficial as civil presences. In the early modern era, they acquired access to individual indoctrination through the beginnings of popular education, mass military conscription, and the printing of gazetteers and newspapers. At that point, the argument for civilizing empire and the media through which the argument was promulgated were identical phenomena. The intensification of the imaginal bond between civilization and empire in the early modern and modern periods was connected to—and reinforced by—additional factors. I have suggested here that the true coherence of the trade and cultural exchange networks on which the emblems of empire had always been suspended was generated by local elites and their perceptions of the degree to which imperial affiliation was beneficial to the stability and enhancement of their wealth. The strategies of imperial representation were in all eras based on a need to accommodate regional and local elite interests, while at the same time struggling to increase central power and contain interference from aristocrats and local magnates (the imperial dynamics that impressed Montesquieu and Zhao Yi). Early modern rulers acquired new struggles against external rivals competing at their borders for resources and the favor of local elites; claiming legitimation for the imperial lineage and the extended imperial court by virtue of unique connections to imperial predecessors was a critical advantage (particularly in an age when inculcating the public in such ideas was newly possible). Finally, national republics found value in adding their own layer to these myths of retrospective legitimation, as they sought criteria for political enfranchisement within and justified expansion without. In the early twentieth century, the narrative that empires had, as Gibbon had described it, caused disparate local cultures to "insensibly coalesce into one great nation" was irresistible, the probabilities of actual history notwithstanding.

Pamela Kyle Crossley is the Collis Professor of History at Dartmouth College. She is author of *The Wobbling Pivot: China since 1800, an Interpretive History* (2010), *What Is Global History?* (2008), *A Translucent Mirror: History and Identity in Qing Imperial Ideology* (1999), *The Manchus* (1997), and *Orphan Warriors: Three Manchu Generations and the End of the Qing World* (1990). She is also coauthor of *The Earth and Its Peoples* (5th ed., 2012) and *Global Society* (3rd ed., 2012).

■ NOTES

For useful reading suggestions over many years, I want to thank Gene Garthwaite, Yü Ying-shih, Charles Wood, Susan Reynolds, David O. Morgan, Peter Bang, Christopher Bayly, and Dominic Lieven and, for comments on this draft, Naomi Standen and Carl Estabrook. The *Verge: Studies in Global Asias* referees have also been invaluable, and I am very grateful for their suggestions. All remaining errors of fact or interpretation are my own.

1. My characterizations of Gibbon's ideas are drawn, when not otherwise indicated, from Gibbon (1782).

2. This is a reference to *De l'esprit des lois,* in which Montesquieu made the point by indicating the antiaristocratic missions of the short-lived Qin and Sui empires in China, whose history he had absorbed from a redaction by Jean-Baptiste du Halde. See Secondat (1748, livre VIII, chapitre VI, "De la corruption du principe de la monarchie").

3. For example, see Trevor-Roper (2010) and Krause (2001).

4. Zhao Yi's most famous historical work is "Notes on the Twenty-Two Histories" (Zhao 1795)—that is, the imperial histories of twenty-two dynasties. See also Tu (1943) and Man-cheong (2004, 71–74).

5. Wang's insistence that the past has no inherent qualities of its own but that present circumstances appear to reveal features of the past to modern observers has suggested to some scholars that he is comparable to early modern European hermeneuticists. See Wright (2000), Teng (1968), and Black (1989).

6. From Han through Qing, imperially generated documents occasionally referred to the regime as "the Great 大 [Han, Tang, Ming, Qing, etc.]"; government or the imperial court were indicated by "our court" (*wo chao* 我朝 or *benchao* 本朝) and the emperor as *huangdi* 皇帝. The word *guo* 國—sometimes following the dynastic designation—was used in documents of the imperial period to mean variously "nation," "lineage," "tribe," "people," "state," or "country." An early discussion was Levenson (1952); more recently, see Gang (2006).

7. On Victorian elaboration of the Roman imperial heritage, see Hingley (1996).

8. For general discussion of the similarities, see the work of Walter Scheidel cited throughout this essay as well as the introduction to Nylan and Vankeerberghen (2015).

9. The imperial history (*Hou Han shu* [Tables of officials of the hundred ranks] 百官公卿表上, part 1, chapter 39), referring to the year 5 BCE, comments 吏員自佐史至丞相十二萬二百八十五人.

10. Other studies of Chinese local administration for Qin and Han

offer similar estimates but often use different methods of deriving them. See particularly Yen (1961; 1963) and Chang (2006).

11. For the problems of defining literacy in Han society, as well as determining the degrees of literacy (if any) needed for various kinds of government service, see Nylan (2000) and Giele (2006). I am indebted to my reviewer for the latter suggestion.

12. With respect to the Roman Empire, there is a very well-developed body of scholarship and interpretation based on this theme. See Barrett (1997, 51–66) and Mattingley (2013).

13. While we have detailed information on the payment of officials for many eras, guessing the general total at any point in time is a sport, most often conducted in verbal presentation and debate. Estimates normally range from fifteen thousand to forty thousand full-time centrally appointed and paid civil officials for the Qing, with the most likely number being around thirty thousand.

14. See also the discussion supporting the comment in Terranato (2008, 239) that "in short, when we look at the culture of the Roman Empire beyond the common data-sets and assumptions, it is hard to describe the process as one of straightforward diffusion of the same universal structure from a centre."

15. This process has been made partly visible by the innovative research of Chang (2007, 59–68), in which the magnified role of aristocrats and gentry in the armies and in the new colonial administration in Hexi is illuminated.

16. See also Bang (2012, 60–75) on the tendency of universalizing rulers (in the Seleucid case) to seek legitimation through submitted elites, producing a variegated imperial presentation in the Greek-speaking world owing a certain amount to acknowledgment of the traditions of Iran and of northern India.

17. In his own time, Ašoka expressed himself in terms of solidarity with the Buddhist community, rather than as their instrument, or as a monarch devoted—in his political person—to any individual religion. See Thapar (1966, 70–75). For uses of the *čakvravartin* ideal in Mongol and Manchu political orders, see Crossley (1999).

18. Modern historians often credit Gibbon with the description of the religious policies of the Mongols as "tolerant," evidently on the strength of this passage: "The Catholic inquisitors of Europe, who defended nonsense by cruelty, might have been confounded by the example of a Barbarian, who anticipated the lessons of philosophy, and established by his laws a system of pure theism and perfect toleration" (LXIV, para. 3). See also Khazanov (1993), Deweese (1994, 90–102), Atwood (2004), and Jackson (2005).

19. For an examination of a similarly described process in additional Muslim empires of the period, see Dale (2011, 77–106).

20. On printing in the Islamic world, see Roper (1999), Boogert (2005), Gencer (2010, 178), and Redman (2010).

■ **WORKS CITED**

Atwood, Christopher. 2004. "Validation by Holiness or Sovereignty: Religious Toleration as Political Theology in the Mongol World Empire of the Thirteenth Century." *International History Review* 26, no. 2: 237–56.

Bang, Peter Fibiger. 2011. *The Roman Bazaar: A Comparative Study of Trade and Markets in a Tributary Empire.* Cambridge: Cambridge Classical Studies.

———. 2012. "Between Ašoka and Antiochus: An Essay in World History on Universal Kingship and Cosmopolitan Culture in the Hellenistic Ecumene." In Bang and Kołodziejczyk, *Universal Empire,* 60–75.

Bang, Peter Fibiger, and Dariusz Kolodziejczyk, eds. 2012. *Universal Empire: A Comparative Approach to Culture and Representation in Eurasian History.* Cambridge: Cambridge University Press.

Barrett, John C. 1997. "Romanization: A Critical Comment." *International Roman Archaeology Conference Series JRA Supplementary Series* 23: 51–66.

Bielenstein, Hans. 1980. *The Bureaucracy of Han Times.* Cambridge: Cambridge University Press.

Black, Alison Harley. 1989. *Man and Nature in the Philosophical Thought of Wang Fu-Chih.* Seattle: University of Washington Press.

Boogert, Maurtis H., van den. 2005. "The Sultan's Answer to the Medici Press? Ibrahim Muteferrika's Printing House in Istanbul." In *The Republic of Letters and the Levant,* edited by Alistair Hamilton, Mauartis H. van den Boogert, and Bart Westerweel, 265–91. Leiden, Netherlands: Brill.

Burke, Peter. 1992. *The Fabrication of Louis XIV.* New Haven, Conn.: Yale University Press.

Chang, Chun-shu. 2006. *The Rise of the Chinese Empire: Nation, State, and Imperialism in Early China, ca. 1600 B.C.–A.D. 8.* Ann Arbor: University of Michigan Press.

———. 2007. *The Rise of the Chinese Empire: Frontier, Immigration, and Empire in Han China, 130 B.C.–A.D. 157.* Ann Arbor: University of Michigan Press.

Cherniavsky, Michael. 1969. *Tsar and People: Studies in Russian Myths.* New York: Random House.

Christensen, Arne Søby. 2002. *Cassiodorus, Jordanes, and the History of the Goths: Studies in a Migration Myth.* Copenhagen: University of Copenhagen Press.

Crossley, Pamela Kyle. 1987. "*Manzhou Yuanliu Kao* and the Formalization of the Manchu Heritage." *Journal of Asian Studies* 46, no. 4: 761–90.

———. 1999. *A Translucent Mirror: History and Identity in Qing Imperial Ideology.* Berkeley: University of California Press.

Dai, Yingcong. 2009. *The Sichuan Frontier and Tibet: Imperial Strategy in the Early Qing.* Seattle: University of Washington Press.

Dale, Stephen F. 2011. *The Muslim Empires of the Ottomans, Safavids, and Mughals.* Cambridge: Cambridge University Press.

Deweese, Devin. 1994. *Islamization and Native Religion.* College Park: Pennsylvania State University Press.

Elverskog, Johan. 2011. *Buddhism and Islam on the Silk Road.* Philadelphia: University of Pennsylvania Press.

Gang, Zhao. 2006. "Reinventing China: Imperial Qing Ideology and the Rise of Modern Chinese National Identity in the Early Twentieth Century." *Modern China,* no. 32: 3–30.

Garthwaite, Gene R. 2006. *The Persians.* Oxford: Wiley-Blackwell.

Gencer, Yasemin. 2010. "Ibrahim Muteferrika and the Age of the Printed Manuscript." In *The Islamic Manuscript Tradition,* edited by Christiane Gruber, 154–93. Bloomington: Indiana University Press.

Gibbon, Edward. 1782. *Decline and Fall of the Roman Empire.* Revised 1845 by H. H. Milman. Annotated 1996 by David Reed. https://www.guten berg.org/files/25717/25717-h/25717-h.htm.

Giele, Enno. 2006. *Imperial Decision-Making and Communication in Early China: A Study of Cai Yong's Duduan.* Wiesbaden, Germany: Harrassowitz.

Graves-Brown, Paul, Sian Jones, and C. S. Gamble. 2013. *Cultural Identity and Archaeology: The Construction of European Communities.* London: Routledge.

Heather, Peter, ed. 2000. *The Visigoths from the Migration Period to the Seventh Century: An Ethnographic Perspective.* Rochester, N.Y.: Boydell and Brewer.

Hingley, Robin. 1996. "The 'Legacy' of Rome: The Rise, Decline, and Fall of the Theory of Romanization." In *Roman Imperialism: Post-colonial Perspectives,* edited by J. Webster and N. Cooper, 34–48. Leicester, U.K.: School of Archeological Studies. https://lra.le.ac.uk/bit stream/2381/28433/1/3%20Hingley.pdf.

Hodgson, Marshal S. G. 1974. *Venture of Islam: The Classical Age of Islam.* Vol. 1. Chicago: University of Chicago Press.

Holcombe, Charles. 1994. *In the Shadow of the Han: Literati Thought and Society at the Beginning of the Southern Dynasties.* Honolulu: University of Hawai'i Press.

Hopkins, Keith. 1980. "Taxes and Trade in the Roman Empire (200 BC–AD 400)." *Journal of Roman Studies* 70: 101–25.

———. 2002. "Taxes, Rents, and Trade." In *The Ancient Economy,* edited by Walter Scheidel and Sitta von Reden, 190–231. London: Taylor and Francis.

Hulsewé, Anthony F. P. 1955. *Remnants of Han Law.* Vol. 1. Leiden, Netherlands: Brill.

Innes, Matthew. 1997. "The Classical Tradition in the Carolingian Renaissance: Ninth-Century Encounters with Suetonius." *International Journal of the Classical Tradition* 3, no. 3: 265–82.

Jackson, Peter. 2005. "The Mongols and the Faith of the Conquered." In *Mongols, Turks, and Others: Eurasian Nomads and the Sedentary World,* edited by Reuven Amitai and Michal Biran, 245–90. Leiden, Netherlands: Brill.

Judt, Tony. 2015. *When the Facts Change: Essays, 1995–2010.* New York: Penguin Press.

Kafadar, Cemal. 1995. *Between Two Worlds: The Construction of the Ottoman State.* Berkeley: University of California Press.

Kang Le 康樂. 1995. *Cong xijiao dao nan jiao: guodia jidian yu Bei Wei zhengzhi* [從西郊到南郊: 國家祭典與北魏政治]. Taipei: Daohe Press.

Keay, Simon, and Nicola Terrenato, eds. 2001. *Italy and the West: Comparative Issues in Romanization.* Oxford: Oxbow Books.

Khazanov, Anatoly. 1993. "Muhammad and Jenghiz Khan Compared: The Religious Factor in World Empire Building." *Comparative Studies in Society and History* 35, no. 3: 461–79.

Kołodziejczyk, Dariusz. 2012. "Khan, Caliph, Tsar and Imperator." in Bang and Kołodziejczyk, *Universal Empire,* 175–93.

Krause, Sharon. 2001. "Despotism in the Spirit of the Laws." In *Montesquieu's Science of Politics: Essays on the Spirit of the Laws,* edited by David Carrithers, Michael A. Mosher, and Paul Rahe, 231–72. Lanham, Md.: Rowman and Littlefield.

Levenson, Joseph R. 1952. "'T'ien-hsia' and *Kuo,* and the 'Transvaluation of Values.'" *The Far Eastern Quarterly* 11, no. 4: 447–51.

Lewis, Mark Edward. 2009. *China between Empires: The Northern and Southern Dynasties.* Cambridge, Mass.: Harvard University Press.

Lincoln, W. Bruce. 2007. *The Conquest of a Continent: Siberia and the Russians.* Ithaca, N.Y.: Cornell University Press.

Loewe, Michael. 1967. *Records of Han Administration*. 2 vols. Cambridge: Cambridge University Press.

Man-Cheong, Iona D. 2004. *Class of 1761: Examinations, State, and Elites in Eighteenth-Century China*. Stanford, Calif.: Stanford University Press.

Mango, Cyril. 1980. *Byzantium: The Empire of the New Rome*. Ann Arbor: University of Michigan Press.

Mann, Michael. 2010. *A History of Power from the Beginning to 1760*. Vol. 1 of *The Sources of Social Power*. 2nd ed. Cambridge: Cambridge University Press.

Mattingley, David J. 2013. *Imperialism, Power, and Identity: Experiencing the Roman Empire*. Princeton, N.J.: Princeton University Press.

Necipoglu, Gulru. 1991. *Architecture, Ceremonial, and Power: The Topkapı Palace in the Fifteenth and Sixteenth Centuries*. Cambridge, Mass.: MIT Press.

Newman, Andrew J. 2008. *Safavid Iran: Rebirth of a Persian Empire*. London: I. B. Tauris.

Niaz, Ilhan. 2014. *Old World Empires: Cultures of Power and Governance in Eurasia*. London: Routledge.

Nylan, Michael. 2000. "The Early Aesthetic Values of Writing and Calligraphy." *Oriental Art* 46, no. 5: 19–29.

Nylan, Michael, and Griet Vankeerberghen. 2015. *Chang'an 26 BCE: An Augustan Age in China*. Seattle: University of Washington Press.

Pitts, Martin, and Miguel John Versluys, eds. 2014. *Globalisation and the Roman World: World History, Connectivity, and Material Culture*. Cambridge: Cambridge University Press.

Redman, James Clyde Allen. 2010. "The Evolution of Ottoman Printing Technologies: From Scribal Authority to Print-Capitalism." In *The Ottomans and Europe: Travel, Encounter, and Interaction from the Early Classical Period Until the End of the 18th Century*, edited by Seyfi Kenan, 495–512. Istanbul: ISAM.

Roberts, Charlotte. 2014. *Edward Gibbon and the Shape of History*. New York: Oxford University Press.

Roper, Geoffrey. 1999. "Muslim Printing before Guttenberg." http://www.muslimheritage.com/article/muslim-printing-gutenberg.

Secondat, Charles-Louis de. 1734. *Considérations sur les causes de la grandeur et de la décadence des Romains*. Amsterdam: Jacques DesBordes. http://gallica.bnf.fr/ark:/12148/btv1b8613371v/f7.image.r=.langEN.

———. (1758) 1995. *De l'esprit des lois*. Paris: Gallimard. http://www.ecole-alsacienne.org/CDI/pdf/1400/14055_MONT.pdf.

Scheidel, Walter. 2013. "The Shape of the Roman World." http://www.princeton.edu/~pswpc/pdfs/scheidel/041306.pdf.

————. 2015. "State Revenue and Expenditure in the Han and Roman Empires." In *State Power in Ancient China and Rome,* edited by Walter Scheidel, 150–80. Oxford: Oxford University Press.

Scott, James. 2010. *The Art of Not Being Governed: An Anarchist History of Upland Southeast Asia.* New Haven, Conn.: Yale University Press.

Shelach-Lavi, Gideon. 2015. *The Archeology of Early China: From Prehistory to the Han Dynasty.* Cambridge: Cambridge University Press.

Skrynnikov, Ruslan Grigorevich. 1986. "Ermak's Siberian Expedition." *Russian History* 13, no. 1: 1–40.

Stein, Peter. 1999. *Roman Law in European History.* Cambridge: Cambridge University Press.

Teng, Ssu-yü. 1968. "Wang Fu-chih's Views on History and Historical Writing." *The Journal of Asian Studies* 28, no. 1: 111–23.

Terranato, Nicola. 2008. "The Cultural Implications of the Roman Conquest." In *The Short Oxford History of Europe,* edited by E. Bispam, 234–64. Oxford: Oxford University Press.

Tezscan, Baki. 2011. "The New Order and the Fate of the Old—The Historiographical Construction of an Ottoman *Ancien Régime* in the Nineteenth Century." In *Tributary Empires in Global History,* edited by Peter Fibiger Bang and Christopher Bayly, 74–95. Cambridge: Cambridge Imperial and Post-Colonial Studies.

Thapar, Romilla. 1966. *A History of India.* Vol. 1. London: Penguin Books.

Trevor-Roper, Hugh. 2010. *History and the Enlightenment.* New Haven, Conn.: Yale University Press.

Tu, Lien-che. 1943. "Chao I." In *Eminent Chinese of the Ch'ing Period,* edited by Arthur E. Hummel, 73–74. Washington, D.C.: U.S. Government Printing Office. http://www.dartmouth.edu/~qing/WEB/CHAO_I.html.

Wang, Yü-ch'üan. 1949. "An Outline of the Central Government of the Former Han Dynasty." *Harvard Journal of Asiatic Studies* 12, no. 12: 134–87.

Wilbur, C. Martin. 1943. *Slavery in China during the Former Han Dynasty, 206 B.C.–A.D. 25.* Chicago: Anthropological Series, Field Museum of Natural History.

Winford, Donald. 2003. *An Introduction to Contact Linguistics.* Oxford: John Wiley.

Wortman, Richard. 2000. *Scenarios of Power: Myth and Ceremony in Russian Monarchy.* Princeton, N.J.: Princeton University Press.

Wright, Kathleen. 2000. "The Fusion of Horizons: Hans-Georg Gadamer and Wang Fu-Chih." *Continental Philosophy Review* 33: 345–58.

Yen, Keng-wang [Yan, Gengwang] 嚴耕望. 1961. *Zhongguo difang xing-zhengzhidushi, jiabu: Qin Han difang xingzheng zhidu* [中國地方行政制度史: 甲部: 秦漢地方行政制度]. Taipei: Academia Sinica.

———. 1963. *Zhongguo difang xingzheng zhidu shi, yibu: Wei Jin Nanbei chao difang xingzheng* [中國地方行政制度史:乙部: 魏晉南北朝地方行政制度]. Taipei: Academia Sinica.

Zhao, Yi. 1795. *Ershi'er shi zhaji* [二十二史劄記; Notes on the twenty-two histories]. Beijing.

DEREK SHERIDAN

"Uncle Sam Said *Very* Clearly You Are Not a Country": Independence Activists and the Mapping of Imperial Cosmologies in Taiwan

IN 2006, a group of three hundred people led by a man named Roger Lin held a demonstration outside the American Institute in Taiwan (AIT), the de facto U.S. embassy in Taipei. The group claimed that Taiwan, governed by the mostly diplomatically unrecognized Republic of China (ROC) and claimed by the People's Republic of China (PRC), had actually been under the legal jurisdiction of the United States since 1945. They demanded the United States to "explain clearly" Taiwan's legal status and to provide them U.S. passports. The group then attempted to sue the U.S. government directly to have it recognize the existence of an entity they called the "United States Military Government" (USMG) (Hsu 2009). Although the U.S. Federal Court of Appeals would decline to decide their case, Lin and his supporters established a Taiwan Civil Government (TCG) in 2008. Rejecting the authority of Taiwan's elected government, they created flags representing the USMG and TCG, selected regional governors for Taiwan, and produced identification cards on the backs of which were printed summaries of their legal argument for the cards' authority. The realization of Taiwan's formal recognition as a separate country from China, they argued, depended on first recognizing Taiwan's actual current status as part of the United States. Although activists associated with the Taiwan independence movement with whom I spoke in 2012 considered Roger Lin a marginal figure who, so they claimed, deceived supporters into believing there was official U.S. backing, one former supporter told me that even if Lin was deceptive, the TCG could "still help" the larger independence movement because it "made something out of nothing [*wú zhōng shēng yǒu*]."

This performed claim to belong to an American empire poses a challenge to critical scholarship, including a politically conscious anthropology that, in the wake of the U.S. invasions of Afghanistan and Iraq, contributed to the scholarship on American imperialism (Hardt and Negri 2000; Johnson 2000; Lutz 2006; Stoler and Bond 2006; Go 2008). Around this same time, Taiwanese scholar Chen Kuan-Hsing produced a study of Club 51, a movement that advocated American statehood for Taiwan. Club 51 preceded, but also laid the conceptual groundwork for, the emergence of the TCG. In his article, Chen emphasized the radical significance of a proposal that abandons aspirations to nationhood and instead seeks annexation into empire. He interprets this aspiration as a symptom of the internalization of imperialist subjectivities in Taiwan (and East Asia more broadly). In the context of his larger critical project of "de-imperialization," he goes on to argue that Club 51 makes explicit "an unspeakable dilemma" for the Taiwan independence movement: "to become independent, Taiwan must depend on the United States militarily, diplomatically, and economically, but to openly admit this fact is contrary to the very idea of independence" (Chen 2010, 162).

In this article, I examine the logics through which grassroots independence activists *map* empire and their place within it. What happens, as social practice, when marginalized political actors imagine imperial communities that do not (yet) exist? I argue that empire is an imagined community, not only in terms of cultural identification but also in terms of the pragmatics through which nationalist activists map their aspired communities into a global order, in this case, one defined by American power vis-à-vis a Chinese nationalist project considered itself to be imperial. The article is based on ethnographic fieldwork with the grassroots activists among whom the TCG emerged. I trace debates and discussions among activists, examining their relationship to theories that place Taiwan within an American empire. Specifically, I trace the epistemological practices through which claims to belong to an American empire emerged.

Recent scholarship on both empire and nationalism has challenged the implicit dichotomy of national self-determination and imperialism. Duara (2004), for example, argues that the Japanese imperial project in the 1930s to constitute "Manchukuo" as a nation-state rather than a colony prefigured the postwar arrangement of American client states in East Asia. Kelly (2003) argues on a broader scale that anti-imperial critiques of American power fail to question the assumptions of the nation-state system as an institutional arrangement that limited political self-determination to the project of the nation-state and limited liabilities for the major powers on whom the new nation-states were still dependent.

Rutherford (2012, 180), arguing that all nations have "extra-national" roots, points out that self-determination in a postcolonial context has been dependent on recognition, particularly the recognition of powerful actors. These considerations lead Kelly to be critical of the use of *empire* to describe the United States. The argument that the United States has maintained an *informal* empire without colonization, however, is an old one. Nonetheless, it is itself significant that so much theoretical work has been devoted to the definition of what is empire or not-an-empire. As Stoler (2006, 94) argues, "the force of imperial macropolities is lodged in and exercised through the ambiguously opaque and creative terms of these vocabularies themselves." It is for this same reason that Lutz (2006) calls for anthropologists to go beyond macrotheories of empire, and to contribute an ethnographic perspective by studying "empire in the details."

The case I present goes beyond theories and definitions of empire and instead examines how the putative subjects of empire themselves construct its outlines and features. I contribute to ethnographic work that has explored how nationalist movements and local political actors theorize geopolitical cosmologies (Tsing 1993; Brown and Theodossopoulos 2003; Rutherford 2012). The concept of "cosmology" that I use here is inspired by Lisa Malkki's (1995, 5) description of the "national order of things" as "a powerful regime of order and knowledge that is at once politico-economic, historical, cultural, aesthetic, and cosmological." I am also inspired by work on what Tsing (1993) calls the "imagination of power," or the vernacular epistemologies through which people map lines of force and hierarchies of power around the globe. Vernacular political theories often appear in the literature as "conspiracy theory," which Boyer (2006, 327) calls a "key mode of cultural knowledge that seeks to reveal and to make locally intelligible the hidden forces and estranging dynamics of modern social experience." Anthropologists have argued that these theories reveal historical memories and moral stakes and that they index the uncertainties and confusion of politics and power themselves (Brown and Theodossopoulos 2003; Smith 2001; West and Sanders 2003). In this article, I go beyond the insight that vernacular political theory is meaningful by bringing an ethnographic lens to bear on the particular epistemological practices through which political cosmologies are constructed.

Taiwan has historically been integrated into multiple imperial formations, creating the conditions of possibility for different people to imagine many different "empires" into which the island might be mapped. These possible belongings are more complex than a simple dichotomy between "Chinese" and "Taiwanese" identities (Wachman 1994; Ching 2001; Simon 2003; Brown 2004). The island has been an outpost of the seventeenth-century Dutch trading empire, a frontier of the Qing Empire, and, after the Treaty of Shimonoseki in 1895, a colony of the Japanese Empire. Although political movements under Japanese colonialism did emerge among Taiwan's elite who sought independence from Japan or eventual reunification with mainland China, the home-rule movement largely accepted the irreversibility of remaining part of the Japanese Empire. When Taiwan was returned to what was now the ROC after 1945, this colonial experience shaped Taiwanese expectations of home rule within a larger Chinese polity (Phillips 2003). Dissatisfaction with the rampant misadministration of the incoming Chinese Nationalist (KMT) government, however, culminated in a 1947 uprising that was suppressed in a massacre that effectively eliminated, exiled, or silenced the Taiwanese elite. The "228 Incident" would become the "founding massacre" for the Taiwan independence movement and (in the beginning) appeals for a United Nations (UN) trusteeship (Corcuff 2002; Kerr 1965). In 1949, however, the Chinese Communist Party defeated the KMT, which then, accompanied by two million mainland Chinese, retreated to the island. Taiwan was reimagined as a temporary base and "model province" within a larger mission to "recover the mainland." The ROC on Taiwan developed into an authoritarian developmental state backed by a far-reaching U.S. military and economic presence that incorporated the island into the Cold War "first island chain" in the Western Pacific and tied the life trajectories of entire generations to the United States.

The Cold War and its aftermath have situated Taiwan on the edge of multiple empires and multiple potential statuses. The PRC imagined the "liberation" (and, later, "peaceful unification") of Taiwan as the final stage of the reunification of a Chinese nation that had been partitioned by Western and Japanese imperialism. During this same period, exiled Taiwanese independence activists, notably Su Beng (1980), reimagined Taiwanese history as a struggle of the island's original Han settlers[1] against the successive colonialisms of the Dutch, Ming loyalist Chen Chenggong, the Qing, the Japanese, and the Chinese Mainlanders who arrived in 1949. Democratization in the 1990s precipitated the popular convergence of the "Republic of China" imaginary with Taiwan, but efforts to remap Taiwan as a sovereign state within the international system have failed largely due to opposition from the PRC, which regards eventual unification as the only acceptable outcome, even if it is only achievable through military force. At the same time, Taiwan is being integrated economically through extensive cross-strait circulations of capital and people. Cross-strait trade agreements have become increasingly controversial in recent years, however, leading to the emergence of new social movements opposed to arrangements that would eventually lead to unification (Rowen 2015).

The imaginative claim that Taiwan might be an unrecognized U.S. possession becomes less absurd in a context where, despite having its own elected president and legislature, bureaucracy, currency, and military, the island is imagined many ways otherwise by other polities, and even by its own government. The Chinese government maintains that the ROC ceased to exist in 1949, and although it has itself never controlled the island, Taiwan is formally spoken of in public contexts as an internal province. The ROC formally maintains that it still retains sovereignty over all of China but effective jurisdiction over the "Taiwan Area." Prior to 1991, this claim was expressed by maintaining the all-China legislature elected in 1947. After 2008, President Ma Ying-Jeou opened negotiations on trade liberalization with "China" under the premise of "One China, Different Interpretations," wherein the ROC formally maintains *itself* to be China and the other side to be the "mainland authorities." Although the opposition Democratic Progressive Party (DPP) maintains that Taiwan is a separate sovereign state with the name of the "Republic of China," independence activists argue that despite popular sovereignty, the ROC remains a colonial government on Taiwan. They advocate forming a Republic of Taiwan. The U.S. government doesn't recognize *any* of these claims but maintains unofficial diplomatic and military ties. Taiwan provides exemplary evidence of the iterative and performative quality of sovereign claims.

In this context, some grassroots activists associated with the Taiwan independence movement attempt to "make things legible" (Scott 1998) by formalizing the terms of informal American empire in Taiwan in ways that seem to promise spaces for political agency otherwise denied. The activists with whom I conducted fieldwork are neither political parties and elites nor "public opinion," usually the focus of studies on Taiwanese identity. Rather, they are leaders and volunteers of the network of pro-independence civil society organizations popularly referred to as *běntǔ shètuán* (localization groups). Their members come from a diverse variety of socioeconomic backgrounds, but at the time of my fieldwork, their most unifying characteristic was that they were either retired or older than the age of sixty. These activists are easily recognizable in Taiwan's public sphere as those who regularly attend Taiwan's frequent political demonstrations and earnestly pursue projects whose goals are taken as quixotic even by Taiwanese who prefer independence. Many of the groups to whom they belong emerged in response to the DPP moving from active support of Taiwan independence to preservation of the status quo. Following the election of Ma Ying-Jeou in 2008 and the opening of controversial negotiations with the PRC to liberalize cross-strait trade, a new wave of organizations emerged to oppose what was seen as the beginning of unification with China. At the time of my fieldwork in 2012, just after Ma's reelection, and still before the Sunflower Movement marked the entry of younger activists into Taiwan independence activism, most of the activists I spoke to regarded themselves as more politically informed than a society they considered "brainwashed." They debated approaches to pursuing independence, with some focusing on how to mobilize other Taiwanese and others focusing on how to realize independence through foreign intervention or international law.

Originally assuming the goals of independence and American statehood to be very different, I initially designed my research as a comparison of the activists who participated in 908 Taiwan Republic (a group founded in 2005 to advocate September 8, 1951, to be Taiwan's "Independence Day" on account of that being the day Japan formally renounced sovereignty) and those who participated in Club 51, now called the Formosan Statehood Movement. Upon beginning fieldwork, however, I quickly discovered that both of these groups were part of a network of individuals and small organizations who participated in an ongoing circuit of rallies, lectures, and casual political discussions around the city. I ended up spending a majority of my time with activists from the Alliance of Referendum for Taiwan (ART), which has been camped outside the legislature in protest of Ma's China policies since 2008, but also spent considerable time in interviews with individual activists. These interviews were really extended lectures that often included other activists and friends whom they would invite when I arrived. As an American, my presence itself was conductive to initiating discussions about the role of the United States in the history of Taiwan.

Based on my participation in these discussions, as I accompanied activists through their weekly activities, I begin by describing the ways American and Chinese empire are interpreted in relationship to each other. I then attempt to retrace the process through which the theory that Taiwan belonged to the United States developed. I do so by both tracing the social life of this claim as it evolved and showing its deployment in the context of everyday political conversation. Finally, I examine the theory's premise of allowing activists to reset history through their creative appeal to notions of empire.

■ THE ENTANGLEMENT OF AMERICAN AND CHINESE EMPIRES

At the beginning of our first interview, David Chou, founder of the Formosa Statehood Movement, took out a blank sheet of paper and drew a map of the Asia Pacific. He explained that Taiwan forms part of the "first island chain" necessary for maintaining American hegemony. I had already entered this interview with Chen Kuan-Hsing's article in the back of my mind. Given Chen's larger purpose of critiquing imperialist thought in East Asia, I was surprised when David brought up the article himself as an introduction to his ideas. Chen had taken him seriously, he felt, and both he and Chen agreed that the United States had become internal to Taiwanese subjectivity. David, however, embraced the label of "pro-imperial," arguing Chen's political–intellectual project of "de-imperialization" (qùdìguóhuà) to actually be "de-American imperialization" (qùměidìguóhuà) and therefore pro-"Chinese imperialism." The indirect exchange I witnessed here illustrates how anti-imperial critiques are contingent on and can themselves become entangled in other imperial projects. Chinese nationalist scholars have long seen Taiwan independence as overdetermined by American imperialism (Nan 1980), but as Shu (2001) argues, this argument overlooks the significance of local political subjectivity in the formation of Taiwanese political projects. The activists with whom I did research contend with two different imperial formations: China and the United States. In their discourse, however, these formations take on different meanings in different contexts.

The broadest set of meanings aligns China and the United States on two poles of an imagined civilizational hierarchy. Activists I spoke with frequently imagined the United States as the ideal realization of the institutions and political practices they saw to be limited in Taiwan. The United States was a "real democracy," unlike Taiwan; the United States "lacked corruption," unlike Taiwan; and American voters would not "put up" with the same mistreatment Taiwanese voters accepted. China, conversely, was invoked as the source of all the negative qualities they found in Taiwan. Although the PRC's stated intention to eventually unify Taiwan was invoked as expected, I was more surprised to find that what the activists referred to as "Chinese" were more often shorthand for various social ills attributed to the arrival of the KMT. A narrative was evident of Taiwan having been better organized under the Japanese prior to 1945, when the "Chinese" came and brought bad habits with them. Chen (2010) identified this discourse, exemplified by Club 51's quest for cultural integration into the United States, as an unmistakable sign of postcolonial consciousness.

On the other hand, the project of modern Chinese nationalism is itself experienced as a form of imperialism. This includes not only the equivalence of "unification" with "annexation" but also memories and legacies of KMT authoritarian rule in Taiwan. A Hakka activist told me that he "hated the Chinese nation [zhōnghúa mínzú]" because of the suppression of the Hakka language by the KMT during authoritarian rule. As Hung and Kuo (2010, 318) argue, the history of modern Chinese nation building is usefully understood as a comparatively successful project to "transform nearly all of [China's] imperial territory into a singular nation-state despite the cultural and ethnic heterogeneity of this geographical space," but one that "is far from complete and uncontested." The KMT pursued this project in Taiwan through the enforcement of Mandarin and the discursive elevation of (Greater) Chinese subjectivities and experiences over (local) Taiwanese subjectivities and experiences (Phillips 2003). The project's methods uncannily resembled the methods of the prior Japanese colonialist project. It is therefore unsurprising that the centering of *Taiwanese* subjectivities during democratization has been positioned against a Chinese empire, regardless of how much Han Taiwanese popular religion and language continued to be informed by an older Chinese imperial cosmology and historical tradition inherited from Taiwan's inclusion in the Qing Empire (Cohen 1991).

These activists also speak of the United States as an empire, but wherein the "Chinese" are associated with KMT colonialism, the United States is imperialist because it is *not imperialist enough.* Activists I knew would occasionally work out the differences in the course of conversation with me. While I was speaking with Mr. Wen in the office of 908 Taiwan Republic, he referred to China as *zhina,* a pejorative Japanese term he preferred to *zhōng guó,* which he emphasized means "center country." After claiming this exemplified the problem with Chinese nationalism, he then added, imitating an American accent, that Americans also probably thought they were the center of the world. Every country thinks they are the center country, he added. He continued, saying that the United States invaded Iraq, but it did not annex it. China, on the other hand, wanted to invade and annex Taiwan because of claims to shared "blood" *(xuètǒng).* But if that was true, he asked, why doesn't the United Kingdom insist that Americans are still part of the U.K.? Wen shifted into a broader set of complaints about the KMT, the 228 Incident, and recent corruption scandals, in the middle of which he suddenly said, "I'm sorry, but Taiwan belongs to you."

Starting with a pejorative term for China inherited from the discourse of Japanese imperialism, Wen, through a series of shifts, identifies imperial affinities between China and the United States that are quickly qualified by significant contrasts. The apology-bracketed claim that Taiwan "belongs" to the United States, however, is different from David Chou's advocacy of statehood. It is a claim, popularized by Lin's lawsuit, that the United States had a special responsibility in Taiwan. I had conversations with other activists in different settings that closely followed my conversation with Wen. For example, I was approached one afternoon while sitting at the ART by a middle-aged man who shared his complaints about the KMT. He then described the KMT and Chinese Communist Party as "brothers" and said that President Ma took orders from Chinese president Hu Jintao. "America is also not good," he added. General MacArthur was to blame for "giving" Taiwan to Chiang Kai-Shek and the KMT at the end of World War II. Chinese and American imperialisms, in other words, are entangled in these narratives of Taiwan's current predicament. Ma Ying-Jeou embodies these entanglements. His Mainlander background, Chinese identity, and policies of opening to China directly challenged Taiwan-centric identities. However, activists frequently accused him of both secretly taking orders from Beijing *and* secretly holding a U.S. green card. One story I heard was that after Ma "sold out" Taiwan to China, he would actually flee to the United States to live with the rest of his family there. The ROC government in Taiwan, U.S. statehood supporter Johnny Huang told me, represented two governments: China *and* the United States. Ma wanted to unify with China but also had to "obey" the United States because, otherwise, he joked once, they "would take away his green card."

While entangled, a clear contrast that emerges is that whereas the KMT are considered to have constructed a colonial regime in Taiwan and to be facilitating unification with China, the United States is invoked to explain how "the Chinese" came to Taiwan in the first place. This is not limited to those espousing statehood or supporting the TCG. Independence activists I spoke to regularly emphasized that the United States had "responsibility" *(zérèn)* for Taiwan's future. One informant, Little Chen, reminded me every time we met that "the most important question" I should answer for him is why the United States supported the ROC. The possibility that it could have acted differently allows some activists to imagine other possible futures for Taiwan. Indeed, some called Americans "imperialist" by virtue of the fact that they had not been imperialist enough and had not done what Chinese nationalists had long accused the United States of plotting to do: establishing the permanent separation of Taiwan from China. Richard Bush (2004), the former head of the AIT, characterized U.S. policy toward Taiwan as having deterred three outcomes: a Chinese invasion of Taiwan, Chiang Kai-Shek attacking the mainland, and Taiwan declaring independence. American leaders maintained deliberate "strategic ambiguity" about Taiwan's status as a tool in managing its relationship with China. However, whereas those like Bush credit strategic ambiguity with maintaining Sino-American peace,

Taiwanese independence activists directly challenge these uncertainties and seek to make them legible.

■ THE SOCIAL LIFE OF IMPERIAL COSMOLOGIES

The recognition of the importance of the United States in Taiwan's recent history leads many activists to question the "strategic ambiguity" of U.S. policy makers. "We are waiting for Uncle Sam to tell us what to do," Johnny Huang told me, "they say we are not a country, but also not a state. It's like saying you can't eat noodles, but you also can't eat rice!" In the absence of legibility, activists attempt to make U.S. policy legible on their own. I encountered frequent debates in meetings among activists about the proper interpretation of policy statements.[2] As an American researcher, some informants assigned me the role of searching for documents that would provide them "evidence" *(zhèngmíng)* for Taiwan's real status. Activists consistently attributed greater veracity and efficacy to the statements of U.S. officials than to the statements of Taiwanese officials. This reflects the historical fact that U.S. declarations and statements regarding Taiwan have exemplified "words that do things" (Austin 1962), but there is also the interpretive logic that U.S. nonrecognition of Taiwan vetoes the existence of a government that otherwise reproduces itself through everyday bureaucratic practices. In everyday discussion about politics, the frequent assertions I heard that the ROC was "not a country" was occasionally accompanied by the statement that "America said *very* clearly!" it was not. Johnny Huang had collected a folder's worth of news stories concerning U.S.–Taiwan relations and quoting the statements of U.S. officials regarding Taiwan, from which he would occasionally proffer theories about an underlying U.S. grand strategy.

It would not be a stretch to argue that making sense of what U.S. policy might actually be encourages exegetical readings of diplomatic texts and statements analogous to the practice of interpreting divine will in religious texts (Bakhtin 1981, 351).[3] The archive of U.S. policy is extensive enough for creative projects of making legible an empire that is deliberately illegible. On the basis of both interviews and conversations I witnessed, I am able to reconstruct here the emergence and social life of theories that Taiwan belonged to the United States. Tracing the everyday practices through which activists developed these reveal that "empire" is as much an emergent construction of its subjects as it is a project of its ostensible architects.

The story begins with the Formosa Statehood Movement. In my conversations with David Chou and Johnny Huang, they directly drew links between their personal life experiences and how they came to either propose or support the possibility of U.S. statehood. They explicitly adopted the language of "empire" to interpret these experiences. David, who, like many Taiwanese of his generation, attended college in the United States, described the experience of being invited to attend Bicentennial celebrations in 1976 as being "like a student from a vassal state coming to see the empire." He added, "I am best return on the investment [the U.S. government made]." Johnny had spent his teenage years working on a U.S. military base as a shoeshine boy, telephone operator, and supply depot manager. If Anderson (1991) has argued that "administrative pilgrimages" have been crucial in the creation of "imagined [national] communities," the legacy of a U.S. military presence in Taiwan and the transpacific pilgrimages that tied generations of Taiwanese to the United States are the conditions of possibility for imagining oneself in a U.S. imperial community. David and Johnny both describe either the moment of creation or support of statehood as the resolution to the dilemma of U.S. "strategic ambiguity" toward Taiwan. Chou described to me how the idea originated from the time he worked as an aide to opposition leader Kang Ning-Xiang in 1988. He often received visiting U.S. politicians and reporters who he said would tell him that the United States "supported democratization in Taiwan, but if you talk independence, we are reserved." David continued:

> At that time I supported independence, but because I kept getting that response, I would ask them with curiosity, "If you Americans don't support independence, then how about this," I came up with an alternative, "how about we just join the United States." At that time, I thought it was a joke, I wasn't serious, but I discovered 20% supported. Half laughed, but did not say whether they supported or not. They were ambiguous [ai mèi].

The ambiguity David perceived was enough to transform a playful idea into a serious proposal. David made an appointment with Johnny in 1994. By this time, Johnny was already well known as an activist for the end of military conscription in Taiwan. He had become involved because of work helping the families of Taiwanese whose sons studied high school and college abroad in the United States. Not only did Taiwan's conscription laws effectively prevent these people from returning home for visits, they also had to appear in court upon their return. After hearing David's proposal, Johnny said he thought, "Hey! It sounds great, because my overseas student families, probably a quarter already had American passports. Why not? Instead of some people having a U.S. passport, why not everybody has a U.S. passport?" Johnny frequently supported statehood in terms of transforming the informal empire into the actuality of formal membership in the United States. For example, he argued that the weapons the United States sold to Taiwan were already a form of taxation for defense, because the weapons in themselves were not capable of defending Taiwan. Johnny framed statehood as the generalization of security (from a Chinese invasion), which he presented as a social justice issue. Telling me that a "U.S. passport means security," he believed that Taiwanese elites, particularly those from families who came over with Chiang Kai-Shek in the 1940s, already had U.S. passports. "Where is my passport?" he would ask me.[4] Statehood was argued both to guarantee U.S. protection and to resolve its unequal application to people in Taiwan by building on relationships that were already analogous to being a U.S. dependency.

David's proposal attracted widespread (and even international) media attention in the 1990s, although much of it with an undertone of amusement. Nonetheless, it had five hundred members at its height, and even in 2012, when I only personally encountered fewer than a dozen, some activists who supported Taiwan independence occasionally mentioned in passing (sometimes in a lighthearted manner) U.S. statehood as the least bad option after unification with China. Although the TCG, which surpassed David in fame in the 2000s, is often popularly associated with him, the claims, logics, and methods of the two groups are very different. Rather than making an argument about the desirability of U.S. statehood, the TCG claimed that Taiwan is *already* part of the United States and that its supporters should act in accordance with this reality. Nonetheless, I found that supporters of both groups begin with the potentiality of American empire (in terms of either informal relationships or legal technicalities) and construct imagined political institutions through which they can exercise agency within it.

It is worth tracing the precise discursive processes through which this happens because doing so reveals both how imperial cosmologies are constructed and how arguments for them obtain legitimacy. Johnny claims that the TCG originated in an offhand comment he made during a conversation with an American expatriate named Richard Hartzell in 1999. The story uncannily reproduces David's own narrative of U.S. statehood beginning as a joke:

> I said, "Hey, Richard, Taiwan is probably already American territory." He said, "How could that be?" I thought it was a joke, I didn't take it seriously. I said, "It doesn't matter, every day, when you have nothing to do, you can go do the research." The result, *unbelievable.* He spent five years doing research. In 2004, one day he calls me and says, "Johnny, it's true! Taiwan is a territory of the United States!"

Hartzell's argument, subsequently published in the *Harvard Asia Quarterly* (Hartzell 2004), makes the claim that when Japan surrendered in 1945, its colony of Taiwan also fell under the legal authority of the United States, the "principal occupying power." General MacArthur issued Order Number 1, instructing Japanese forces in Taiwan to surrender to Chiang Kai-Shek, but because the order was never rescinded and because the final status of Taiwan was never formally determined, Taiwan remains an unacknowledged overseas possession of the United States. Hartzell's article attracted the attention of former president Lee Deng-Hui, who publicly recommended it. Hartzell was then approached by former businessman Roger Lin, leading to the events spoken of at the beginning of the article: a strategy of suing the U.S. government to have it recognize its jurisdiction over Taiwan and to provide the passports due to a people living in an American territory. In 2009, the United States Court of Appeals declined the case on the grounds that a judicial decision would infringe on a "question the Executive Branch intentionally left unanswered for over sixty years: who exercises sovereignty over Taiwan" (*Lin v. US,* 561 F.3d 502 [D.C. Cir. 2009]).

One might end the story there, but the discourse and activism generated around and in response to Lin illustrate the extent of the creativity involved in imagining and constructing imperial cosmologies and the purposes these projects are imagined to serve. Consider the following examples of Mr. Lee and Mr. Wang. Both started as supporters of Lin but subsequently became disillusioned with him and developed their own interpretations of Taiwan's status. Mr. Lee was a pharmacist who, being "very worried about the future of Taiwan," had donated money to various pro-independence causes, including Mr. Lin. As often happened during interviews, Mr. Lee invited a friend of his to join us: an English teacher who was herself not yet familiar with Mr. Lee's theories. When we got to the café, he began to describe all the changes in Taiwan's legal status since 1895. Lin's mistake, he argued, was to only discuss the San Francisco Peace Treaty and not the 1979 Taiwan Relations Act (TRA). Whereas I had previously understood the act to allow "unofficial" diplomatic ties between the United States and Taiwan following the recognition of Beijing, Lee explained that, within the logic of the TCG's theory, the act gave Taiwan independence:

> Inside the Taiwan Relations Act, you need to understand, none of us understand the Taiwan Relations Act, if you look, you would be surprised! It says very clearly in Article 2 that what the United States used to refer to as the Republic of China was now to be referred to as the "governing authorities in Taiwan" [*Táiwān tŏngzhì dāngju*]. On that day, the Republic of China ended.

Lee argued that it was unnecessary to "nation build" *(jiàn gúo)* because the TRA already recognized the "people of Taiwan" as a foreign country. Instead, all Taiwanese needed to do was "set up" *(chéng lì)* a country by creating an "applicable law of the Taiwanese people" *(Táiwān rénmín shǐyòngfǎ)*. He continued, "I did not understand the Act before, but when I did, I was shocked! Wow! So Taiwan was like this all along!" The United States, he added, should not allow the governing authorities in Taiwan to continue "deceiving" *(piàn)* the Taiwanese by telling them that the ROC is a government.

His friend intervened at this point and asked what is wrong with the status quo.

"There is no Republic of China," Mr. Lee responded. "Ma Ying-Jeou is just a governing authority." People in Taiwan use the ROC because they had been "brainwashed."

"I've been brainwashed by you all afternoon!" his friend responded, smiling.

"I'm not brainwashing," Lee responded. "I'm just explaining clearly [*shuō dé qīngchǔ*]."

The owner of the coffee shop, who had been listening to us nearby, intervened, saying, "It's a shame [*kělián*] when my children ask about Taiwan's status, why we are not allowed to fly our flag [overseas]. What thing are we [*wǒmen shì shénme dōngxī*]? A country, an American state? Quickly establish what we are. Taiwan is a country, or it is a state, OK, neither matters. Tell our children so that they are not confused."

Mr. Lee discovered an alternative interpretation of Taiwan's status, "speaking clearly" in contrast to the "brainwashing" of the KMT. Although his friend questioned the utility of reimagining Taiwan's status, the coffee shop owner posed clarity regarding Taiwan's identity in terms of avoiding shame. Many (but not all) of Mr. Lee's ideas were inspired by Wang Yun-Cheng, a businessman whose involvement in politics began when he heard Lin and Hartzell's theory discussed on the radio. He subsequently wrote a book intended to help explain the theory in an accessible question-and-answer style (Wang 2005). He then began to undertake his own research on sovereignty disputes around the world and eventually wrote a two-volume book (Wang 2007) that came to different conclusions.

I was introduced to Mr. Wang by Mr. Lim, another businessman who was an active supporter of independence groups. The three of us met in Mr. Lim's office. Wang described to me a three-tiered structure where, historically, "the UN gave [occupation authority] to the United States, and the United States gave it to Chiang Kai-Shek." The ROC constitution was not really a Chinese constitution, he said, but a "civil affairs document." Above this, the United States used the TRA to "manage" the ROC. It was similar, Wang said, to the way the federal government is above a state government in the United States. The United States did not possess sovereignty, however, but held it in trust for the UN. Short of war, he added, there were no means available for resolving Taiwan's situation, but it was nonetheless important to pass down the knowledge of Taiwan's "true" status so that it would still be useful several hundred years in the future. On one hand, this elaborate yet elegant theory represents a kind of long return to a "status quo" argument. On the other hand, no one else I have met or read expressed Taiwan's status in precisely these terms. The formalism of the model is Wang's creation. He said that he developed his theory to tell people "you have a status!" and thereby assuage the anxiety he felt among independence supporters.

■ PERFORMING THE EMPIRE

The theories and their presentation described herein evince political imaginations not well captured by the concept of nationalism. The theories *do* construct imagined communities and retrospective historical narratives, but rather than stories of nationalist subjectivity, they are stories of historical contingency that reimagine the acts of powerful external actors into a basis for political community. Activists debate which date (1895, 1945, 1952, 1979, etc.) can be retroactively considered the basis for pursuing a legal claim about Taiwan's status. This often entails repurposing the intentions of powerful actors for the intentions of Taiwanese political agency. For example, in the same café where I regularly met Johnny to talk about Taiwan as a U.S. state, I found banners and fliers placed by the boss advertising a campaign to formally establish Taiwan as a "neutral country." The fliers identified the 1895 "internationalization" of the Taiwan Strait (by virtue of Taiwan's transfer to Japan) as the "First Stage" of Taiwan's neutralization and Truman's 1950 order to neutralize the Chinese Civil War in the Taiwan Strait as the "Second Stage." Establishing Taiwan as a neutral country was the "Third Stage." The projects associated with Lin, however, make the claim that the Taiwanese can "travel back in time" (Taiwan Civil Government 2010) to the postwar moment, vetoing sixty years of history. And if not 1945, maybe 1979, as Mr. Lee argues. The efficacy of these projects are widely contested within the independence movement, but their very existence, and the extent to which groups like the TCG went to realize them, demonstrates the agentive appeal of imagining empire.

I often found arguments presented in the style of a claim to redo history correctly following the revelation that it had been done incorrectly. During a visit with 908 Taiwan Republic, a volunteer showed me a small booklet in which was printed the 1960 UN resolution on decolonization. "It says right here, see!" he yelled. "Why then has it taken sixty-five years? America should help! Will we be independent?" I replied that it would probably take a lot of effort. He got angry and told me there was no need for effort, that it was "very simple," pointing again to the 1960 resolution. I encountered similar themes of revelation both in the life stories of activists and in the techniques they used to propagate their theories. David discovers that a joke about being a state may not be a joke; Hartzell discovers that Taiwan may already be U.S. territory; Mr. Lee discovers that the United States "gave" Taiwan independence in 1979. These revelations follow having been "deceived" by the KMT to believe that the ROC was a country, or even deceived by the theories of other activists. I frequently encountered activists who explained that the facts they were telling me were not known by many Taiwanese because of KMT "brainwashing."

The propagation of alternative theories sometimes employed the use of techniques seemingly intended to surprise and lead one to reimagine oneself in a different political reality. On a few separate occasions, I was provided a pocket-sized photograph of the Japanese surrender ceremony on October 25, 1945. The significant information in the photo is the presence of the Allied flags at the ceremony, equally positioned above the dignitaries. The photo indexes the fact that Japan technically surrendered to Chiang Kai-Shek, representing the Allies, rather than to China. The photo is intended to argue that Taiwan never legally returned to China and to suggest alternative possibilities for determining Taiwan's future.

Resisting placement within China, but unable to achieve recognition within an international community of states, activists imagine a place within an American empire. Because this empire is ambiguous and disavowed, however, activists attempt to formalize its terms themselves. Statehood, David and Johnny told me, would remove ambiguity about whether the United States would defend Taiwan. Independence activists who distance themselves from U.S. statehood or the Civil Government nonetheless map Taiwan (and China) into an imagined global community whose institutional contours have been historically shaped by the United States (Kelly and Kaplan 2004). This is the case of the man who showed me the UN resolution on decolonization. One informant who supported a Republic of Taiwan liked to tell me and other activists that "it's not China's Taiwan, but the world's Taiwan [bù shì Zhōngguó de Táiwān, shì Shìjiè de Táiwān]," and that the activists should not be afraid because it was not "Taiwan against China, but China against the world." Wu (2004) argues that an anti-imperial strategy of appealing to Western universalism was also found in the Japanese period, when Japan's anti-imperial "oriental colonialism" justified itself in part as resistance to Western imperialism. Rutherford (2012, 189) argues that the "performative creation of a nation has long entailed the conjuring of transcendentally extra-national points of view."

The particularity of the preceding theories, however, is the emphasis placed on international law, rather than nationalist subjectivity, as the basis for political community. The argument that Taiwan is *actually* part of the United States is close to the argument of some Hawai'ian independence activists that the "Kingdom of Hawai'i" is *actually* still in existence. Although the political aims may seem opposed, both engage in what Philips (2005, 407) calls "a common U.S. colonial legal discourse about the nature of these entities and about their mutability. . . . Part of this discourse on political entities entails an assumption of the mutability of these units or of the capacity of one kind of unit to become another kind." In both cases, activists are "strategically using law to both preserve and create the kind of political entities that will help them maintain and further the social identities they value" (407), in other words, to "have a status."

The appeal to the idea of impartial international law, however, goes beyond whether these interpretations are legally "correct" and entails certain assumptions about how one exercises agency in a field of powerful geopolitical actors. Lin was unsuccessful, after all, in using the U.S. legal system to resolve Taiwan's status. Within the independence movement, activists disagreed over *who* had the greater agency in determining Taiwan's future. One activist took me aside one night and told me,

> I don't like [the people you talk to]. They waste time looking at history, at treaties. They confuse people about what they want. The United States didn't care about history when they invaded Afghanistan. Might makes right! When I was young, I supported unification, and opposed independence. Now, I support independence and oppose unification. Theory can be thought, but it can't lead [*lǐ lùn kěyǐ cān kǎo, bù kěyǐ lǐng dǎo*].

The activist's criticisms fit into a larger debate within the pro-independence community about whether the movement depended more on the mobilization of a pro-independence "voice" *(shēngyīn)* in Taiwan or the support of powerful foreign actors. Given the inability of even pro-independence presidents to realize formal independence, what do these projects accomplish? The activists associated with the TCG went beyond lawsuits. The United States did not recognize jurisdiction over Taiwan, so they performatively extended the jurisdiction themselves by establishing the TCG. The group created flags for the military and civil governments, divided Taiwan into different "states," and selected governors from among its members. The TCG produced letters, flags, identification cards, and travel documents issued for residents of the U.S. "Formosa Cession." The story becomes murky here, as I encountered frequent accusations that Lin posited these flags and documents as being officially endorsed (at least covertly) by the U.S. government. Lin eventually revised the TCG's theory to argue that Taiwan was actually still legally part of the Japanese Empire, a position I was told aligned more closely with the affinities of elderly Taiwanese nostalgic for Japanese colonialism.

In the course of talking to informants about the claims of Roger Lin, I encountered divergent interpretations about what exactly was being claimed or the kind of work that was being done. Criticisms of Lin centered on the claim that he exploited patriotic elderly Taiwanese worried about the future of the island by making them believe the United States had given him covert backing. Supporters of Lin, conversely, even when acknowledging that he may have engaged in fraud, defended the larger project. As Rutherford (2012, 182) argues, "in a world where diplomatic acknowledgement is the *sine qua non* of legitimate statehood, nationalists are particularly dogged by the specter of iterability." In this case, however, what is being iterated is the assumed responsibility of an empire that has deliberately extricated itself from the imperial relationship. During a dinner in which a former supporter of Lin described how she was increasingly uncomfortable with what Lin was doing, another man responded, "It doesn't matter if [Lin] deceives. Explaining the history has advantages for Taiwan. It doesn't matter who says he is a fraud. What matters is explaining Taiwan's status. Saying the Republic of China is fake is what's important!"

The iterations of Lin contended with the iterations of other independence groups, which contend with the iterations of the ROC, the PRC, the United States, and the international community about Taiwan's status. Rutherford, writing on similar practices of raising independent West Papuan flags, argues that such claims "afford a fleeting experience of supremacy that may feel just like sovereign power. Don't be mistaken; it takes a strict sense of geopolitical conditions to make a declaration of independence stick. But there is always something seductive in voicing an utterance that creates its own truth" (21). This is indeed how one former supporter of Lin described the TCG. "Lin lied to us," he said, but then he added that even if the U.S. Military Government flag was fake, it "could still help us." It was the strategy of "making something out of nothing [*wú zhōng shēng yǒu*]." TCG supporter Mr. Yang explained the group's strategy by saying, "We are not a toy given to us by our father. We are people making our own toys." Whereas other groups engaged the

ROC government given to them by the United States, he argued, they created their own government for engaging with the United States. Unlike standard claims to be an independent country, however, they were performatively expanding American empire in formal ways that U.S. policy makers themselves did not. This was not necessarily only about cultural identification, but the promise of revealing spaces for political agency otherwise denied.

■ CONCLUSION

The case presented here demonstrates how "empire" is a political cosmology that has to be imagined, mapped, and sometimes even performatively created. The mapping of American empire by Taiwanese independence activists and the emergence of projects like the Formosan Statehood Movement or the Civil Government pose a challenge for anthropologies of empire that start from macrotheories formulated in the context of anti-imperial movements. Looking at empire through the eyes of local political struggles reveals the importance of historical contingency in shaping not only geopolitical affinities and antagonisms but also the mode in which imperial politics are interpreted. The manner in which Taiwan's international status has been regularly transformed through the diplomatic maneuvers of imperial powers explains epistemological practices that seek legibility and avenues for repurposing these maneuvers to work in the interest of local political actors.

Projects like these, however, pose a challenge for progressive projects premised on what Chen calls "de-imperialization" because they challenge mappings of empire that assume popular bases for regional solidarity against a singular "Empire." Indeed, the definition of *empire* in this situation is complicated by the fact that American and Chinese geopolitical self-definition in East Asia is based on contrasting the self against the "imperialism" of the other. The case of Taiwan highlights the broader entanglement of "anti-imperial" movements in East Asia with putative imperial movements of another kind. American imperialism in East Asia cannot be historically disentangled from Asian imperialisms, and Asian imperialisms in turn cannot be historically disentangled from the Western imperialisms to which many of them responded. To argue this is not to make an argument that these different imperialisms are equivalent; they are in fact of different scales and reach. However, they mean different things to Taiwanese political actors than they do to, for example, anti-militarist activists in Okinawa who experience American empire in the form of military bases and their negative social effects (Lutz and Enloe 2009). The goal of this article has been to provoke discussion about how people talk about "empire," its historical contingency, and the political stakes involved. This is a necessary intervention for a situation like in Taiwan, where one's positionality within entangled and/or competing imperial projects can overdetermine one's political affinities and antagonisms vis-à-vis *multiple* empires.

The geopolitics of critique, however, often overdetermine the implicit maps that people adopt. Through examining the elaborateness of the political discourse of Taiwan independence activists, I hope to have shown just how constructed these maps of world order can be. The purpose here is not to deny the significance of macrotheories of empire or the importance of anti-imperial movements but rather, as the counterintuitive cases here suggest, to suggest more cognizance of the geopolitically contingent, emergent, and overdetermined sources and types of political subjectivity within contemporary formations of nation-states and empire.

Derek Sheridan is a PhD candidate in the Department of Anthropology at Brown University. His current research concerns the experiences of Chinese migrant entrepreneurs in Tanzania and the everyday negotiation of "(non-)imperial" relationships.

■ NOTES

I would like to thank Catherine Lutz, Keith Brown, Lina Fruzzetti, Daniel Smith, Bhrigupati Singh, Shih Shu-Mei, Shu Wei-Der, Chang Mau-Kuei, Antonia Chao, Shinju Fujihira, Vazira Zamindar, and Ching-Fang Hsu for their thoughts on this article. I would especially like to thank five anonymous reviewers whose comments were invaluable in bringing this article to completion.

1. This narrative excluded the indigenous Austronesian peoples of Taiwan, although other nationalist narratives emerged that drew on these histories to make claims that the Taiwanese were not Han (Brown 2004). Indigenous-led projects themselves, however, have their own histories and contexts that are unfortunately beyond the scope of this article.

2. For example, U.S. "acknowledgment" of the China's claims on Taiwan in the 1972 Shanghai Communique has different meaning than U.S. "recognition," although in Chinese, both can be translated as *chéngrèn*.

3. In several conversations, the United States was spoken of jokingly by statehood supporters and detractors as being "like a God."

4. Johnny Huang maintained the possibility of eventual independence after statehood, whereas David Chou advocated full integration into the United States.

▪ WORKS CITED

Anderson, Benedict. 1991. *Imagined Communities: Reflections on the Origin and Spread of Nationalism*. London: Verso.

Austin, John L. 1962. *How to Do Things with Words*. Cambridge, Mass.: Harvard University Press.

Bakhtin, Mikhail. 1981. *The Dialogic Imagination*. Translated by Carolyn Emerson and Michael Holquist. Austin: University of Texas Press.

Boyer, Dominic. 2006. "Conspiracy, History, and Therapy at a Berlin 'Stammtisch.'" *American Ethnologist* 33, no. 3: 327–39.

Brown, Keith, and Dimitrios Theodossopoulos. 2003. "Rearranging Solidarity: Conspiracy and World Order in Greek and Macedonian Commentaries on Kosovo." *Journal of Southern Europe and the Balkans Online* 5, no. 3: 315–35.

Brown, Melissa J. 2004. *Is Taiwan Chinese? The Impact of Culture, Power, and Migration on Changing Identities*. Berkeley: University of California Press.

Bush, Richard C. 2004. *At Cross Purposes: U.S.–Taiwan Relations since 1942*. Taiwan in the Modern World. Armonk, N.Y.: M. E. Sharpe.

Chen, Kuan-Hsing. 2010. *Asia as Method: Toward Deimperialization*. Durham, N.C.: Duke University Press.

Ching, Leo T. S. 2001. *Becoming "Japanese": Colonial Taiwan and the Politics of Identity Formation*. Berkeley: University of California Press.

Cohen, Myron L. 1991. "Being Chinese: The Peripheralization of Traditional Identity." *Daedalus* 120, no. 2: 113–34.

Corcuff, Stéphane. 2002. "Introduction: Taiwan, a Laboratory of Identities." In *Memories of the Future: National Identity Issues and the Search for a New Taiwan,* edited by Stéphane Corcuff, xi–xxiv. Armonk, N.Y.: M. E. Sharpe.

Duara, Prasenjit. 2004. *Sovereignty and Authenticity: Manchukuo and the East Asian Modern*. Lanham, Md.: Rowman and Littlefield.

Go, Julian. 2008. "Global Fields and Imperial Forms: Field Theory and the British and American Empires." *Sociological Theory* 26, no. 3: 201–29.

Hardt, Michael, and Antonio Negri. 2000. *Empire*. Cambridge, Mass.: Harvard University Press.

Hartzell, Richard W. 2004. "Understanding the San Francisco Peace Treaty's Disposition of Formosa and the Pescadores." *Harvard Asia Quarterly* 8, no. 4: 1–12.

Hsu, Jenny. 2009. "Taiwan Part of US since World War II: Protestors." *Taipei Times,* September 9. http://www.taipeitimes.com/News/taiwan/archives/2009/09/03/2003452676.

Hung, Ho-fung, and Huei-ying Kuo. 2010. "'One Country, Two Systems' and Its Antagonists in Tibet and Taiwan." *China Information* 24, no. 3: 317–37.

Johnson, Chalmers A. 2000. *Blowback: The Costs and Consequences of American Empire.* New York: Metropolitan Books.

Kelly, John Dunham. 2003. "U.S. Power, after 9/11 and before It: If Not an Empire, Then What?" *Public Culture* 15, no. 2: 347–69.

Kelly, John Dunham, and Martha Kaplan. 2004. "'My Ambition Is Much Higher Than Independence': US Power, the UN World, the Nation-State, and Their Critics." In *Decolonization: Perspectives from Now and Then,* edited by Prasenjit Duara, 131–51. London: Routledge.

Kerr, George. 1965. *Formosa Betrayed.* Boston: Houghton Mifflin.

Lutz, Catherine. 2006. "Empire Is in the Details." *American Ethnologist* 33, no. 4 : 593–611.

Lutz, Catherine, and Cynthia Enloe, eds. 2009. *The Bases of Empire: The Global Struggle against US Military Posts.* New York: NYU Press.

Malkki, Liisa H. 1995. *Purity and Exile: Violence, Memory, and National Cosmology among Hutu Refugees in Tanzania.* Chicago: University of Chicago Press.

Nan Fang-Shuo 南方朔. 1980. 帝國主義與台灣獨立運動 [Imperialism and the Taiwan independence movement]. Taipei: Four Seasons.

Philips, Susan U. 2005. "U.S. Colonial Law and the Creation of Marginalized Political Entities." *American Ethnologist* 32, no. 3: 406–19.

Phillips, Steven E. 2003. *Between Assimilation and Independence: The Taiwanese Encounter Nationalist China, 1945–1950.* Stanford, Calif.: Stanford University Press.

Rowen, Ian. 2015. "Inside Taiwan's Sunflower Movement: Twenty-Four Days in a Student-Occupied Parliament, and the Future of the Region." *The Journal of Asian Studies* 74, no. 1: 5–21.

Rutherford, Danilyn. 2012. *Laughing at Leviathan: Sovereignty and Audience in West Papua.* Chicago: University of Chicago Press.

Scott, James C. 1998. *Seeing Like a State: How Certain Schemes to Improve the Human Condition Have Failed.* New Haven, Conn.: Yale University Press.

Shu Wei-Der 許維德. 2001. "中國民族主義‧帝國主義‧台灣獨立運動：評三本 90 年代中國出版的 [台獨研究] 專書" [Chinese nationalism, imperialism, and the Taiwan independence movement: A critical review of three books conducted by Chinese scholars regarding the Taiwan independence movement]. 思與言： 人文與社會科學雜誌 [Thought and word: A magazine of the humanities and social sciences] 39, no. 2: 89–164.

Simon, Scott. 2003. "Contesting Formosa: Tragic Remembrance, Urban Space, and National Identity in Taipak." *Identities: Global Studies in Culture and Power* 10, no. 1: 109–31.

Smith, Daniel Jordan. 2001. "Ritual Killing, 419, and Fast Wealth: Inequality and the Popular Imagination in Southeastern Nigeria." *American Ethnologist* 28, no. 4: 803–26.

Stoler, Ann Laura, with David Bond. 2006. "Refractions off Empire: Untimely Comparisons in Harsh Times." *Radical History Review* 95: 93–107.

Su Beng [Sú-bêng]. 1980. *Tai-oan-lang Si Pah Ni Su* [Taiwan's 400-year history]. San Jose, Calif.: Paradise Culture Associates.

Taiwan Civil Government. 2010. *The Taiwan Civil Government in D.C.* DVD.

Tsing, Anna Lowenhaupt. 1993. *In the Realm of the Diamond Queen: Marginality in an Out-of-the-Way Place.* Princeton, N.J.: Princeton University Press.

Wachman, Alan. 1994. *Taiwan: National Identity and Democratization.* Armonk, N.Y.: M. E. Sharpe.

Wang Yun-Cheng 王雲程. 2005. 佔領與流亡-台灣主權地位之兩面性 [Occupation and exile: The dual character of Taiwan's sovereign status]. Taiwan: Jing Yi.

———. 2007. 放眼國際: 領土地位變遷與台灣 [Looking internationally: Transformations in territorial status and Taiwan]. 2 vols. Taiwan: Jing Yi.

West, Harry G., and Todd Sanders, eds. 2003. *Transparency and Conspiracy: Ethnographies of Suspicion in the New World Order.* Durham, N.C.: Duke University Press.

Wu Rwei-Ren. 2004. "Fragment of/f Empires: The Peripheral Formation of Taiwanese Nationalism." *Social Science Japan* 30: 16–18.

SONY CORÁÑEZ BOLTON

Cripping the Philippine Enlightenment: *Ilustrado* Travel Literature, Postcolonial Disability, and the "Normate Imperial Eye/I"

WHAT MIGHT IT MEAN to speak of colonialism as systematic mass disablement? In this essay, I use *debility/capacity* somewhat interchangeably with the more common *disability/ability* to engage other histories not often addressed under the rubric of disability critique.[1] Doing so allows me to prioritize other global contexts that don't "count" as disability in the phenomenological sense (Erevelles 2011). I translate these concepts to the realms of postcolonial criticism and Spanish-language writing from the Philippines under U.S. occupation. I am particularly interested in the ways in which disability critiques of self-determining autonomy—the constellation of political, affective, and social attitudes that have shaped our ideas of normal embodiment and mental ability—can be rearticulated with the historical preponderance of colonial projects that have routinely found political justification based on the presumptive mental inferiority of the colonized.

"Disabling postcolonialism," a foundational move made by postcolonial disability theorists, urges postcolonial criticism to reframe colonialism as a systematic imposition of mass disablement through the technologies of economic exploitation, metroimperial governance, and enduring racialized notions of cognitive and physical ability (Barker and Murray 2013). Scarcely have disability theories considered histories of imperialism wherein the physical and cognitive capacities for autonomous self-government were denied to the colonized. Neither has postcolonial theory adequately addressed ability/disability as guiding instantiations of coloniality. Indeed, "proving" the colonial subject's physical and cognitive incapacity lies at the heart of the colonial project. While initial forays into postcolonial disability critique mainly focus on physical impairment, I also extend such figurations to elaborate the discursive connections between mental in/capacity and colonial race relations. Philippine and Filipino American historiography have examined this "cognitive tension" in the critiques of U.S. colonialism as a project of "benevolent assimilation" (Rafael 2000; Kramer 2006). U.S. empire benevolently rehabilitated the Philippine native into the mores of the civilized world, thus aligning whiteness with robust cognitive capacity and the Philippine native with an enduring cognitive underdevelopment. Such a reframing of U.S.–Philippine colonial relations demonstrates, I argue, how the Philippines is one site wherein theories of race and postcoloniality can be reconciled with crip theory. Therefore my site of intervention lies in a postcolonial understanding of ability/disability through the frame of the Philippine postcolonial nation-building project that hagiographically has been called the "Philippine Enlightenment," which I explain more fully in the following pages. For now, think of the Philippine Enlightenment as a historical securing of male autonomy through a long conversation across time *between men*. The homosociality of postcolonial enlightenment, perhaps surprisingly, inspires my turn to crip theory.

Crip theory has sought to connect discourses of able-bodiedness as unspoken norm to those of compulsory heterosexuality (McRuer 2006). In similar moves connecting race and disability, histories around the scientization of homosexuality as pathology can be understood in tandem with those of disability. According to Alison Kafer (2006, 15), "disability studies and crip theory differ in orientation and aim: crip theory is more contestatory than disability studies," as it seeks to critique the modes of reformist state recognition on which disability activism has relied. To "crip" a text or period of history cannot be reduced to "finding the cripple" or disabled body. Much the same can be said for "queering" a text.[2] Crip and queer are modes of reading that are not invested exclusively or even at all in locating subjects that would confess to disability or queerness per se. Rather, both are about locating regimes of regulation that discipline bodies, rendering that regulation obvious and, finally, destabilizing it for more than just political ends and a more ethical distribution of resources. Crip theory's importance in understanding Philippine intellectual histories cannot be overstated.

I argue that under the orchestration of the imperial benevolence of U.S. occupation, the colonial debilities that routinely attached to the Filipino male body were sublimated to an Asian female body symbolically and literally disabled by the practice of foot-binding—a reformation of the Philippine Enlightenment through the symbolic deformation of

Chinese Woman. This is where the homosociality of enlightenment enters as an instructive analytic. The homosocial conversation "between men" canonically chronicled in queer theory I reinterpret to understand how postcolonial autonomy for Filipino intellectuals materializes through the conduit of a disabled Asian female body engulfed by the particularity and savagery of her "pies aprisionados" or bound feet (Sedgwick 1985).

Because of the atavist stasis that foot-binding comes to represent in Philippine enlightened resignifications of Asia, I privilege the often-studied colonial genre of travel literature—writing predicated on the literal physical capacity to travel and the cognitive capacity to represent what is apprehended by what Mary Louise Pratt (2008) calls the "imperial eye/I." I align postcolonial critique with crip theory to advance a "postcolonial crip critique"; that is, I align postcolonial criticism that has thematized the enlightened Subject at the center of travel/touristic narration with crip theory's formidable critiques of the constellation of assumptions around the mental and physical capacities that serve as the underlying yet often unspoken mode of production for the rational powers of the Subject (Da Silva 2007).

■ THE "NORMATE IMPERIAL EYE/I" AND THE *ILUSTRADO*'S TRANSNATIONAL MATERIALIST VISION OF ASIA

Teodoro Manguiat Kalaw (1884–1940) was one of an emergent class of new Filipino intellectuals who came of age in the years just following the Philippine wars for independence, otherwise known as the Spanish–American (1898) and Philippine–American (1899–1902) wars. Kalaw represents a "new" Filipino intellectual, or *ilustrado,* in the sense that his prolific work in Spanish proceeds and is epistemologically indebted to late-nineteenth-century anticolonial writings. Despite following in the intellectual patrimony of intellectuals like José Rizal, Kalaw differed; he was partially the product of the U.S. colonial enterprise of "benevolent assimilation" rather than the Filipino anticlerical discourse of the late Spanish colonial period. Philippine historiography has assiduously detailed a late-nineteenth-century movement of Filipino intellectualism that produced a textual nucleus through which the Philippine nation became "enlightened" and thus marked the formation of a nationalist intellectual worldview.[3] Anticolonial enlightenment was the agitation for epistemological and political sovereignty—the articulation of a Philippines to a self-determining future animated by democracy. Under U.S. colonial occupation, the anticlerical enlightenment discourse that once agitated for Philippine sovereignty was reformulated to navigate and, in some cases, accommodate U.S. empire.[4] For my purposes, I analyze

Kalaw's reinscription of an occupied enlightenment as part of articulating a history of postcolonial disability as integral to global imperial histories and U.S. empire in the Philippines.

Toward this end, I center Kalaw's Spanish travel narrative *Hacia la Tierra del Zar* (Toward the land of the czar, 1908), written at the beginning of his political career. By tracking his representations of colonial debility, I aim to crip the genre of colonial travel writing. Such an endeavor intervenes in the ways in which many scholars in disability studies have framed Enlightenment ideals of autonomy and self-determination that elaborate disability as lacking, diseased, and nonnormative configurations of bodily and mental capacity. To be fully human under the long shadow of the Enlightenment, one must approximate a white, male, able-bodied norm. Disability studies and its queerer discourse, "crip theory," have remained largely U.S.- and European-based theorizations of culture and history. Only recently have scholars started to intervene to articulate postcolonial theory with disability theory. My objective is to extend the productive disability critiques of Enlightenment sovereignty to the cultural field of postcolonial enlightenment movements that relied on such normative discourses to attain recognition, political power, and self-determination.

Kalaw's historical positioning vis-à-vis intellectual canonicity brings us irrevocably into an American-occupied Philippines and, unpredictably, into a Russian-occupied Manchuria, a Japanese-occupied Taiwan, and a bucolic Russian countryside—all "cuadros de miseria," or "portraits of misery," he depicts on his colonial travels. His work in a Philippine Spanish written under the duress of American imperialism is an affirmation of intellectual sovereignty that simultaneously ponders the state of colonial debilities and disabilities orchestrated by both Philippine Enlightenment and American colonial discourse. In this article, I gesture toward an understudied "tradition" of "American" Hispano-Philippine writing in the twentieth century through the work of Kalaw given his prolific textual production. In fact, Kalaw's writing was so prolific that historian Teodoro Agoncillo (2003, 3–29) would forgive students of Philippine historiography for calling the American colonial period the "Age of Kalaw"—a period of writing roughly encompassing 1900–40. His work actually ponders the position of the Philippines and Filipinos as what he calls a "race that is destined for death"—a discourse of colonial debility he renders through the prism of post–Boxer Rebellion Manchuria and Czarist Russia. More specifically, this article engages in a postcolonial disability studies reading of Kalaw's navigation of American and Japanese imperialism as he travels throughout Asia, ultimately ending up under the steps of the Kremlin.

I suggest that the early American imperial period saw the protraction rather than the decline of the Hispanic modernity of the *ilustrado* typically ignored in Filipino American studies. The protraction of Hispanic modernity is of interest to global theories of disability. In Kalaw's travel narrative *Hacia la Tierra del Zar*, I suggest that Hispanic Philippine sovereignty relied on debilitated and disabled renderings of Chinese femininity and the backward-Asian cultures that fetishize the impairment of foot-binding. The gendered readings of a monolithic "Chinese" culture figuralized in the bound feet of Chinese Woman (capitalized, as she is only operative as symbol) become an othered Asia buttressing the economic success of imperial Japan and the intellectual capacity of the Filipino *ilustrado* to reform a modern Asia—a reformation that hinged on the racialized gendered deformation of the Chinese female body. Following in line with a postcolonial disability studies critique, I "disable postcolonialism" by centering the genre of travel writing that Kalaw participates in, which actively produces a cognitively able-minded and able-bodied itinerant traveler "erased" from the atavist Asias through which Philippine Enlightenment propagates. This Spanish-language discourse becomes articulated as a feature of American imperial benevolence. Thus such representational gestures in Kalaw's travelogue, I further claim, cannot be taken outside the framework of imperial capitalism assiduously and ambivalently analyzed by Kalaw as, on one hand, an economic boon for a modern Asia (particularly in the case of Japan) and, on the other, coming at a high cost particularly for what Kalaw comes to call a "bloody Manchuria" at the mercy of a supposedly "barbaric" and "superstitious" Russia.

By establishing Kalaw's travel writing as a map of the circulation of transnational capital in American transpacific expansion, Japanese militarized economic imperialism, and the failed imperial decadence of Czarist Russia, I show how the able-bodied/able-minded itinerant *ilustrado* projects the debilities of imperialism and Orientalism onto the body of Chinese Woman to (1) rehabilitate her as an able-bodied laborer, (2) position the *ilustrado* as the enlightened steward of an Asia with cognitive and physical capacity, and (3) reinscribe the enterprise of "benevolent assimilation" as a racialized gendered discourse on colonial cognitive capacity and debility. This postcolonial disability optic mirrors *ilustrado* touristic itinerancy to "crip" the genre of colonial travel writing, arguing that Hispanic Asian modernity is propagated as itself a discourse on colonial impairment and global disability under empire—such a vertiginous reading takes us from the colonially occupied Philippines to the Japanese sugar plantations of Formosa (Taiwan) to the immiseration of a war-torn Chinese Manchuria post–Boxer Rebellion. It should not surprise us that the "pies aprisionados" of the Chinese Woman would appear alongside travels into an immiserated China; the stasis of China serves to orient the movement of the *ilustrado* as a participant in colonial travel narration.

The colonial travel narrative has been theorized as a space where intellectuals have gained access to the sovereign tools of Enlightenment. This access is predicated on disembodiment—what Pratt (2008) has called the "erasure of the human from nature." Put simply, the observer is erased as an active participant in the "Nature" that he shapes and documents. Pratt has argued that this erasure both invisibilizes the debilitating effects of colonialism in travel literature under the guise of scientific objective "Truth" and absolves the colonial traveler from ethical responsibility for imperialism. Indeed, the "totalizing project lives *in* the text, orchestrated by the infinitely expansive mind and soul of the speaker" (109). Colonial travel writing is another of the ableist and debilitating architectures of representation that produces what literary theorist of disability Rosemarie Garland-Thomson has called the "normate" subject. Postcolonial theorist Ato Quayson defines and extends Thomson's concept into the realm of postcolonial literary aesthetics; the "normate" is a colonial aesthetic produced from "the cluster of attitudes that govern the nondisabled's perception of themselves and their relations to the various 'others' of corporeal normativity. . . . There are complex processes by which forms of corporeal diversity acquire cultural meanings that in their turn undergird a perceived hierarchy of bodily traits determining the distribution of privilege, status, and power. . . . Corporeal difference is part of a structure of power, and its meanings are governed by the unmarked regularities of the normate" (Quayson 2013, 203). Extending disability as a colonial aesthetic into realms of the cognitive, I capture the intersection between the critiques of the "expansive mind and soul" of the colonial traveler and the "normate" aesthetics of postcolonial literature as articulating what I call a *normate imperial eye/I*.

The normate imperial eye/I positions the travel narrative as space for the "postcolonial" Filipino *ilustrado* to access the transparent status of sovereign subject—an able-bodied and itinerant eye/I physically able to cross borders and cognitively capable of representing what he sees, in Spanish—the language of Philippine Enlightenment. The appearance of the Chinese Woman operates as symbol engulfed by the spectacularization of her savage impairment:

> Pero estas chinas, estas pobres chinas, con sus pies aprisionados, muy diminutos, ¿en qué piensan, qué hacen, por qué están tristes? Nunca una

sonrisa amable asomó a sus caras pintadas de rosa, nunca. Y si alguna vez lo hicieron fue porque, queriendo dar señales de alegría, no tuvieron más remedio que abrir sus bocas pequeñas y hacer brillar sus dientes marfileños.

But these Chinese girls, these poor Chinese girls, with their imprisoned feet, so diminutive; what are they thinking, what do they do, why are they sad? Never does a smile appear on their rose-colored faces. Never. And if they do occasionally smile, wanting to give signs of happiness, they had no remedy but to open their small mouths and let their ivory teeth shine. (Kalaw 1908, 17)[5]

The spectacle of racialized gendered impairment not only adumbrates the *ilustrado*'s travel itinerary as unbound savant but also emphasizes a boundless cognitive interiority mapped through Spanish. The representation of bound feet highlights how the Chinese Woman's "cultural visibility as deviant obscures and neutralizes the normative figure that [she] legitimates" (Garland-Thomson 1997, 8–9). Indeed, according to Garland-Thomson, "disabled literary characters . . . operate as spectacles. . . . Main characters almost never have physical disabilities" (9). Readers should note that the logics of visibility and erasure in literary representation coincide with those logics germane to travel narrative. Again, what Louise Pratt names the "erasure of the human" from the nature that the travel writer documents is functionalized as the colonial traces of ability left in the wake of colonial travel narration and the impairments produced by the movements of imperialism. It is curious that Kalaw's grand tour toward the "land of the czar" is made possible in the wake of the colonial devastation of the Spanish–American and Philippine–American wars. "Nature," or what Kalaw homosocially comes to call "cuadros de miseria" (portraits of misery), becomes the raw material that is made flexible for disposal by postcolonial enlightenment culture. This exploitation is the logic of capitalist colonialism. Such transparency (or invisibility), however, is traversed by a U.S. colonial gaze by virtue of both the American absent presence throughout *Zar* and the political support offered by American colonial embassies. Kalaw demonstrates that his travels coincide with the movements of capital that he documents coevally. The question of the restructuring of epistemology in the "Philippine Enlightenment" during the early twentieth century is not disentangled from economic restructurings occurring in Asia writ large. Kalaw's normate eye/I documents the "pies aprisionados" of the Chinese Woman to posit an atavist Asia as a racialized gendered discourse on female impairment. Significantly, this body is one that is at odds with transnational capitalist designs on a perfectible laboring Asian body. That is, this colonial genre is a materialist cartography opening up entry points for the penetration of capital through the representations of bodies, vast material wealth, and natural resources and the extension of American "benevolent assimilation" rehabilitating the Filipino intellectual as civilized colonial subject.

Nevertheless, before the estrangements enacted upon and through the "Chinese Woman" as symbol of a debilitated Asia can properly orient a postcolonial disability reading of the *ilustrado* as cognitive figure, I establish *Hacia la Tierra del Zar* as protracting Philippine Enlightenment through a homosocial continuum between an American empire and a Filipino nation. It is through this continuum that we can understand this Filipino travel narrative as a racial materialist survey of the economic developments in and around Asia at the turn of the twentieth century—an Asia that the Philippines as colonial satellite and sovereign national project gets to reform and subsequently deform.

■ THE *MILAGRO JAPONÉS*: MOBILE ASIAS, PHILIPPINE HOMOSOCIALITY, AND AMERICAN IMPERIALISM

Significantly, one of Kalaw's closest friends and confidants accompanied him on his Filipino grand tour—perhaps the most famous Filipino politician in the history of the country: Manuel Quezon.[6] Kalaw details their travels to an international congress on navigation held in St. Petersburg in 1908. Quezon and Kalaw were the then First Philippine Assembly's representation at the congress to be held in Russia. Though St. Petersburg was their main destination, their travels took them through Tokyo, Hong Kong, Shanghai, Formosa, Moscow, Paris, and Port Said. Significantly, Quezon is one of the central figures of Kalaw's touristic impressions, as evidenced by his homosocial dedication:

> el que ha sido testigo personal de estas impresiones de viaje; el que ha visto, a lo largo de las estepas rusas, cuadros de miseria; el que ha sentido simultáneamente, en su paso breve por pueblos, el ambiente de la libertad y el ambiente de la opresión; el que sabrá recoger, en una palabra,—porque es inteligente y porque es joven,—de las ciudadespopulosas, enseñanzas para *su pueblo sometido*, dedica cariñosamente este libro.
> ... Manila, 10 de septiembre de 1908

> the one who has been a personal witness to these travel impressions; the one who has seen, through the Russian steppes, portraits of misery; the one who has simultaneously felt, in his brief passage through villages, the feelings of liberty and oppression; the one who will know how to apprehend,

in one word,—because he is intelligent and because he is young,—from these populous cities, teachings for *his own subdued nation*, [I dedicate] this book affectionately.

. . . Manila, 10 September 1908 (xv)

Quezon and Kalaw are the "personal witness[es]" to the "cuadros de miseria" represented in *Zar*. In the analyses that follow, Kalaw refers most notably to post-Boxer Chinese Manchuria and bucolic subproletariat Russia. The dedication speaks fascinatingly to the historical positioning of *Zar*, most notably to a homosocial relationship *between men* as this kinship extended across othered Asias.

Asia comes to be othered by Kalaw as the sovereign *ilustrado* representing, redrawing, and critiquing its borders muddled the transparent referent that we might call "Asia." Kalaw leverages the description of a flexible "Asia" where "enlightened" Filipino writers negotiate a complex domain of intersecting imperial projects. Indeed, *Zar* indexes major literal and imaginative shifts in the geopolitical arena of Asia as the United States acquired its first Asian colony. Japan becomes a sign of Asian economic success and, by proxy, scaffolds the Philippines, as recipient of American imperial largesse, as a civilization worthy of racial uplift. In this formulation, however, Kalaw indexes that Japan has its own colonial goal of uplifting an economically potent Asia. In Formosa, what today is known as Taiwan, "toda la atención se puso entonces preferentemente en el azúcar . . . crearon un sub-departemento del azúcar" (23).[7]

Japanese-occupied Taiwan is transformed into a sugar plantation. The transformation is so complete that, indeed, "they created a sub-department" dedicated entirely to the cultivation and exportation of sugar. Kalaw's description of Japanese economic agricolonialism admires the shrewd and efficacious uptick represented in the "milagro japonés." He writes, "La primera medida es ayudar a los capitales particulares: a los que adquirían máquinas modernas para el beneficio del azúcar el gobierno ayudaba con una donación de un 20 por ciento del capital invertido. Ya, con este emolumento, muchos se sintieron con deseos de emprender el negocio. Actualmente la isla cuenta con 10 máquinas modernas como las que se encuentran en Cuba y Hawaii" (23).[8] Significantly, this economic "miracle" is measured in U.S. terms: agricolonial development of Cuba and Hawai'i. These parallel imperial projects are an interesting read in the historical context of the post–Russo-Japanese War. Japan triumphs over the nation characterized by Kalaw as a "mediaeval" violent empire given its martial exploits in Manchuria that leave it "bloody" beyond recognition. The transformation of Taiwan into an economic hub that helps to fund Japanese imperial expansion cannot, then, be separated from the very visible militarization marked by Kalaw as he travels through the miraculous modern renovation effected by the Asian empire, which has built "fortificaciones y obras de defensa que se construen desde Ki-lung [hasta Tai-pé]" (22).[9]

The connections between the sugar economics of Japan are not distanced from similar economic militarism undertaken by the United States "que se encuentr[a] en Cuba y Hawaii." The United States's sugar plantations have been documented to have prompted and benefited from a massive migration of Filipino laborers (Baldoz 2011). One might wonder, because the United States is sponsoring and providing interpretive support for this trip, what is it that it wants these *ilustrados* to see? How do the sites of U.S. imperialism shape the sight of the normate eye/I? The fact that this implicit triangle between a Japanese-occupied territory and the U.S.-occupied territories of the Philippines and Hawai'i is deemed by Kalaw to be a political success perhaps suggests mainly that the "consul americano" succeeded in convincing some *ilustrados* of the benefits of their own assimilation. Indeed, "según los datos que nos facilita el consul americano, antes de la ocupación japonesa, la isla sólo producía 10 mil toneladas de azúcar al año. Hoy, bajo el dominio de los nipones, produce 70 mil. Y tan grande es la esperanza para el porvenir, que los severos y sabios directores del sub departamento, en un momento de legítima fe en su obra, han dicho que dentro de 5 años ellos esperan una producción de 250 mil toneladas" (23).[10] The assiduous attention given to the governmental organization of sugar economies in Formosa transpires in the name of maximizing the latter's production. This suggests that the pattern of coloniality characterized by imperial agricolonial development represents a possibly pivotal step in eventual postcolonial sovereignty *for the Philippines*. Within this literal and symbolic economy, Kalaw's travelogue can be read as an important historical index of the material economic transformations that transpired at the turn of the century in Asia. Additionally, the positioning of the text between multiple imperial projects (Japan, Russia, the United States) speaks to the ways in which Filipino Enlightenment is scoped in the crosshairs of these competing imperialisms. All this before Kalaw's critique of imperialism inches closer and closer to Russia by way of Manchuria! I suggest that Manchuria stands as a bloody allegory of a hotly contested Asia—a "contact zone" between an American-occupied Philippines and Russian imperial China. We are left to ponder productively, Which Asia are we seeing as we read *Hacia la Tierra del Zar*? Which Asia does the *ilustrado* want us to see? What are the representational strategies of the normate eye/I as an active shaper of debilitated and capacitated Asias?

One of the tactics that Kalaw employed in his adaptation to American imperial rule was the ambivalent deployment of Orientalist imagery. To demonstrate the shifts, translations, and mutations that the Philippine Enlightenment (and, by extension, "Asia" itself) experiences, I turn to a scene from Kalaw's travel diary where multiple Orients converge with and upon U.S. empire:

> A la hora de la cena, instintivamente, por impulso "racial," los cinco Filipinos quisieron encontrarse en una sola mesa y dialogar sobre las tristezas de la Patria. Considero a [Theo] Rogers, con criterio liberalmente cosmopólita, un Filipino. Somos: Salvador Roxas, Narciso Alegre, [Manuel] Quezon, Rogers y el que escribe estas cuartillas. Los americanos que, al principio, se sentaban con nosotros, viendo nuestro amable intimismo y nuestros alegres corazones nos dejaron, por completo, el control de la mesa. Es pues, en medio del exótico ambiente, una mesa Filipina.

> During dinner, instinctively, due to a "racial" impulse, the five Filipinos decided to meet at a single table and discuss the tragedies of the Homeland. I consider [Theo] Rogers, with liberally cosmopolitan criteria, a Filipino. We are: Salvador Roxas, Narciso Alegre, [Manuel] Quezon, Rogers and the one that writes these very lines. The Americans who, at first, sat with us, seeing our friendly intimacy and our happy hearts, left us total control of the table. Hence, in the middle of this exotic environment, [there was] a Filipino table. (4)

Discourses of benevolence become central to the normativities crystallized by the eye/I. The *ilustrado* becomes the benevolent subject extending Philippine citizenship to the American. This "Filipino American" moment should not be considered outside of the framework of Orientalism. "La mesa Filipina" is where "unos chinos sacerdotales, con sus amplias túnicas blancas, misteriosos dentro de su orientalismo, nos sirven ceremoniosamente, con parsimonia mandarinesca" (4).[11] "La mesa" is oriented within the modern scene of the Japanese gunboat "el Hong Kong Maru," representative of an economic and martial change for the Philippines as it finds articulation within a shifting frame of reference that is "Asia." Whose Asia is being represented (And, who's Asia?) in such an imperial patchwork becomes an increasingly important question as Kalaw continues. Although these travel diaries begin in Asia, the reader is confronted with the instability of such a geopolitical referent. Various "Orients" converge at "la mesa Filipina," unraveling any monolithic image of Asia that we might entertain reading Southeast Asian literature. These "chinos sacerdotales" are represented as vicars of an oriental essence that comes to circumscribe their "parsimonious" service to the future Philippine heads of state who consort momentarily with their American diplomatic attachés before conversing alone. Yet even as this essential "parsimonia mandarinesca" is held up as fulfilling an austere Orientalist stereotype undoubtedly assumed to be circulating in the mind of Kalaw's imagined reader, the *ilustrado* at the center of the production of Asianness in this sentence (indeed, *served* by it: "nos sirven ceremoniosamente") subverts, while also dining on and furthering, the "mystery" of Orientalism. This subversion is articulated through the crossroads of the Orient that is represented vis-à-vis (cultural) capital and its attendant privileges, enjoyed by Kalaw as Asian author with the powers to perform such a representation. Such subversion, I argue, transpires through the transparency of enlightenment—the ability to represent as a threshold subject within and without Asia as a Filipino through the medium of Spanish. It is this threshold "Asian" sovereign that can not only exploit Chinese labor through an Orientalist racialization but also invite Americans to the table, as it were, by redefining "Filipino" with "criterio liberalmente cosmopólita." I suggest that the *ilustrado* profits from the erasure of U.S. imperialism via the surprising assimilation of white Americans *into* the Philippines. Indeed, it is the invitation of "America" to the table that elaborates one re-formation of who composes Asia. Here the Philippines is symbolically part of the United States.

The pliancy of "Asia" as an unstable referent simultaneously connoting Orientalist savage and savant demonstrates that Kalaw's *Hacia la Tierra del Zar* evokes the colonial travel narrative as the racial materialist representation of the movement of global capital. For instance, the colonial subject (yet emancipated intellectual) of the *ilustrado* repeats a "postcolonial" Enlightenment project as the very mechanism through which American imperial and economic interests ramify through the flexibly redefined "Asia" that Kalaw himself maps out. This cartographic imperative transpires through the homosocial continuum (the table conversation between illustrated men discussing "las tristezas de la Patria") of the Philippine Enlightenment. However, there are several episodic interventions that Kalaw stages in his narration that shift the homosociality of the Enlightenment to allow a consideration of the genre of the travel narrative itself through a postcolonial disability studies lens of imperial benevolence and "white love."

■ CRIPPING ENLIGHTENMENT: THE ABLE-MINDED
ILUSTRADO'S WHITE LOVE

The representation of Russian-occupied Manchuria serves as the literary mechanism through which Kalaw politically reimagines "Asia." Such reimagination of the space of "Asia" endows it with a sense of pliancy that can be understood in the context of the itinerancy of the *ilustrado* traveler and power to represent such a space through Spanish under the beneficent tutelage of American empire. The ruination of Manchuria after the Boxer Rebellion (1899–1901) and the subsequent Russian occupation of China are understood through the framework of a failed Philippine insurrection against the United States (1899–1902). Surprisingly, the destination that makes sense of these intersecting colonial conflicts is the bucolic Russian countryside; Kalaw presents the material effects of poverty that the Russian state has all but ensured for its citizens. The impoverished Russian hinterlands is also where the thread of the Filipino homosocial brotherhood between Kalaw and Manuel Quezon is substantiated further:

> Ayer, en uno de esos villorrios obscuros en donde los trenes hacen paradas momentáneas, mi compañero, Quezon se acercó a un grupo de emigrantes que acababan de llegar al pueblo, queriendo contemplar de cerca a aquellas pobres víctimas del hambre. Indudablemente, serían miembros de una familia. El compañero llamó a un mugriento niño de 5 años, enclenque y tímido, figura del hambre y del esclavo, con un abriguito que era un trapo, le dió una monedita rusa. La madre que lo vió, no pudiendo ocultar su satisfacción y su gratitud, ordenó al hijo, en lengua moscovita, que besara la mano del buen extranjero.
>
> Y el niño, educado en la sumisión de todo un pueblo, se acercó con mucho miedo al dadivoso compañero y le besó la mano generosa.
>
> Ese cuadro simbólico representa la educación social de una raza.

> Yesterday, in one of those obscure hamlets where trains make but fleeting stops, my friend, Quezon, approaches a group of emigrants that were just arriving to the village, with the desire to inspect these poor victims of famine. Undoubtedly, they were members of one family. My friend called to a filthy boy of 5 years, sickly and shy, the figure of hunger and poverty, with a rag for a coat, he [Quezon] gave him a Russian coin. The mother saw it; unable to hide her satisfaction and her gratitude, ordered her son, in Russian, to kiss the hand of the kind foreigner.
>
> And the boy, brought up in the submission of an entire people, fearfully approached my generous friend and kissed his benevolent hand.
>
> This symbolic portrait represents the social education of a race. (Kalaw 1908, 87)

In this scene, Quezon, the future first president of the Commonwealth of the Philippines, is represented as a "kind foreigner" extending his "benevolent hand" to a poverty-stricken Russian boy. Quezon charitably gifts him a "Russian coin." In the context of the "benevolent assimilation" of American imperialism in the Philippines, this encounter between the white Russian impoverished boy and the Filipino intellectual takes on a special meaning. One can observe in the preceding passage one of the "cuadros de miseria," or "portraits of misery," that Kalaw alludes to in his dedicatory remarks to the star of this particular scene, Quezon. The benevolence in this scene should not shock those familiar with the discursive arrangements that organized the affect of American imperialism in the Philippines as one of "white love" (Rafael 2000). Indeed, couched in the affect of "love" for the Americans' "little brown brother" was the white man's burden to educate the Filipino in the ways of the civilized world. The polarity between civilized American and barbaric Filipino is upended in this representation of *ilustrado* charity to the white boy, ruined by the imperial despotism of Russia—a decadence only amplified by the Manchuria "ensangrentada" (bloody) preceding such descriptions of white poverty.

A whiteness ruined by imperialism is saved by the *ilustrado*. The political reversal here is that of the erudite *ilustrado* benevolently extending his "mano generosa" to the "mugriento niño." This scene of "white love," or, rather, love for the white boy, speaks to the racialized gendered and sexualized encounter between the "white daddy–native boy"—indeed, the pivotal frame through which I suggest we should understand the reversal that Kalaw stages for his reader. It is through such a reversal that we can note the strategy through which Kalaw represents "Asia" as a site for reclamation and reimagination vis-à-vis the "civilizing" discourse of Filipino Enlightenment.

The reclamation of "Asia" is the keystone of an intersectional paradigm in which discourses of race, gender, sexuality, ability, and class innervate the twentieth-century Philippine Enlightenment. The repetition of such a paradigm through the medium of travel narration gains its iterative power through the staging and restaging of the colonial encounter— encounters in which the *ilustrado* performatively gains power as agentive subject. The stage in which these colonial encounters between Self and Other reside can be theorized as a *contact zone*. Contact zones describe the highly syncretic space where "disparate cultures meet, clash, and grapple with each other, often in highly asymmetrical relations of domination and subordination" (Pratt 2008, 7). Queer of color theory has examined how such encounters are steeped in various gendered and sexualized histories of colonial relations refracted through the paradigm of the "white man–native boy" (Lim 2013). The repetition of coloniality in Filipino intellectual discourses demonstrates both the constrained agency of the *ilustrado* and the problematic limitations of sovereign cognition (Kramer 2006). The "benevolent assimilationist" protocols of U.S. imperialism in the Philippines similarly gain traction as an intellectual project of colonial benevolence in Kalaw's staging of Quezon and the white Russian boy. In much the same way Filipino *ilustrados* reformulated and iterated a Philippine Enlightenment when confronted with American empire, scholars like Lim understand the dyad of the white man–native boy as a repetition of an "unhomely" trope that always already reads racialized gender and sexuality in colonialism (Bhabha 2004). Such a paradigm consolidates for analysis the ways in which racialized gendered relations are constitutive of a Filipino (anti-)colonial intellectual project at the turn of the twentieth century.

In one sense, we can read as already a factual state of affairs that the very production of this travel narrative is a repetition of the native boy–colonial father dyad that Lim gets at. The historiographical precedent in Filipino study's analyses of "white love" has concluded as much. A crucial difference is the subtle and overt ways in which "Asia" is itself a fertile and shifting ground of contested meanings that is resignified depending on the colonial project described in the journey toward the Kremlin. Cultural productions such as these leverage themselves on a polysemous "transnational and sometimes unruly itinerary . . . meant to trouble the ascribed unidirectionality of critical and complicit energies and logics that often accompany the provenance of 'Asia' as a stable and static category in [the] twentieth century" (Lim 2013, 11). Lim takes to task the "classic colonial/native encounter of post-Enlightenment modernity" wherein the product of structural colonial seduction is a rational colonial white subject that is fully formed and agentive and thus "inspires a biography," whereas the native, brown bottom is infantilized, bounded, and fetishized by/as tradition, thus "disappear[ing] into a mob" (8). I add to this dyadic paradigm by considering the contributions of postcolonial enlightenment movements in a supposedly "post-Enlightenment modernity" that Lim's homosocial/homoerotic encounter takes as its historical and temporal assumption. *Hacia la Tierra del Zar* is a crucial text detailing the beginning of U.S. imperial power's relationship with a "post-Enlightenment," post-(Spanish)-colonial Filipino *ilustrado* that repeats the dyadic native boy–white daddy colonial encounter with a difference: it is the biography of enlightened "postcolonial" brown boys that we consider as they simultaneously center and disappear their white men (both Spanish and "American").

What does this have to do with postcolonial disability? The "white boy" recipient of *ilustrado* benevolence is actually part of the debilitated landscape uplifted by *ilustrado* enlightenment—a "cuadro de miseria." The white daddy–brown (native) boy dyad (what in Filipino American critiques of U.S. empire is read as a fraternal, if tacitly sexualized, relation of white male anti-imperialist to "little brown brother") helps us to understand not only the gendered and racialized components of American empire in the Philippines but also the ways in which problematic gender and sexual politics come to underwrite the Filipino Enlightenment. As we see in the colonial encounter between Quezon and the Russian boy, there is a powerful political reversal of the trope that Lim offers us. Instead it is the *ilustrado* extending his benevolent colonial hand to the white child ruined by a failed antimodern Russian empire. However, the failures of another "Asian" imperialism in this scene are a foil for the success of the benevolent assimilation of these Filipinos into a U.S. imperial imaginary of racial uplift for the Philippines. That is to say, the success of the *ilustrado* in this scene only makes sense given his receipt of American imperial largesse—the little brown boy grown up. Therefore, the cursory liberating potential of the dyadic "brown *ilustrado* man/off-whitish child" gains traction in its underlying mode of production: manhood and masculinity attained through the tutelage of a "disappeared" white daddy.

▪ THE NATIVE DISABLED GIRL

Taking Lim's productive queer of color framing of the erotics of colonialism, there is one other such staging of colonial encounter that is enabled by the homosocial enlightenment logics proliferated by Kalaw: where the cognitively able-minded *ilustrado* meets the native disabled girl. The disappearance of the "white daddy" is complicated by the conjuring of a symbolically iterated impaired figure of the Asian woman as articulated and temporally bound by the social practice of foot-binding. This figure is disabled through the discursive exclusion from enlightened cognition that characterizes the masculinist domain of Enlightenment proper as well as its postcolonial rearticulations. Additionally, the re-presentation of the figure of "Woman" as literally physically impaired provides another vista through which to view the discourse of Yellow Peril that characterizes Kalaw's appraisal of China as a "mancha negra, sucia, ululante" (black, dirty, wailing stain) and "ensangrentada." The "black bloody stain" emerges, I suggest, through the misshapen feet of Chinese Woman. The emergence of this figure, which precipitates the colonial encounter of *ilustrado*–disabled girl, begins in Manchuria, where Kalaw poses the question, "¿Hay razas destinadas a morir?"

"Are there races that are destined to die?" he asks in a chapter titled "La

Mandchuria Sangrienta," or "Bloody Manchuria," highlighting the high costs of imperial war (83). Nirmala Erevelles argues that "disability and war" should be a crucial framework through which "feminist disability studies and third world feminism" understand the production of disability through the machine of imperialism. I suggest that the exploitative dynamics of imperial capitalism intersects with the propagation of global disabilities. A "bloody Manchuria" exists in an asymmetrical cripped relationship to Russia, Japan, and the United States. Such a bloody state of affairs leads the enlightened Filipino subject to ponder the whether some "races" exist on the "horizon of death" (Da Silva 2007). Nevertheless, within the same breath, we can observe that the bloody state of Manchuria coincides with the racialized colonial uplift of Formosa as a sugar plantation under Japanese imperialism. Erevelles (2011, 132) pushes for a materialist understanding of disability as a condition, response, and sign of the proliferation of war since imperial conflicts historically are "one of the largest producers of disability." Disability, then, whether it takes the form of economic debility, bodily harm, environmental devastation, "slow death," or the colonial presumption of incompetence, testifies to the widespread precarity orchestrated in colonial relations. The Philippines is a vital site to understanding the propagation of global impairments through the circulation of transnational capital; the Hispanized imposition of Philippine Enlightenment in other kinds of Asias (Japanese imperial Asia, colonized Taiwan, bloody Manchuria) exists alongside the persistent discourse of "benevolent assimilation" that has come to historically mark American–Philippine colonial relations. It has been suggested that "benevolent assimilation" of the Philippines into the more enlightened domain of U.S.-sponsored racial uplift depended on the presumption of incompetence of the Filipino to truly self-govern. In this sense, "benevolent assimilation" aspires to reshape the very cognitive landscape of the Filipino mind, thus making colonial racial uplift also always a cognitive relation. The racialization of the Filipino in U.S. imperial expansion relied on the cognitive impairment of the Philippines to participate as a fully sovereign democratic subject. The travel narrative is an important genre in this context, as it relies on the able-bodied and able-minded itinerancy of the colonial traveler to cross borders and represent them.

Disability, I suggest, systematically defines the "asymmetry" in power relations constitutive of the "contact zone" in which travel narrative representations circulate. The process of racialization in which imperialism is thoroughly embedded utilizes disability tautologically as a major technology for justifying its own existence. Put bluntly, the brown mind is too stupid for imperial war against the brown body to ethically count as violence. I suggest that imperialism gains moral traction insofar as it articulates itself as a project that restores the battered brown body to approximate the "normate" white (imperial) body (Garland-Thomson 2013, 333–53). Violence against the brown body doesn't meet the threshold of ethical harm if the brown mind is recipient of the rehabilitative civilizing influence of American imperialism. Kalaw takes up the presumption that such benevolence is a constitutive aspect of any successful empire. For Kalaw, more specifically, his rhetorical question about the horizon of death that colonial conflict inevitably hails is posed as part of an ongoing reflection on the presence of Russia in Manchuria as testament to what failed imperialism looks like—an "Imperio moscovita" "despótica" "pan-eslavista" succumbing to a base "idolatría" "ortodoxa" that proves that "en la Santa Rusia hay más ignorancia que religión" (78, 143–44, 188).[12] Indeed, when in Russia, Kalaw exclaims, "Eso no es Europa, eso es Asia" (143–44). The representation of Russia as a "Europe" that is really "Asia" is difficult to read outside of the devastation of China wrought after the Boxer Rebellion. While Russia as a European nation is rendered barbaric given both its proximity to and imperialism of Asia, the Philippines attains cultural capital as an Enlightened Asia given its rehabilitation as a domain of American empire.

China is scripted into the savior complex constitutive of the *ilustrado*'s redefinition of Asia. China is discursively "saved" through a critique of a Russian imperial project. However, the critique of Russia as antimodern depends on an Orientalist vision of China. China becomes the Orientalist and barbaric substrate on which the Philippine Enlightenment relies. In an earlier reflection on his voyage through Hong Kong, Kalaw observes that from the first to the last moment, the only sensational observation that injures and captivates is of those black, dirty, wailing stains that are called "the Chinese . . . the first thing one smells is Chinese" (7). Significantly, the description of a Chinese essence as a "black, dirty, wailing stain" precedes a section titled "Peligro Amarillo" or "Yellow Peril." However, as we will observe, it is not simply the national space of China that serves as the atavist catalyst of a new, better Asian enlightened subject. Rather, what's more interesting here is China's corporal and material representation as the racialized gendered disabled figure vis-à-vis its practices of foot-binding. Hence the question of "are there races destined to die?" that began this section can refer to the supposed slow death of the racialized gendered figure of the Chinese Woman whose feet are bound in space and time. Again, "these poor Chinese girls, with their imprisoned feet, so diminutive; what are they thinking, what do they do, why are they sad?" (17).

A discourse of foot-binding and the construction of Chinese feminin-ity represented through the trope of "pies aprisionados" is a crucial mo-ment in Kalaw's writing. Kalaw deploys the iconic image of bound feet to mark Chinese antimodernity vis-à-vis a Western definition of civilization. Dorothy Ko exhaustively has studied the cultural and historical underpin-nings around the social practice of foot-binding. She argues that there exists many foot-bindings, not just one (Ko 2007). That is, it is impossible to understand such a geographically and temporally pervasive cultural practice through one framework; instead, we must be historically specific in any analysis or supposedly "moral" claim about gender asymmetries in Chinese society. Ko situates herself "outside the anti-foot-binding enlightenment discourse" that only ever ensures Western modernity as the arbiter of gender parity. Like Spivak, she objects to the paradigm of "white men saving brown women from brown men" (Spivak 1988, 296–97). Yet, what is to be made of brown men saving brown women from brown men?

A native disabled girl–native enlightenment boy dichotomy frames Kalaw's travel narrative, the arc of his journey to the heart of (Russian) "darkness." This colonial encounter, I argue, is foundational to the nor-mate eye/I's perception of reality. A connection exists between Kalaw's depiction of the material division of international labor and the cogni-tive division of intellectual capacities intrinsic to postcolonial enlighten-ments. The *ilustrado*'s touristic itinerary as portrayed in *Zar* mirrors and relies on the movement of capital; indeed, the *ilustrado* border crosses as a liberal subject of enlightenment due to the liberalizing of borders to facilitate the movements of transnational capital at the turn of the twentieth century. This movement, however, ironically relies on the stasis of "Asia" flexibly reinterpreted—an Asia literally and figuratively bound. The static image that constrains and enables the duality of the "Asia" that Kalaw articulates is the racialized gendered (and inevitably sexualized) image of Chinese foot-binding. It is through the disabled Asian female body that a cognitively judicious and able-minded Filipino *ilustrado* can critique failed imperial projects in and around Asia (Russia) while simul-taneously, albeit ambivalently, manipulating American imperial interests to promote Filipino sovereignty. But, following Ko, what kind of foot-binding in particular does Kalaw describe?

What I claim via this illustration of "pies aprisionados" is that the social integuments of disability are rooted in enlightened postcolonial cognition. The interiority of the Chinese Woman debilitated by the erotic gaze of Chinese men (and alternatively aestheticized by the enlightened gaze of the *ilustrado*) is never really considered. The Chinese Woman is only operative as a symbol evacuated of interiority. She ornaments Kalaw's travel narrative through the spectacle of her impairment. Here the colonial gaze of the Philippine Enlightenment maneuvers through and functions as the "stare" dehumanizing the disabled body foundational to Western modernity's constitution of "normate" bodies (Erevelles 2011). "Saving" the native disabled girl does not involve a robust consideration of her interior life, her subjective experience, or the material conditions in which foot-binding operates. Instead, we receive a line of questioning from Kalaw: "what are they thinking, what do they do, why are they sad?" Robust answers to these questions never materialize in Kalaw's Orientalist impressions. Instead, a remark on their smile of "ivory teeth" from a moment of provisional happiness is rendered, repeating the ornamental image-conscious discourse that could be said to have imprisoned her feet in the first place. Chinese Woman's experiences are never truly elaborated in order to buttress Western rationality as the most desirable human and gender rights model. Kalaw subscribes to a Western model of gender parity and the normative body to become the master of subjectivity in this instance. In the same vein, Chinese Woman's entire corporeal (and cognitive) existence, impossible insofar as she remains symbol, is subsumed by the fetishization of her impairment.

The female body is functionalized as a machine whose purity is not to be disturbed by the earthly barbaric practices of a backward culture. This reading corroborates Ko's excavation of the historical roots of the anti-foot-binding movement in British missionary culture. According to Ko, the "body as machine" as a theological concept cannot be fully explained through a supposedly divine law that could never really secure the gender equality upheld in the theoretical by Western societies—the language of parity is a convenient cloak for Orientalist discourse that also masks British imperial projects in China. The real "sin" of the practice of foot-binding is that it hinders the productivity of the body. The disabled body hinders full incorporation into capitalist systems of labor exploitation. It takes a cognitive "enlightenment discourse," such as that exemplified by "anti-foot-binding" societies and what I have been calling the "Philippine Enlightenment," to secure the liberal humanist discourse that ensures the proper "democratic" protection of bodies from debilities and impairments that would halt the movement of transnational capital. Kalaw's racial materialist grand tour affirms cognitive capacity through the impaired ornamentalization of these "pobres chinas" "aprisionadas." I agree with Ko's gesture that Enlightenment discourses can be seen as trafficking in a "loathing for the stagnant female body," one whose impairment is at odds with the sovereign cognition that serves capitalist penetration into Asia—a capitalist penetration that is venerated earlier in Japanese-occupied Taiwan and tacitly in the U.S.-occupied Philippines (Ko 2007, 27).

■ CONCLUSION: TOWARD A POSTCOLONIAL DISABILITY STUDIES

I have argued that the homosocial continuum gains traction through variously staged colonial encounters in which the *ilustrado* "inspires a biography"—a representational impulse that allows for a materialist redefinition of Asia. Initially, I established the Philippine Enlightenment as a homosocial continuum that traverses from the United States *through* the Philippines, thus ramifying American imperial power through the Asia that Kalaw pliantly redefines. Homosociality is concretized through the colonial reversal of "white love" performed in Quezon's patronizing uplift of the Russian white boy in the depressed countryside rendered as a "cuadro de miseria." This scene adds additional nuance to the queer of color critique of the colonial encounter thematized as a discursive repetition of the white daddy–native boy dyad. Kalaw's travel narrative disappears this white daddy, thus resignifying "white love." However, the underlying substrate on which these resignifications and disidentifications with white imperial paternalism occur is the colonial encounter between the cognitively capacitated *ilustrado* and the native disabled girl. This girl is wholly embodied by and subsumed into the fetish of her impairment—the symbol of Chinese Woman and her bound feet. Her appearance in the travel narrative is crucial to reinterpreting this colonial genre through a postcolonial disability studies optic.

The cognitive itinerancy and *literal* border crossing of the *ilustrado* are secured through the stasis and literal binding of the impaired Asian female body. Because the movements of the *ilustrado* reflect the movement of transnational capital in Asia, disability (and the cognitive capacity that is immanent in disability's transcendence) becomes the node through which capital can "burrow into the body," to paraphrase Neferti Tadiar (2009). While this argument certainly mimics the itinerant subjectivity constantly in flux and moving in *Hacia la Tierra del Zar,* I formulate it as part of a broader critique in this essay to continue the nascent intellectual project of a postcolonial disability studies or a postcolonial crip theory. Given this context, I suggest that the material histories of transnational capital as mapped by the movements of *ilustrado* travel writing make two main interventions I'd like to highlight here: (1) challenging the rather obscurantist trajectory of a Filipino American cultural studies that privileges Anglophone and largely U.S.-based renderings of "Filipino experience" and (2) how U.S. disability study's deconstructive moves problematizing the primacy of the able body (in its liberal humanist or biomedical configuration) can abstract such critiques from colonial history.

The point that I would like to make here is that postcolonial enlightenment projects should be arenas where crip theory's critique of the Western Enlightenment and Filipino American studies can ponder the extent to which ability and disability should become part of our theoretical strategies. I would go as far as to say that all postcolonial enlightenment projects following in the "tradition" of the Haitian Revolution are anticolonial disability critiques. Such gestures toward the emancipatory protocols of enlightened cognition are a means of discursively articulating a notion of citizenship that results from "disputes regarding the best way to discern the field of not-disability." That is, anticolonial revolutionary struggle demonstrates that black and brown bodies can also become fluent in the political language of sovereignty as it is tied to the nation-state. Such moves toward the epistemic sovereignty of Enlightenment, however problematic or ableist such a move by the *ilustrado* may be, cannot be disarticulated from the screen of colonial violence, which constitutes manifold projects of mass disablement through war, poverty, and categorical exclusion from the "human"; indeed, such *ilustrado* discourse is itself a "dispute" of the systematic mass disablement that Spanish and U.S. colonial projects have enacted. Postcolonial Enlightenment, then, is an insistent corroboration of *capacity* under the duress of genocidal imperial violence.

I gesture toward the complications entailed in the "situated" critiques of disability as proffered by an incipient postcolonial disability studies. What constitutes "ability" and "disability" radically shifts, depending on context. Dis/ability radically shifts definition in the context of colonial histories of disablement. We might critique Filipino Enlightenment for subscribing to the very cognitive ableism that excluded the Philippine nation from humanity in the first place. However, in that critique, I would be hesitant to begrudge or efface the revolutionary movements that such epistemic sovereignty inspired and the revolutionary potential incumbent in such anticolonial histories. But my project here is not to fully redeem the Philippine Enlightenment, ironically through a disability studies optic—such a project has major limitations. One such limitation is that it renders opaque various kinds of feminized labors that ensure the construction of masculinist cognition as the underwriting protocol of the postcolonial Filipino nation. In this analysis, the site of both cognitive extraction and generation of surplus value is the symbolic Chinese Woman and her deformed body. However, in a postcolonial critique of disability or a move to "disable postcolonialism," we can more fully interrogate what a disability studies critique of postcolonial Enlightenment looks like.

Sony Coráñez Bolton is a C3-Mellon Postdoctoral Fellow in the Departments of Spanish and Portuguese and of Gender, Sexuality, and Feminist Studies at Middlebury College in Vermont.

NOTES

1. Jasbir Puar (2012) expands the terms *ability* and *disability* with the illuminating *capacity* and *debility*. As a result, other historical dimensions of difference can be articulated to rhetorics and histories of ableism. For instance, histories of scientific racism are predicated on the proximity of cognitive impairment and the racial science of eugenics, even though one's color does not connote mental disability in a phenomenological sense. However, the historical proximity of blackness and mental retardation can be captured more readily by talking about race/racism as a debility vis-à-vis an able-bodied, white norm endowed with unquestioned and, as we will see, infinite cognitive capacity.

2. That is, queer theory is not invested in excavating sociological subjects that would confess to the truth of being LGBT as much as it is invested in critiques of normativity. Crip theory shares this political orientation: to critique the regulatory structures that discipline bodies rather than finding positivist accounts of disability.

3. Several scholars have written about the "Propagandist Movement" and Philippine Enlightenment. See Anderson (1990; 2007), Thomas (2012), Ileto (1997), Mojares (2008), and Reyes (2008).

4. However, rather than claim that Filipino *ilustrados* were American apologists, their intellectual production was articulated within the constrained field of agency of imperialism.

5. My translation from the original Spanish. All translations throughout this article are mine.

6. Actually, several future Filipino statesmen accompany Kalaw. He writes while on the Japanese gunboat the *Hong-Kong Maru* that "Salvador Roxas, Narciso Alegre, [Manuel] Quezon," and he are participating in this tour of Asia and Russia. He also acknowledges the presence of a Russian-language interpreter and of U.S. diplomatic attaché Theo Rogers.

7. "All attention and preference was placed on sugar . . . they created a sub-department of sugar."

8. "The first step is to aid in particular capital developments: to those that would acquire modern machines for the benefit of sugar production

the government provided a donation of 20 percent of the total capital invested. So, with this stipend, many felt motivated to pursue this business venture. Today the island [Taiwan] possesses 10 modern machines like those found in Cuba and Hawaii."

9. "Fortifications and defenses are being constructed from Ki-Lung [to Taipei]."

10. "According to the information provided by the American consul, before the Japanese occupation, the island only produced 10 thousand tons of sugar per year. Today, under the dominion of the Japanese, it produces 70 thousand tons. So large is the hope for the future, that the strict and wise directions of the sub-department [of sugar], in a moment of supreme faith in their work, have stated that within 5 years they expect an output of 250 thousand tons."

11. "Some priestly Chinese, with their ample white robes, mysterious in their orientalism, serve us ceremoniously, with Mandarin parsimony."

12. A "despotic" "Slavic [nationalist]" "Moscovite Empire" succumbing to a base "orthodox" "idolatry" that proves that "in Holy Russia there is more ignorance than religion." My translation.

WORKS CITED

Agoncillo, Teodoro. 2003. "Philippine Historiography in the Age of Ka-law." In *History and Culture, Language and Literature: Selected Essays of Teodoro A. Agoncillo,* edited by Bernardita R. Churchill, 3–30. Manila: University of Santo Tomas.

Anderson, Benedict. 1990. *Imagined Communities.* New York: Verso.

———. 2007. *Under Three Flags: Anarchism and Anti-colonial Imagination.* New York: Verso.

Baldoz, Rick. 2011. *The Third Asiatic Invasion: Migration and Empire in Filipino America, 1898–1946.* New York: NYU Press.

Barker, Clare, and Stuart Murray. 2013. "Disabling Postcolonialism: Global Disability Cultures and Democratic Criticism." In *The Disability Studies Reader,* edited by Lennard J. Davis, 61–73. New York: Routledge.

Bhabha, Homi. 2004. *The Location of Culture.* New York: Routledge.

Da Silva, Denise. 2007. *Towards a Global Idea of Race.* Minneapolis: University of Minnesota Press.

Erevelles, Nirmala. 2011. *Disability and Difference in Global Contexts: Enabling a Transformative Body Politic.* New York: Palgrave Macmillan.

Garland-Thomson, Rosemarie. 1997. *Extraordinary Bodies: Figuring Physical Disability in American Culture and Literature.* New York: Columbia University Press.

———. 2013. "Integrating Disability, Transforming Feminist Theory." In

The Disability Studies Reader, edited by Lennard Davis, 333–53. New York: Routledge.

Ileto, Reynaldo. 1997. *Pasyon and Revolution: Popular Movements in the Philippines, 1840–1910.* Manila: Ateneo de Manila Press.

Kafer, Alison. 2006. *Feminist Crip Queer.* Bloomington: Indiana University Press.

Kalaw, Teodoro. 1908. *Hacia la Tierra del Zar.* Manila: Librería Manila Filatélica.

Ko, Dorothy. 2007. *Cinderella's Sisters: A Revisionist History of Footbinding.* Berkeley: University of California Press.

Kramer, Paul. 2006. *The Blood of Government: Race, Empire, the United States, and the Philippines.* Chapel Hill: University of North Carolina Press.

Lim, Eng Beng. 2013. *Brown Boys and Rice Queens.* Durham, N.C.: Duke University Press.

McRuer, Robert. 2006. *Crip Theory: Cultural Signs of Queerness and Disability.* New York: NYU Press.

Mojares, Resil B. 2008. *Brains of the Nation.* Manila: Ateneo de Manila Press.

Pratt, Mary Louise. 2008. *Imperial Eyes: Travel Writing and Transculturation.* New York: Routledge.

Puar, Jasbir. 2012. "The Cost of Getting Better: Suicide, Sensations, Switchpoints." *GLQ: A Journal of Lesbian and Gay Studies* 18, no. 1: 149–58.

Quayson, Ato. 2013. "Aesthetic Nervousness." In *The Disability Studies Reader,* edited by Lennard Davis, 202–13. New York: Routledge.

Rafael, Vicente. 2000. *White Love and Other Events in Filipino History.* Durham, N.C.: Duke University Press.

Reyes, Raquel. 2008. *Love, Passion, and Patriotism in the Propagandist Movement, 1882–1892.* Seattle: University of Washington Press.

Sedgwick, Eve Kosofsky. 1985. *Between Men: English Literature and Male Homosocial Desire.* New York: Columbia University Press.

Spivak, Gayatri. 1988. "Can the Subaltern Speak?" In *Marxism and the Interpretation of Culture,* edited by Cary Nelson and Lawrence Grossberg, 271–316. Urbana: University of Illinois Press.

Tadiar, Neferti X. 2009. *Things Fall Away: Philippine Historical Experience and the Making of Globalization.* Durham, N.C.: Duke University Press.

Thomas, Megan. 2012. *Orientalists, Propagandists, and Ilustrados: Filipino Scholarship and the End of Spanish Colonialism.* Minneapolis: University of Minnesota Press.

DAVID S. ROH

Kaneshiro Kazuki's *GO* and the American Racializing of *Zainichi* Koreans

PART OF A LONG TRADITION of *zainichi bungaku* (Korean Japanese literature), Kaneshiro Kazuki's *GO* is an accessible rendering of *zainichi* (resident Korean in Japan) alienation and subjectivity in a familiar Japanese
genre—the chronicle of a schoolboy brawler. I do not mean to characterize
Kaneshiro's 1996 novel as necessarily representative of the tradition of
zainichi fiction that has preceded him; indeed, his work has been criticized
for its problematic depictions of nationality and gender. This essay views
GO through a transnational studies lens to articulate the importance of
tertiary national sites in considering domestic and international minority discourse. Whereas Asian American studies scholars may focus on
domestic Asian diasporic literatures, I look abroad to uncover connections to expose the collaborative—and knotty—formulation of these
communities through politics, history, and culture in both the United
States and Japan.

The plot of *GO* is as follows: Sugihara, a *zainichi* Korean high schooler,
struggles to find his place in a Japan that discriminates against *zainichi*
Koreans, who are considered alien residents despite being born and raised
in Japan. Sugihara falls in love with a Japanese girl named Sakurai, who
is oblivious of his Korean heritage. During their courtship, Sugihara, who
passes for Japanese, struggles with the decision to reveal his ethnicity
to Sakurai. Meanwhile, Sugihara's father chooses to switch nationalities from North Korean to South Korean, ostensibly for the purpose of
vacationing in Hawai'i—a move that sends Sugihara spiraling down an
existential hole. Sugihara then decides to transfer from his North Korean state-affiliated school to attend a Japanese high school, where he
has to contend with bullying. It is only before they consummate their

relationship that Sugihara admits to Sakurai that he is *zainichi*. She initially rejects him, but the novel concludes with their reconciliation when she finally accepts him, absent labels.

Complicating the standard high school romance between our protagonist and love interest are subtextual plotlines centered on racial anxiety, national politics, intergenerational conflict, and social discrimination. Beneath the surface of *GO* are several sites of discourse wrestling with the ethnonational politics of Japan, Korea, and the United States in formulating a *zainichi* minority subjectivity. This essay argues that the novel struggles with formulating an epistemology for *racial* rather than national or ethnic subjectivity beyond the ken of Korea and Japan; to do so, it imports racial discourse through the vehicle of American popular culture.[1]

I engage with both Asian and Asian American studies as part of a longer conversation on transnational, multidisciplinary, and multilingual studies. Disciplinary boundaries in area studies have traditionally precluded meaningful dialogue, but there have been attempts at rectification, with scholars moving across Japanese, Korean, and Chinese studies (Ching 2001, 30). Studies of *zainichi* history and literature, for instance, lend to an alignment between Korean and Japanese studies. Likewise, Asian American studies has made concurrent shifts; however, that dialogue has been largely unidirectional. Elaine Kim and Lisa Lowe (1997, viii) write, "There will need to be a variety of connections between Asian studies and Asian American studies, though these encounters will surely have to take account of the long history of dissymmetry between the two fields." The dialogue they call for is in the hope of creating a more comprehensive critical framework to account for an influx of new immigrants from Asia to America, which has the secondary effect of altering the makeup and character of Asian America. However, this still adheres to a framework of a "homeland–destination binary" centered on the United States as the final resting place of inquiry (Koshy 1996, 338). This essay takes the opposite tack by calling for dialogue between Asian studies and Asian American studies to account for immigrants in Asia who have been indelibly affected by American political interventions, cultural imports, and racial discourse. I hope to rectify the fact that there is little consideration for mediating tertiary spaces to critically account for the presence of American cultural and racial discourse in the literary constructions of race in Asia.

▇ TRANSPACIFIC CULTURAL MEDIATION

A comparative transnational approach is essential to creating a comprehensive understanding of not only minor literatures in Asia but Asian American literature as well. An Asian Americanist should go beyond domestic minority fiction to account for the specter of empire, both American and Japanese, as Shu-mei Shih and Francois Linnonet (2005, 11) argue in *Minor Transnationalism*:

> When non-U.S. forms of transnationalism and transcolonialism are brought into play, the "minority discourse" model is helpful only to a limited extent. Not all minorities are minoritized by the same mechanisms in different places. . . . By looking at the way minority issues have been formulated in other national and regional contexts, it is possible to show that all expressive discourses . . . are inflected by transnational and transcolonial processes.

That is, to understand Asian American fiction—Korean American in particular—a transnational approach to comparative minor literary studies is not only justified because it "refutes any notions of a natural and wholly bounded national identity while simultaneously iterating the historic and material power of the nation-state" but is also necessary as "a critical methodology that mediates interpretation, counseling deliberate disruption of normative understandings of nationhood and social subjectivity, and that insists on recognizing the ideologies conditioning national identity formation" (Chuh 2001, 280). Threading the needle between two traditions of minor literature across the Pacific enriches our comprehension of both.

Asian studies scholars generally approach *zainichi* subjectivity as a matter unique to the area's particular history and circumstance. Sonia Ryang argues that the prevailing approach by Western scholars is to treat *zainichi* as Japan's foreign minority, which tacitly internalizes a Japanese monoethnic logic (Ryang and Lie 2009, 2). Instead, Ryang argues for the reframing of *zainichi* in discourses of diaspora. In her formulation, there are two models of diaspora: the *classical* and the *cultural*. The classical model, best exemplified by the Jewish Diaspora, is premised on several traits: an ethnic persecution causing the dispersal and loss of the homeland, a sense of collective connection to the homeland, a nostalgic sentimentality and desire to return, and an emphasis on phylogeny (collective genesis) of diaspora. The cultural model, conversely, is less bound by physical space. Instead, it is more concerned with a general state of instability and crisis of identity related to loss of the homeland (real or imagined) and a self-labeling as displaced and dislocated.[2] The most decisive criterion for identifying diaspora is "an irreducible diasporic consciousness or state of mind," with an emphasis on ontogeny (individual genesis) of diaspora (Ryang and Lie 2009, 2). Ryang argues that while first-generation *zainichi* may be best articulated by the classical model, subsequent generations are more accurately described by the cultural model. Thus, even within the same ethnic group, generational differences may affect their racial-ized subjectivity. Furthermore, the complicated politics and history of citizenship creates a web fraught with tension, creating multiple modes of statelessness in one ethnic group.

Yet, according to Lisa Lowe (1996, 22), those legal constructions of the Asian Other can be contested and refined by subsequent cultural forms: "if the state suppresses dissent by governing subjects through rights, citizenship, and political representation, it is only through culture that we conceive and enact new subjects and practices in antagonism to the regulatory *locus* of the citizen-subject." In *Immigrant Acts,* Lowe (1996, 2–3) posits that the state produces one definition of race through *legislation,* but Asian American communities can seek to challenge and question those definitions through culture, which parallels Ryang and Lie's (2009, 6) articulation of *zainichi* diasporic discourse:

> Culture is the medium of the *present*—the imagined equivalences and iden-tifications through which the individual invents lived relationship with the national collective—but it is simultaneously the site that mediates the *past....* It is through culture that the subject becomes, acts, and speaks itself as "American."

I would add that first-generation Asian American immigrants may be disproportionately defined by juridical machinations, which Lowe charac-terizes as a mechanism for reproducing capital labor structures; however, if culture is the central means by which Asian Americans can contest legal definitions, then culture would be largely the arena of subsequent generations.

Although Ryang and Lowe speak to different inflections of culture with respect to diaspora and minoritization, they are intimately related with the "memory work" evinced in Lisa Yoneyama's (1999) critically comparative *Hiroshima Traces.* Speculating that "the Korean resident aliens' reality in Japan appears perhaps as fragmented as that of the 'Asian American'" (183), she discusses how a memorial to the Korean victims of the atomic bomb in Hiroshima crystalizes several lines of negotiation in forming ethnic subjectivity against the backdrop of a competing national project. Most compellingly, Yoneyama's broader argument acknowledges the plas-ticity of ethnic subjecthood in the national imaginary through dialectic memory work. Similarly malleable, Sugihara grapples with his cultural diaspora, inherited from the first-generation *zainichi,* by sifting through imported cultural objects through which he can redefine *zainichi* in Japan.

It is for these reasons that I propose reading *GO* through what I call *transpacific cultural mediation,* extending Ryang and Lowe's theoretical emphasis on culture as a means of self-definition, in the sense that Sugihara's relationship to the homeland is largely imaginative and negotiated through tertiary national spaces. As second-generation *zainichi,* Sugihara contests his father's more classical model of diasporic subjectivity (though not without its own plasticity) and appears to operate under the cultural model; he rejects legislative and political mobilization for a cultural means of self-determination. Situated at the nexus of Japanese, North/South Korean, and American politics, the second-generation *zainichi* subject's pathway for a self-constructed racialized subjectivity is quite narrow.[3] The emphasis on culture as a means of contesting and defining the citizen-subject is central to my thesis with regard to younger *zainichi* subjects; it is a strikingly postmodern approach to racialization that is afforded to a *specific* vector of a *specific* minority group in Japan at a *specific* time.[4]

Kaneshiro's novel and Sugihara's search for selfhood are culturally mediated not only through Japanese and Korean ethnonational politics but also through American racial discourse and popular culture. That is, in the process of negotiating a *zainichi* identity for himself outside an either-or dichotomy, Sugihara must detour through another cultural space—in this case, American cultural and racial discourse—to find the latitude to break free from reified cultural identities that have been thrust upon him. John Lie argues that the meaning of Korea for *zainichi* cannot be considered without Japan, and vice versa (Lie 2008, 177–78); in fact, *zainichi* ideology's totalizing politics brooks no path for even considering the formation of an ethnic minority subjectivity (116). In Sugihara's rejection of alien resident status and heretofore absent ontological construction of *zainichi* as minority subject, I posit that a triangulation of Japan, Korea, and the United States as political, cultural, and racial intermediary must be considered.

■ **THE MYTH OF MONOETHNICITY AND AMERICAN INTERVENTION**

Beyond racial formation theory, there are tangible historical connections between the United States, Japan, and the *zainichi* population. In a sense, the Allied occupation and Allied powers had a hand in the reemergence of Korean as an ethnic and national category. Koreans were legally considered Japanese citizens until Japan's surrender, after which they suddenly found themselves in a stateless legal limbo.[5] That is not to say the matter of citizenship was clearly delineated; as Erin Aeran Chung shows, the question of the Korean population's "contingent citizenship" was quite complicated. Initially, the Supreme Commander for the Allied Powers (SCAP) decided to repatriate all Koreans; consequently, it did not concern itself with clarifying the legal status of *zainichi* Koreans (Chung 2009, 153). This would prove to be problematic for the six hundred thousand who remained behind, finding themselves somewhere between second-class Japanese and foreign nationals with murky legal status (Mitchell 1967, 107–8). It was a position that was embraced at the time, because to be "foreign" in the moment meant to be a member of the Allied forces during the occupation; and as newly minted foreigners, Koreans openly rejected the legitimacy of Japanese law (Chung 2009, 155). In fact, an early *zainichi* Korean organization called Joryeon, perhaps sensing the power disparity of "foreignness," would try to take an active hand in reshaping Japanese politics (eventually, Joryeon was dissolved by SCAP for its work with the Japanese Communist Party) (Chung 2009, 156).

If the Japanese Empire considered its colonized subjects lesser beings, why grant citizenship to the colonies? A closer look at the particulars of the imperial project shows how a myth of monoethnicity—necessitating citizenship—was integral to its success. Japan sought to create Japanese subjects of its colonized peoples, not out of any benevolent intent, but as a consequence of its peculiar position in very material conditions. Having recently modernized in relatively short order, it had to somehow reconcile its lack of resources with its ambitions of becoming a global power; its extreme shortage of capital created unique conditions for its imperialist project (Ching 2001, 21). Japan had to accrue land, labor, and capital quickly, so unlike most European projects that reached into distant lands, Japan's empire was circumscribed to neighboring regions—essentially, the northeastern Asian continent. That brought about a particular dynamic, because, according to Western classifications, Japanese imperial subjects shared a common cultural heritage and were ethnically similar in appearance.[6] That allowed Japan to exercise a rhetoric of inclusiveness, even as it subjugated its colonies. Moreover, this allowed Japanese nationalists to describe their colonial practices as more "humane" (Ching 2001, 27). The push toward enfolding the colonial subject into itself, then, stemmed from its material and practical goals: to integrate the colonized into the imperial project quickly, but at arm's length, and distinguish their empire from Western nations as humane and superior, with an eye toward defending against, or expanding into, the West.

What is interesting is that in formulating its colonial policies, Japan studied European and American models of empire and assimilation (Caprio 2009, 17). Mark Caprio articulates three broad levels of colonial administration: external, internal, and peripheral. External colonial administration entailed handling distant territories with racial and geographic differences from the homeland—which would apply to many European colonizing projects. Internal best describes the U.S. condition, which was mostly a nation-building project whose primary concern was securing the political allegiance of the people, requiring the installation of a hegemonic culture and the dismantling of local, social, and cultural barriers. Japan, however, would adopt the peripheral model for colonial administration—a policy promising the colonized assimilation into the interior but, in reality, practicing marginalization. Japan's project required its colonies to buy in to the monoethnic argument as an incentive for participating in empire—ultimately, its goal was to use their suzerain states to protect the colonial center from the West.

Thus the relationship between the United States and Japan, with the *zainichi* population caught between, informed their definition as colonized subjects, their ephemerality as citizens, and, finally, their formulation as resident aliens. The particularities of the *zainichi* colonial status may explain the move toward cultural mediation. First, citizenship for *zainichi* Koreans is a sensitive matter, for the aftermath of the postwar period was occupied with vehement opposition toward their categorization as Japanese citizens—a label not of inclusion but of exclusion. Second, for first- and even second-generation *zainichi,* citizenship was not to be sought after but categorically rejected for a favored state of "foreignness," because that included a recognition of their existence as liberated people. Still, living in Japan as an ethnic minority and permanent resident alien enables the perpetuation of discrimination and disenfranchisement. Third, in conjunction with a gradual shift in attitude toward Japanese citizenship, it is necessary for the *zainichi* Korean imaginary to construct a strong racial subjectivity that goes beyond nationality and ethnicity— the most effective theater being cultural. Still, culture cannot be created in a vacuum, and so Sugihara must negotiate something between Japan and Korea, which he feels he cannot do unless he travels through another cultural space—America.

■ HYPERMASCULINITY AND RECOVERY

GO has been subject to critique for its hypermasculine bent and emphasis on individuality. As others note, the novel can be read as a rejection of *zainichi* identity politics. Sugihara's proclamation at the novel's dénouement rejects labels, names, and categories, taking to task the very label of *zainichi.* In a reading of both the text and the film adaptation, Ichiro Kuraishi (2009, 117) points out that

> Sugihara's claim, repeated in the movies, that he dares to erase the national borders . . . in this sense embodies the zainichi generation gap, with the younger generation's eye on the possibility of going beyond the homeland orientation, as if to forget about the lost homeland, colonial history and diasporic reality. But this desertion of the past obviously carries a conservative, almost reactionary message of antidiaspora and antiethnicity.

Kuraishi's reading appears to have a strong case: Sugihara's denial of national circumscriptions might appear to transcend the limits of a state-inflected *zainichi* identity, but by failing to embrace and redefine *zainichi*, he reverts to a default Japanese identity. Indeed, his reformation is in the mold of the student archetype—studying for exams so that he may eventually become a professional salaried worker and follow the standard path toward economic stability and success.

Moreover, in a rather worn fashion, Sugihara's coming to terms with himself is predicated on the romantic acceptance by a "native" female character. Sugihara and Sakurai's initial attempt at sexual congress takes place at Imperial Hotel (Teikoku Hoteru), where Sugihara reverses the naming dynamic by giving Sakurai a pseudonym on the hotel registry.[7] Within the confines of the room, Sakurai finally reveals her first name (Tsubaki), whose conventional Japaneseness embarrasses her. Sugihara decides to reciprocate by revealing his ethnicity, which results in Sakurai rejecting him. It is only at the end of the novel, when they reconcile, that he comes to terms with his racial identity. Thus Sugihara's resolution depends on the conquest of the feminized Japanese figure—a simplistic reversal of the colonial dynamic. Melissa Wender (2005) reads the resolution as disappointingly heteronormative—Sakurai confesses that she loves him for his fierce passion, his skill as a fighter, and his leaping ability.[8] Thus, it is through Sugihara's "male hetereosexuality . . . that this book proposes [he] define his relationship to his identity" (200; see also Tomonari 2005).

Yet Kuraishi's and Wender's readings of *GO*'s heteronormative underpinnings and exultation of typical Japaneseness are predicated on the finality of Sugihara and Sakurai's reconciliation. However, I read the text as having an ironic position on Sugihara and Sakurai's relationship. Similarly, Christopher Scott's queer reading of *GO* attempts to recover the novel's ambivalence and contradictory vacillations on racism and homophobia as a reflection of the peculiar positionality of *zainichi* Koreans in Japan (see Scott 2006). I am skeptical of Kuraishi's argument that Sugihara's polemic betrays an "antiethnic" message, for Sugihara never considers sublimation to pass as Japanese. Instead, it is important to him that Sakurai acknowledge his Korean background before they further their relationship.

Rather, I would argue that something much more complicated and ambivalent is at play here—that Sugihara's inelegant diatribe is a stumbling first step toward bridging the gap between *zainichi* as racial minority and as Japanese subject. In truth, I am more interested in the means and process of Sugihara's journey. He does not have the sophistication or knowledge to formulate, from the ground up, his own racial ontology. Instead, his is a generation of *zainichi* that, while acutely aware of the history and trauma of Japanese colonialism, is acculturated to, and speaks the postmodern language of, popular culture; thus, he references music, television programs, literary works, and a sundry list of cultural imports to process and negotiate space for himself. In short, he occupies each space, taking anything that might be of use in formulating his own racialized alterity.

■ NATIONALITY, ETHNICITY, RACE, THE "THIRD WAY," AND BEYOND

Sugihara's haphazard search for an ontology beyond the Korean–Japanese binary reflects a complicated institutional and historical legacy. First-generation *zainichi* considered themselves temporary guests in Japan and had every intention of returning to Korea. Second- and third-generation *zainichi,* however, were more interested in permanent status in Japan. With first-generation *zainichi* intellectuals largely dictating the terms of a *zainichi* subjecthood in Japan, a conflict between generations was inevitable if any move toward settlement in Japan were to be considered assimilation (and, implicitly, collaboration). As a possible answer, *zainichi* intellectual Kim Tong Myung introduced a "third way" *(daisan no michi)*:

> The third way was a way to live in Japan as home, without being totally Korean or Japanese but by being "zainichi" (resident in Japan). In other words the third way was the creation of a space for multivocal negotiation away from dominant notions of identity located in hegemonic definitions of nationhood to a space where new identities could be imagined. (Chapman 2004, 34)

However, there are limits to the third way. For example, there is little room for discourse in addressing patriarchal issues within the *zainichi* community, and the third way accepts a colonizer–colonized binary, which, as Shih and Lionnet argue, can be limiting (Chapman 2006, 354–57). Consequently, the "fourth way" *(datsu zainichi-ron,* the "discourse of abandoning *zainichi*"), according to Jeffry Hester, addresses these limits by acknowledging the slippery nature of defining a *zainichi* subjectivity dependent on so many moving parts, caught between the trauma and history of empire, racialization, and popular culture (Hester 2008, 144–45).

It is within this generational tension that the novel contests identity according to three vectors familiar to ethnic studies scholars with respect to the particular history and placement of *zainichi*: nationality, ethnicity, and race. The novel first dismantles nationality as laughably fluid, particularly in the case of *zainichi*, with its "contingent citizenship" legacy, which produces "residents" rather than subjects of Japan that can apparently switch nationalities at will. Next, Sugihara attempts to challenge ethnicity with a discourse on genetics, which he ultimately abandons. Finally, culture is the site for much of Sugihara's intellectual and emotional labor in constructing a racialized self. He understands that despite their shared ethnic heritage, he shares little with both North and South Koreans—underscored by his rejection of North Korean ideology and South Korea.[9] He must dwell in a tertiary cultural space to process and formulate a cultural identity outside the bounds of nationality and ethnicity.

Opening with a desire to vacation abroad, the novel quickly unravels the bundled lines of tension surrounding the subject of *zainichi* nationality. The Sugihara family wants to go to Hawai'i but cannot because of their North Korean citizenship:

> It was New Year's and I was fourteen when my old man started muttering about "Hawaii." . . . Up until then, Hawaii had been a symbol of capitalist decadence in our house. At the time, my old man was fifty-four, had North Korean citizenship (in other words, a *zainichi chosenjin*) and was a Marxist communist. . . . I think an explanation is in order. Why is it that my old man, who was born in Chejudo, Korea, has North Korean citizenship? And why is it that to go to Hawaii, he has to change his citizenship to South Korean? This might be a bit dry, but I'll try to explain as simply as I can.
>
> When the old man was a kid—that is, during the war—he was *Japanese*. The reason's simple. It's because back then, *Chosen* (Korea) was a colony of Japan. Supposing he grows up, the old man—who's had Japanese citizenship, a Japanese name, and the Japanese language forced on him—was to become a soldier for the [Japanese] Emperor. . . . Being in Japan was good, but as the decision to decide on citizenship got closer, my old man picked Chosen (North Korean) citizenship. The reason is, North Korea subscribed to Marxism, which was supposed to be better for the poor, cared more for the zainichi Koreans than the South Korean government did. (9–10)

Unlike in the United States, Japanese citizenship is not determined by place of birth; so despite the fact that Sugihara was born in Japan and had never set foot in North Korea, because his parents chose North Korean citizenship upon their liberation, he inherits North Korean citizenship.[10] In the eyes of the Japanese government, he is *zainichi chosenjin* (North Korean resident in Japan), an alien resident. Therefore he has no right to vote, is discriminated against by businesses and universities, and has limited mobility.[11] And so, Sugihara Sr. decides to switch from North Korean to South Korean. Nationality, then, in the context of the beginning frame of the novel, is quickly dismissed as a farce. It is a means to an end; to change one's nationality is not seen so much as a betrayal as a pragmatic move. In the end, Sugihara's father bribes officials of Mindan—a South Korean *zainichi* group—to change the family nationality to South Korean, at which point, he turns to Sugihara and quips, "You can buy nationality. Which one do you want?" (12). Their insouciant attitude toward nationality is reinforced when Sugihara, after revealing his ethnic heritage to Sakurai, jokes, "I was *Chosen* [North Korean] until the eighth grade. Maybe I'll become Japanese in three months. Maybe I'll become American in a year. Maybe Norwegian by the time I die" (186). The move Kaneshiro makes here is not insignificant. For preceding generations of *zainichi,* national citizenship was integral to subjectivity. Koreans had their national and ethnic identities systematically dismantled by the Japanese and fought, bled, and died for the sake of nationhood. This discourse would leave a lasting effect on *zainichi* politics, as many early efforts of organizing tended to focus on South Korean and North Korean politics rather than on domestic *zainichi* affairs. But Kaneshiro dismisses nationality as a consequence more of practical affairs and politics than of destiny or essentialism.

If nationality or citizenship is no longer a deciding factor of *zainichi* subjectivity, Sugihara has to next address ethnic determinism, which he believes to have solved. At one point, Sugihara attempts to reconcile ethnic difference based on a television program discussing the tracing of human genetics. He explains to Sakurai that DNA can be traced to a single line originating in present-day Africa and that all of the permutations of human genes were rooted there (174–75). He finds comfort in a scientific narrative that accounts for the shared genetic ancestry of Koreans and Japanese but fails to recognize that racial discrimination is not about genes. Tracing mitochondrial DNA shows how everyone is related—a merging of the "pollution" and "purity" ideology (176). At the end of his explanation, Sakurai, missing the point, asks him what he's really trying to say. Still anxious about revealing his ethnic heritage, Sugihara simply states that he admires the bravery of the early travelers who spread out through the various continents. When he finally does confess his Korean ethnicity to Sakurai at the hotel, he returns to this line of thinking in a lengthy cross-examination:

> "How do you tell the difference between a Japanese, Korean, or Chinese person?"
> "How do I tell the difference . . . ?"
> "Nationality? Like I said before, citizenship can change."
> "Birthplace then, or language . . ."
> "Okay, then, what about returnees with foreign citizenship who were born and educated abroad because of their parents' work? They're not Japanese?"
> "If their parents are Japanese, then I think they're Japanese. . . ." (188–89)

Having pointed out that nationality is no determinant of Japaneseness, Sugihara proceeds to dissect Sakurai's ethnicity rationale—that Japaneseness is determined by parental lineage. He points out that genetic forensics traces DNA in Japanese back to China, and going back far enough, Korean and Japanese share the same ethnic heritage. Intellectually, Sakurai understands the logic of Sugihara's argument, but an inarticulable barrier remains:

> Sakurai sighed deeply: "You really know a lot. But that's not really the issue. I understand the reasoning behind everything you say, but that's not good enough. It's scary . . . the thought of you inside me is scary." (190)

Thus, regardless of the logic and reasoning behind Sugihara's DNA thesis, Sakurai finds his blood *kitanai* (dirty). Sugihara's mistake is in thinking that rationality and reason are enough to overcome racialization.

Both nationality and ethnicity take a figurative beating when Sugihara's long-festering resentment toward his father comes to an explosive head. Oyaji (Old Man) has been on a bender, distraught and wracked with guilt over the news that his brother has passed away in North Korea. In his despair, he wallows in guilt over the fact that he had not fulfilled his familial obligations in sending enough money back to his brother, and because he has switched nationalities, he is not able to visit North Korea to bury him. Sugihara, however, has little sympathy for Oyaji or his late uncle. Much to Oyaji's astonishment, Sugihara rails, "If North Koreans want to eat [well], then they should bring the revolution. What are those bastards doing?" (221). Sugihara expressly rejects the idea of feeling obligated to North Korea—that the people are responsible for their own fates. This does not go over well with Oyaji, and they spill out into a small park, where they have a brutal boxing match, which Oyaji wins by spitting blood into Sugihara's eyes. Sugihara thinks, "This blood, my old man's blood, won't get out of my eyes," perhaps reflective of Sugihara's futile efforts at washing away ethnicity (226). Later, Oyaji confesses that he realizes that he is of an older generation and that Sugihara will have a very different relationship with nationality and the idea of the homeland; he switched nationalities to liberate Sugihara, but he cannot help but conflate kinship with the nation. The same blood that is key to Sugihara's universalizing DNA argument is the cause of his downfall. Oyaji's blood cannot be scrubbed away or made benign through a scientific rationale— it has been racialized.

■ RACIAL FORMATION AND AMERICAN CULTURAL IMPORTS

Racial formation, which Sugihara belatedly stumbles upon, is the arena in which his subjectivity is both based and contested. In some ways, part of Sugihara already knows that his DNA thesis will fail to reconcile ethnic difference; and he has always known how little nationality matters in terms of his acceptance by Japanese society. It is with the third and final vector that Sugihara carves space for himself to formulate a cohesive *zainichi* subjectivity, but this cannot happen without several U.S.-based intermediary steps moving from nation- and DNA-based racial formation toward culture and discourse—the putative transpacific cultural media- tion. Stuck between the binary of Korean and Japanese, Sugihara must try to formulate an ontological space between, but that cannot occur in a vacuum. Instead, he temporarily enters a tertiary cultural space as a means of negotiation—a mode of being outside the domestic realms of power to rehabilitate, reshape, and revise.

The first move toward tertiary spaces comes in the aforementioned vacation to Hawai'i. While Sugihara does not accompany his parents to Hawai'i, his father's change in nationality, he later realizes, was more for Sugihara than for himself: "I understood why this asshole-of-an-old man suddenly changed nationalities to South Korea. It wasn't for Hawaii. It was for me" (227). Going to Hawai'i, then, is more than an ideological break; it is the beginning of Sugihara's entrance into Japanese institutionalism, for he uses the money that would have been used to fund his Hawai'i trip to take the entrance exam to enter a Japanese school. It is significant, then, that his family does not choose to go to Okinawa, a similarly tropical vaca- tion spot with a large U.S. military presence that would have been much easier—it must be Hawai'i. His father returns from Hawai'i and places their vacation photo in the *genkan* (hallway entrance) as a declaration of the family's break from totalizing North Korean politics and ideology; and Sugihara embarks on his journey toward racial formation. It is also significant that this is not a permanent space—Hawai'i is a fantasy vacation space, a construct of American empire—that Sugihara's parents visit. It is a pattern that is to be repeated; tertiary national spaces (both geographic and cultural) are a means rather than ends—a place to occupy temporarily to renegotiate the domestic self.

American cultural references are not particularly unusual in Japanese fiction, and indeed, allusions to other cultural sites, such as *Romeo and Juliet,* pepper the novel. But Sugihara's intertextual travels often return to a narrative theme—the transformation and construction of the racialized American. For example, he is fascinated by the film series The Godfather; he describes the scene in which Vito Corleone arrives to Ellis Island, gazing upon the Statue of Liberty, as his favorite, indicative of how appealing he finds the American immigrant narrative (131). However, he also betrays an acute cognizance of the dark side of American racial discourse. At one point, he expounds upon phrenology and how it was used to persecute Native and African Americans, and how the same logic could be used against Koreans (80).

It is through popular culture—with the attendant political and racial underpinnings—that Sugihara negotiates a pathway for *zainichi* subjectivity. Christopher Scott (2006, 175) notes that *GO* appears to be unusually "infatuated with American culture, particularly that produced by African Americans." For example, Sugihara ponders how African American culture has produced a rich array of musical genres, such as jazz and hip-hop, but nothing analogous has been produced by *zainichi* culture (Scott 2006, 134). Scott reads these cultural references as evidence of Kaneshiro's own anxieties regarding *zainichi* culture and perhaps as a circuitous way of layering a possibly queer framework in Sugihara's relationship to his best friend, Jong-il. I, too, note their conspicuous presence but suggest that the intertextuality goes beyond a simple expression of *zainichi* anxiety; Sugihara actively adapts American cultural discourse for his own ends. For instance, the first chapter closes with Sugihara reworking lyrics from Bruce Springsteen's "Born in the USA":

> Born in a rich home and country
> I did bad and got kicked by my old man
> You lose sight and end up like a dog that's been beat too much
> Even though you spend most of your life in style
> I was born in Japan
> I was born in Japan (19–20)

Here Sugihara rewrites the subtext of Springsteen's lyrics, a lamentation over the plight of the working class in the richest nation in the world with imperialist ambitions in Vietnam, by inserting himself as the subject in a Japanese context.[12] His intertextual framing begins with a universalist undercurrent—that of the struggling worker in an exploitative system—but he also positions Oyaji as part of a larger system of oppression, perhaps representative of the totalizing politics of his *zainichi* heritage. Later in the text, Sugihara ruminates on the life and times of Jimi Hendrix:

> After wrapping up an hour and a half of practice, I listened to a CD of "The Star Spangled Banner" by Jimi Hendrix at Woodstock—a half Cherokee, half black rock star. Hendrix played in protest of how minorities were being sent to the frontlines of the Vietnam war. . . . No matter how many times I hear it, it still kills me. There's no way for minority voices to get through to the establishment, so they've got no choice but to be as loud as they can by any means necessary. There might come a day when I want to play the Japanese national anthem in protest. I'm practicing my guitar for when that day comes. (97–98)

This time, Sugihara explicitly identifies with the positionality of the mixed-race Hendrix and his attempt to give a voice to the voiceless through his instrument. Betraying a sharp awareness of the injustices suffered by African and Native Americans, Sugihara envisions a time when he would be able to follow in their footsteps. Both musical performances in their original contexts are attempts to negotiate and redefine the meaning of the United States according to blue-collar, working-class, and racial struggles, to take ownership through extralegal means. In each case, Sugihara internalizes their historical and political contexts and negotiates a language and space for himself; his cultural travels are a form of "practice" for the day when he will have to assert his subjecthood as *zainichi*.

Using culture to mediate relationships is not limited to ethnonational politics. Even Oyaji is not immune; he croons "Silent Night" in the style of Bing Crosby. Perhaps unamused by his father's ironic appropriation of the all-American singer's image, beset by violent tendencies, Sugihara thinks to himself, "Aren't you supposed to be a Marxist?" (243). Another evening, Sugihara watches *Star Wars* with Oyaji, who nods approvingly at the training sequence between Yoda and Luke Skywalker. Afterward, Oyaji quips that Sugihara should refer to him as Yoda—to which Sugihara mutters that he's more Darth Vader than Yoda (66). The text layers and complicates their relationship through ironic intertextuality as a means of negotiating an understanding that cannot be captured in their "native" (or adopted) language of Japanese, let alone Korean. In a moment of vulnerability, Sugihara Sr. empathizes with Sugihara when he sarcastically mentions his plans for moving to Norway to become Norwegian; Oyaji reveals that he once harbored a similar dream of moving to Spain to become Spanish (101).

It is significant that the majority of cultural imports are American in origin, which I posit to have precedence in the United States's postwar function as SCAP. The *zainichi* Koreans initially greeted SCAP as the harbinger of their release as liberated people. However, that relationship would deteriorate rapidly, as SCAP's priority was the rebuilding of Japan's government and people. For example, when the *zainichi* population began to organize with Communist labor forces, SCAP quickly turned on them, as they considered them to be ideological enemies and hindrances to rebuilding Japan (Chung 2009, 153). SCAP would at times intervene on the behalf of *zainichi* Koreans, who were subject to discrimination and intimidation by Japanese authorities (154). Thus, in the *zainichi* consciousness, U.S. occupational forces, despite their at times oppositional stances, would be considered an external tertiary force that may be used to the *zainichi* population's advantage when dealing with a discriminatory Japanese government. Extending this dynamic to American culture, I would argue that there is a similar dynamic at play in *GO*—the use of U.S. intervention in cultural form to liberate the *zainichi* from the shackles of ethnonational inferiority. Thus negotiation of a *zainichi* subjectivity in Japan has always been mediated by external tertiary forces, for it was the arrival of SCAP that enabled *zainichi* Koreans to escape Japanese citizenry, and it was SCAP's status as an arbiter of universal human rights—at least, perception-wise—that afforded *zainichi* some leverage, however tenuous, to struggle for positionality. For better or worse, I suggest that a very similar dynamic is at play in *GO,* with Sugihara wallowing in American culture as a neutral zone while he grapples with his *zainichi* subjectivity in a *racial* rather than ethnonational sense.

I recognize that this is a problematic formulation, for it buys in to the global hegemony of the United States as military power and cultural dominant. By undermining Japan's imperial project of placing itself as the gleaming metropole of modernity, the novel necessarily accepts the United States as the political and cultural arbiter of modernity, which manifests in a distinctively hypermasculine bent in the novel—collectively detected and criticized by Wender, Kuraishi, and Scott. However, Sugihara eventually learns to tap in to American racial discourse, particularly African American culture, as a means of contextualizing his usage of tertiary national space that both acknowledges the complicated history of racial discrimination in the United States and highlights similarities in Japan, while at the same time still taking advantage of its most favored status as cultural dominant. The conflation between culture and politico-militaristic force is made most apparent when Sugihara faces several metonymic discriminatory forces.

For example, when Sugihara confronts bullies at his Japanese high school, he quotes a recent cinematic rendition of Billy the Kid: "I'll make you famous" (22). Invoking the rugged individualist image from the American West fits into the archetype that Sugihara seems intent on emulating; the romantic image of the cowboy rebelling against the rule of law and making his way in the Wild West appeals to Sugihara's rebellious streak. His prowess as a fighter notwithstanding, Sugihara attempts to transcend his status as racialized pariah at school by fighting his way to the top. By miming Billy the Kid, he imagines himself rising above his outlaw status, as part of an American cultural tradition.

When faced with a domestic juridical disciplinary force, the novel's solution is to basically offer the same radical individualism that resolves Sugihara's relationship with Sakurai, mediated once again by American cultural forms. *Zainichi* subjects, as alien residents, are required to carry their Alien Registration ID cards with them at all times; failure to produce identification upon request by the authorities can result in heavy fines or jail time. After Sugihara leaves the hotel, he spies a policeman approaching by bicycle, upon which he begins to ventriloquize Raymond Chandler's hard-boiled private eye Philip Marlowe: "No way has yet been invented to say goodbye to the cops" (194). The officer stops Sugihara, who, upon being questioned, channels detective noir: "I was irritated, angry, and annoyed. If I were Philip Marlowe, I'd make some crack and somehow get myself out of this, but instead I went with The Continental Op and decided to hit and run" (196). Sugihara pushes the officer, who is knocked out when he hits his head on his bicycle. In a curious scene, after returning to consciousness and realizing that a remorseful Sugihara poses no threat, the young officer laments that he is not very good at his job. Sugihara responds, "There's no way you could've avoided that . . . nobody's ever dodged it. It's a technique taught in hand-to-hand combat by the U.S. military" (199). And so Sugihara not only expresses his discontent internally by channeling American detective noir fiction but physically lashes out using U.S. military tactics, presumably learned from training sessions with Oyaji. It is a fearful symmetry between the cultural and methodological that results in self-destructive acts of anger.

While prone to violent outbursts, Sugihara still evinces an understanding that there should be a purpose driving it. Lest he be judged as a mindless brute, Sugihara proves more thoughtful at times in his choice of cultural and political avatars, at one point tapping in to the legacy of another American icon and trailblazer, Malcolm X:

> The black civil rights leader Malcolm X said, "I don't even call it violence when it's in self-defense; I call it intelligence."
>
> I despise violence too, just like Malcolm X. But there are times when there's no choice. If my left cheek gets hit, should I turn the other cheek? No way. There are guys out there who don't go for the cheek, they go for more vital regions. (24–25)

Here Sugihara aligns himself with the civil rights movement, in apparent parallel with his burgeoning consciousness as *zainichi*. He is not a mindless outlaw but a champion of racial equality, even if his methods call for violence. He considers himself the subject of discrimination, fighting to be recognized and acknowledged as a human being; thus his acts of aggression are justified. This is not the first or last time that he betrays a distinct awareness of American racial discourse.

■ A SPECTRUM OF PATHWAYS

Yet there are limits to how far transpacific cultural mediation can travel; it is more a means of negotiation than a permanent solution. Sugihara's abilities as a brawler give him little satisfaction, and even then, he understands that fighting his way to the top of the heap will be pyrrhic. For instance, when confronted by a racist bully named Kobayashi at Kato's birthday party, he rejects Kato's invitation to go into business together. Upon being called *chonko* (a racial slur for Korean) by Kobayashi, Sugihara wearily proceeds to pummel him, but not before pointing out that there will always be a difference between Kato and him, despite both being social outcasts (143–45). Sugihara's immediate regret and shame at knocking out the young officer demonstrate that his acts are not productive. His anger dissipates as soon as he hears the officer's bike crash to the ground, and he returns to check his injuries. And his admiration of Malcolm X's defense of violence speaks more to his fascination of African American culture, which has carved out a strong identity for itself in its struggle.

The impracticality of Sugihara's strategy is made all the more clear when juxtaposed against other exceptional *zainichi* characters' methods of subject formation. Tawake is perhaps the most tragic figure, a superb physical specimen and natural-born leader who should have excelled but is nevertheless constrained by systematic discrimination. Tawake shares much of Sugihara's anger and recounts an episode to Sugihara in which that anger went unfulfilled. At the age of sixteen, *zainichi* Koreans are required to have their fingerprints registered at the ward office (a subject of much protest by *zainichi* organizations in the 1980s and 1990s); when Tawake's day finally arrived, he found that his anger was disarmed by the human face of the city employees, an apologetic, middle-aged man who apologized profusely and a nervous young woman (73–74). He confesses to Sugihara that he had fully intended on confronting the injustice of the exercise and disrupting the bureaucrats' office, but when caught up with the ritual exchange of apologies, he could not help but respond to the woman's stream of *gokurōsama* (my apologies) with *sumimasen* (pardon me). Juridicial dehumanization comes in the form of a low-intensity, diffused, and nebulous bureaucracy immune to individual action. Frustrated, Tawake recedes from view to live out his days as a subaltern who, despite his individual exceptionalism, cannot defeat systematic racial discrimination.[13]

Jong-il, Sugihara's former classmate and best friend, is a soft-spoken intellectual, deeply invested in the *zainichi* community, with the acumen to improve the *zainichi* condition. Perhaps foreshadowing the specter of doom that haunts Sugihara and Sakurai's relationship, Jong-il intervenes in a farcical mirror courtship on a train station platform. A young Japanese student, spurred on by his classmates, approaches a female *zainichi* student—marked by her wearing a *chima jeogori* (traditional Korean dress) instead of a Japanese school uniform. There is no "passing" here, and the Japanese student approaches the Korean student with a butterfly knife for "courage" hidden in his pocket. Conditioned by the political and social context, the girl mistakes the boy's approach as an act of aggression, and Jong-il intervenes, only to find himself stabbed by the boy's knife, which has been reflexively thrust into him. Faced with the naked politics of *zainichi* and Japanese conflict, these bodies are forced into a combative space with their roles predestined, regardless of their individual desires. The Korean girl mistakes the boy for an aggressor, the Japanese boy moves his arm without thinking of killing, and Jong-il, the intellectual, ends up killed.

Finally, the third exceptional *zainichi* Korean character to reach beyond the Japanese–Korean dialectic is Naomi, a manager-owner at the *yakiniku-ya* (Korean BBQ restaurant) where Sugihara's mother works. Naomi stands apart for several reasons. A former fashion model, she naturalized to Japanese citizenship because her North Korean status occluded international modeling jobs. Furthermore, her distinctly Japanese name made her a target for bullying at the North Korean school she attended with Sugihara's mother. Despite her beauty, she retires from modeling before the age of thirty, explaining in vague terms that "there were some things" causing her retirement (87). She returns to take over her father's restaurant and eventually exits by marrying an American man who works at an international trade firm. At the conclusion of Sugihara's journey, he runs into Naomi again:

> "Missing your front teeth—it's very *cute*," Naomi said, brushing my cheek. If you become *cute*-er, then you can *get* a good girlfriend. And, more than anyone else, you'll be *happy*."
> I nodded, and said: "You know, English pops up when you talk."
> Naomi's cheeks turned red, and then, she smiled coyly. (235–36)

Again, it is a problematic formulation for Naomi's means of extrication to depend on an agent of American capital—to "marry out" as a means of legitimating her hybridity. As a *zainichi* Korean with a Japanese name in a North Korean school, Naomi was subject to ridicule, and as an international model, she had to give up her North Korean citizenship to fulfill her professional goals. Stuck between, she has no real means of reaching beyond until she meets and marries a U.S. citizen, whose access to capital—both financial and cultural—allows her to revel in heterogeneity.

Both Tawake and Jong-il purport to rail against discrimination by ensconcing themselves in their identities as *zainichi* Koreans, yet they fail to recognize the degree to which they are Korean *and* Japanese. That misrecognition causes Tawake to freeze when confronting the ward office bureaucrat and Jong-il's death by his assuming the mantle of racial defender in a terrible misunderstanding. Naomi's marriage latches on to social and cultural capital of American-ness that fails to negotiate space for *zainichi* subjectivity. All three critique the myth of individual exceptionalism absent hybridity.

It is for these reasons that I am troubled by the prevailing criticism of the much-maligned conclusion of *GO,* which ends with Sugihara and Sakurai's reconciliation after they both denounce ethnic and racial difference and reconnect based on a nearly primal attraction contingent on their individuality. According to that reading, after all his introspection, Sugihara finally renounces his efforts to find a rationale for equalizing the national, ethnic, and racial differences between Japanese and Korean, only to find that his physicality and raw animal magnetism transcend those categories. It is a troubling and weak resolution, if indeed that is what occurs.

However, I argue that their reconciliation is one idealistic track of several that the text seems to offer with regard to formulating *zainichi* selfhood. Sakurai confesses that she was attracted to Sugihara's primal anger—but where was the anger directed, and where did it come from?

It seems odd and facetious that Sakurai would decouple that anger from Sugihara's racial angst. It is a bizarre courtship, as if they agreed to efface all that has occurred between them and regress to another point in time. In the end, it is precisely because of Sugihara's rage against discrimination and racial anxiety that Sakurai is drawn to him. To read their reconciliation as the disavowal of race would have to include ignoring the entirety of the text and the journey they take to get to that point.

Indeed, another *zainichi* character on a similar path presents another means of achieving something akin to a "third way."[14] Politically conscious and socially active, Miyamoto "outs" himself as *zainichi* to Sugihara, articulating a similar awareness of American racial discourse, particularly Korean American subjectivity (212). He tries to recruit Sugihara to form a unified *zainichi* group beyond the nationalist politics of Mindan or Soren—his interest is in creating a *zainichi* identity endemic to their lives in Japan. Sugihara declines Miyamoto's invitation not because of any ideological opposition but because he has another project in mind—he struggles for a *zainichi* subjectivity so that he can find love.[15] Miyamoto understands, but his project is larger in scope and scale—they come to a sympathetic understanding that they are on similar sides working toward similar goals, if by different means. However, they hold in common a third national referent—in the form of American racial and cultural discourse—as a means of negotiating their space between Korea and Japan. Transpacific cultural mediation is the means by which both *zainichi* characters, Sugihara and Miyamoto, navigate the lines of tension running in multiple directions to embark on their push for a way beyond a Korean–Japanese dialectic. They are two subjects working for similar ends—a distinctive *zainichi* subjectivity—by sympathetic means; to uphold one method as superior to or independent from the other would be incomplete.

It is for similar reasons that I frame my reading of *GO* through an Asian American critical lens; though the novel's cultural and political context falls within the purview of Asian studies, neglecting American racial discourse results in an incomplete and two-dimensional picture. *GO* engages in an interminority and transnational cultural dialogue as a means of rehabilitating a fragmented history, generational alienation, and political absence. Transpacific cultural mediation, then, resolves how East Asian minor literatures speak to diasporic subjectivities in the United States and elsewhere. Asian American scholars looking beyond domestic literature might detect how American racial and cultural discourse is integrated in diasporic communities abroad; and conversely, Asian studies scholars might perceive connections to minority fiction in the United States as well as the attendant scholarly body of work. It may be that, in the future, as the multitude of bodies and capital flows through porous national borders, a truly comprehensive picture cannot be drawn without an engaged, sustained conversation between the two disciplines.

David S. Roh is assistant professor of English at the University of Utah. He is the author of *Illegal Literature: Toward a Disruptive Creativity* (Minnesota, 2015) and coeditor of *Techno-Orientalism: Imagining Asia in Speculative Fiction, History, and Media* (2015).

▪ NOTES

1. I use several terms that need clarifying. *Nationality* refers to citizenship of the state; *ethnicity* refers to cultural lineage usually associated with a geographic location; and *race* refers to a power inequality based on socially constructed differences mapped onto bodies.

2. See also Bhabha (2004) and Tölölyan (2007).

3. Indeed, John Lie (2008) protests that the search for a universal definition is facetious, for the *zainichi* are too fractured and fragmented. "The persistent flaw," he writes, "of essentialism—seeking the least common denominator, or essence of a group—is that its presumption often turns out to be empty" (xi).

4. For example, first-generation *zainichi* intellectuals like Kim Sok Pom refuse to acknowledge the bifurcation of North and South Korea and instead adhere to a prewar imaginative citizenship—*chosen seki*.

5. Although they were technically considered "citizens," the reality was more complicated. Mitchell (1967, 93) notes that "few Koreans in the peninsula gained full equality as Japanese citizens. Koreans in Japan were in a more favorable position, but even they had attained only semi-citizen status. Koreans were sometimes paid less than Japanese, barred from certain Japanese schools, and forbidden to serve in the military."

6. Unlike European imperial powers, Japan had just recently modernized and did not accrue enough capital to facilitate expansion. Marxists argue that empire is the logical outgrowth of capitalism—as a nation reaches maturity, it will reach outward for resources. However, Ching (2001, 23) contends that Japan actually expanded rapidly to compete with other developing nations for its "place in the sun."

7. *Zainichi* Koreans were encouraged to assimilate by adopting Japanese names, to erase their ethnic difference.

8. Tomonari (2005) argues that Kaneshiro and fellow *zainichi* author

Yan Sogiru's works highlight the physicality of the body as a reflection of the consequences of colonial trauma on *zainichi* male subjects, something that was once prevalent in Japanese fiction writ large, which denies female *zainchi* subjectivity. Tomonari writes, "His [Kaneshiro's] resort to the conventional notions of masculinity perpetuates them, thereby strengthening the perceptions of masculinity and gender divisions that are still hegemonic in Japan today. . . . Kaneshiro's stories do not necessarily support such empowerment" (262). Kaneshiro's adherence to heteronormative patterns, then, not only glorifies violence but "enables Sugihara to construct a common ground with the heterosexual, non-zainichi Japanese men who share a similar view of gender, while keeping this world of masculinity off-limits to women" (262).

9. Sugihara recalls a traumatic encounter with a prejudiced South Korean taxi driver who treats him in a brusque and gruff manner for being *zainichi* (88–90).

10. I use *citizenship* loosely in this context; in actuality, North Korean citizenship in Japan does not truly exist, because Japan and North Korea do not have a normalized relationship. It would be more accurate to say that North Koreans in Japan are stateless peoples, with citizenship largely in their imaginary.

11. North Korean schools were not recognized or accredited, although graduates presently have more opportunities than before.

12. For a thematic reading of Springsteen's song, see Cowie and Boehm (2006).

13. Sminkey (2002, 16) reads Tawake and Wonsoo as representative of "two possible responses to discrimination: escaping the problem by running away or attaching one's self to a group that defends one from the discrimination."

14. Though not quite beyond the Korean–Japanese dialectic; Miyamoto declines to procure Japanese citizenship, which he sees as defeat (212).

15. Sminkey (2002, 14) notes that "intelligent and physically powerful, he is portrayed as a superhuman hero doing solitary battle against all odds. Indeed, one might argue that such an approach is beyond ordinary Korean-Japanese, and that Kaneshiro's apparent rejection of the group in favor of the individual is mistaken: socially active groups are needed, not for people like Sugihara, but for ordinary people incapable of fighting on their own. Kaneshiro's response to this criticism is that 'I am a novelist, not an activist, and it is my job to give illusion' (*Chuokoron* 329–330). In other words, he hopes to inspire ordinary Korean-Japanese through his portrayal of Sugihara."

■ **WORKS CITED**

Bhabha, Homi K. 2004. *The Location of Culture.* London: Routledge.

Caprio, Mark E. 2009. *Japanese Assimilation Policies in Colonial Korea, 1910–1945.* Seattle: University of Washington Press.

Chapman, David. 2004. "The Third Way and Beyond: Zainichi Korean Identity and the Politics of Belonging." *Japanese Studies* 24, no. 1: 29–44.

———. 2006. "Beyond the Colonised and the Colonisers: Intellectual Discourse and the Inclusion of Korean-Japanese Women's Voices." *Japanese Studies* 26, no. 3: 353–63.

Ching, Leo T. S. 2001. *Becoming Japanese: Colonial Taiwan and the Politics of Identity Formation.* Berkeley: University of California Press.

Chuh, Kandice. 2001. "Imaginary Borders." In *Orientations: Mapping Studies in the Asian Diaspora,* edited by Kandice Chuh and Karen Shimakawa, 278–93. Durham, N.C.: Duke University Press.

Chung, Erin Aeran. 2009. "The Politics of Contingent Citizenship: Korean Political Engagement in Japan and the United States." In *Diaspora without Homeland: Being Korean in Japan,* edited by Sonia Ryang and John Lie, 147–67. Berkeley: University of California Press.

Cowie, Jefferson R., and Lauren Boehm. 2006. "Dead Man's Town: 'Born in the U.S.A.,' Social History, and Working-Class Identity." *American Quarterly* 58, no. 2: 353–78.

Hester, Jeffry T. 2008. "*Datsu Zainichi-Ron*: An Emerging Discourse on Belonging among Ethnic Koreans in Japan." In *Multiculturalism in the New Japan: Crossing the Boundaries Within,* edited by Nelson H. H. Graburn, John Ertl, and R. Kenji Tierney. 139–50. New York: Berghahn Books.

Isogai, Jirō. 2004. *Zainichi Bungaku Ron* [A theory of *zainichi* literature]. Tokyo: Shinkansha.

Kaneshiro, Kazuki. 1996. *GO.* Tokyo: Kodansha.

Kim, Elaine H., and Lisa Lowe. 1997. *Positions: East Asia Cultures Critique.* Durham, N.C.: Duke University Press.

Koshy, Susan. 1996. "The Fiction of Asian American Literature." *The Yale Journal of Criticism* 9, no. 2: 315–46.

Kuraishi, Ichiro. 2009. "Pacchigi! And Go: Representing Zainichi in Recent Cinema." In *Diaspora without Homeland: Being Korean in Japan,* edited by Sonia Ryang and John Lie, 107–20. Berkeley: University of California Press.

Lie, John. 2008. *Zainichi.* Berkeley: University of California Press.

Lowe, Lisa. 1996. *Immigrant Acts: On Asian American Cultural Politics.* Durham, N.C.: Duke University Press.

Mitchell, Richard H. 1967. *The Korean Minority in Japan*. Berkeley: University of California Press.

Ryang, Sonia, and John Lie. 2009. *Diaspora without Homeland: Being Korean in Japan*. Berkeley: University of California Press.

Scott, Christopher Donal. 2006. "Invisible Men: The Zainichi Korean Presence in Postwar Japanese Culture." PhD diss., Stanford University.

Shih, Shu-mei, and Francoise Lionnet, eds. 2005. *Minor Transnationalism*. Durham, N.C.: Duke University Press.

Sminkey, Paul. 2002. "Korean-Japanese Identity in Kaneshiro Kazuki's *GO*." *Gakujū kenkyu kiyō* [Scholarly research bulletin], no. 28: 11–22.

Tölölyan, Khachig. 2007. "The Contemporary Discourse of Diaspora Studies." *Comparative Studies of South Asia, Africa, and the Middle East* 27, no. 3: 647–55.

Tomonari, Noboru. 2005. "Configuring Bodies: Self-Identity in the Works of Kaneshiro Kazuki and Yan Sogiru." *Japanese Studies* 25, no. 3: 257–69.

Wender, Melissa. 2005. *Lamentation as History: Narratives by Koreans in Japan, 1965–2000*. Stanford, Calif.: Stanford University Press.

Yoneyama, Lisa. 1999. *Hiroshima Traces: Time, Space, and the Dialectics of Memory*. Berkeley: University of California Press.

MARGARET MIH TILLMAN

Laboring between Empires: Coolie Solidarity and the Limits of the Chinese Civic Association in Havana, 1872

IN 1872, a year before the Qing court delegated an Imperial Commission to survey the conditions of Chinese contract laborers in Cuba, free Chinese men *(asiáticos libres)* gathered in Havana for collective legal action. They determined, never again, to be thrown into Cuban prisons without due cause. Their Chinese Civic Association *(huiguan)*[1] provides evidence for labor solidarity. Legal documents from 1847 to 1878, collected in the James and Ana Melikian Collection and digitally archived at Arizona State University, illuminate stories of contract laborers who responded to the degradations of the coolie system by repeatedly appealing to the law, even in the midst of Cuban insurrections against the Spanish Empire. Chinese historiography has emphasized Qing efforts to enter international diplomacy to aid overseas Chinese; Cuban historiography has celebrated the Chinese revolutionaries who contributed to Cuban independence (see, e.g., Yan 1985; Irick 1982; Yu and Chen 2013; López 2008). However, the leaders of the Chinese Civic Association were neither passive victims nor the heralded revolutionaries who fought outside of the system in order to break it but ordinary men who struggled legally for change within the system. This article will present the neglected story of their persistent efforts and the violent obstacles they repeatedly encountered and thus suggest that their ultimate failure exposes the institutional limitations of the coolie system to provide a transitional springboard for free labor.

Historians rightly contextualize contract labor at the intersections of the Qing's Confucian empire, the Anglo-American "informal" empire, and Spain's "second empire" after the South American revolutions. Underlying competition between "the Latin race and the Anglo-Saxon race" in the New World complicated British diplomatic pressure to eradicate slave traffic (Corwin 1967, 69–92; Schmidt-Nowara 1999, 15, 113). Spanish colonial authorities, negotiating with the Cuban plantation class, were also caught between economic interests and political fears that abolition might erode white hegemony on the island (Schmidt-Nowara 1999, 50; Scott 1985, 39). After failing to attract European immigration, plantation owners turned to so-called coolie labor "perhaps in time to solve the great question of slavery" (Nicasio Cañete y Moral, cited in Corbitt 1971, 32). Between 1847 and 1876, former slave shippers imported roughly between 124,873 and 150,000 coolies to Cuba.[2] Although coolie traders asserted that contract labor would incrementally transition to wage labor, critics claimed that the coolie trade was "tainted with slavery" (*MS British Cabinet Papers* 1907, 87, 11; *Lloyd's Weekly Newspaper* 1856; *New York Evangelist* 1860; Powers 1953).[3]

International debates over the legality of the coolie trade and the evolving status of the coolie workers produced conflicting historical materials.[4] Many Chinese pointed to instances of kidnapping or deceit that challenged the integrity of legal contracts (China 1970, 37–42). According to the Chinese, colonial guards demanded bribes in exchange for withholding false accusations of gambling and opium use, and unjust policing should cast some doubt on the veracity of investigations.[5] The *Cuba Commission Report* may also be questioned on the basis of the suspected criminality of coolies and a predetermined agenda to document the mistreatment of coolie labor in Cuba (Irick 1982, 34–35). Both Chinese and Spanish accounts indicate Chinese resistance to assimilation in Cuba.

The recently discovered bylaws of the Chinese Civic Association corroborate both the Commission Report and Spanish colonial archives. Its story seems to conjoin Chinese perspectives with Spanish materials in a legal system that encouraged compliance. The coolie system afforded just enough flexibility to encourage laborers to undertake an extended and expensive application process, and many persisted through a series of setbacks dealt by imperial law and local rebellion. This story illustrates the formidability of the coolie system, trapping the workers through reindenture while promising eventual termination, which helped to commit some Chinese to the flawed legal tools of the coolie system and complicated their protests against that system.

■ INTRODUCTION: NATURALIZATION VERSUS REINDENTURE

In keeping with Qing discouragement of out-migration, the *Qing Commission Report* presents a grim picture of the near-slave conditions on Cuban sugar plantations (Yan 1985, 77). Of particular interest to this story is a group of Cantonese men who contributed to the Chinese Civic Association of 1872. Heading the commission, official Chan Lan Pin (pinyin: Chen Lanbin 陳蘭彬, 1816–95) interviewed the Cantonese coolies, from the Longmen district, on April 24, 1874, in Cienfuegos (China 1970, 33). In the resulting Petition 23, they recount their backstory. Claiming to have been lured to Macao during the Xianfeng emperor's reign (1831–61), they were then shipped to the Spanish colony Luzón in the Philippines. (Although coolies included Filipinos and even Indians indigenous to Mexico [Reid-Vazquez 2011, 157], the coolie trade tapped into long-standing patterns of circular migration between China and Southeast Asia [Viraphol 1977], and even some of those recruited in Southeast Asia may have originally hailed from China.) In Luzón, the Cantonese men were reportedly forced to sign eight-year contracts indenturing their work in exchange for passage and some advanced payment (Corbitt 1942, 302). Probably arriving in 1853, they fulfilled their first contracts in 1861. (At least fifteen workers in Cienfuegos were recorded as completing their contracts in 1861 [Melikian Collection (MC) 1861]; their names, listed only in Spanish, are impossible to cross-reference with the names, listed in Chinese only, on Petition 23.) On the completion of their first contracts, the contract laborers should have ideally been able to negotiate for better terms.

If contract labor truly represented a transition to wage labor, as some plantation owners argued, then it stood to reason that the colonial government would provide institutional means to graduate to wage labor. With the Royal Decree of 1854, the Spanish Crown had outlined provisions for the naturalization of aliens, including Chinese contract workers (Meagher 2008, 209). According to the law, they would submit materials, including their contracts and baptismal records, to the *capitán de partido,* who then remitted applications to the lieutenant governor, as the district supervisor under the Spanish colonial governor (García Triana and Herrera 2009, 201). Even after obtaining a *carta de domicilio,* resident aliens needed to renew their status annually with costly residency permits (*cédulas de vecindad*); after five years, legal residents qualified to apply for a *carta de naturaleza* to become Spanish subjects (Helly 1993, 25; MC 1868a; 1871).

Even more important than legal documentation was social assimilation to maintain peace (Corbitt 1971, 67).[6] For example, even after losing his original contract and baptismal certificate, Ysidro Cabradilla, thirty-eight years old and a native of Macao, successfully became a permanent resident of Guarrabaca in 1867 (MC 1872a). At court, the judge asked local residents to vouchsafe that Ysidro would become a law-abiding member of the community. Ysidro took his Spanish surname from his godfather, the paterfamilias of the Cabradilla family. A member of that household, the ironworker Vicente, swore that for the previous six years, Ysidro had proven "to be a very good honorable man." Likewise, thirty-five-year-old Miguel Pérez "believed the Asian knew how to comply with the laws of the government" and "would be able to follow the laws of our nation." By describing Ysidro's character as "simple and docile and very tranquil" (MC 1872a), these witnesses echoed positive stereotypes about Asians (Narváez 2010, 399). On May 7, 1867, Ysidro was granted a *carta de domicilio*. Identified as "the Asian" throughout the documents as a marker of his race, despite his otherwise Hispanic name, the final permit called him, for the first time, "Don Ysidro."

The possibility for such upward mobility, allowing for a departure from the sugar plantation system, made it much more reasonable, than otherwise, for Chinese to invest in the complicated process of naturalization. The first cohort of Chinese, having arrived in 1847, fulfilled their contracts by 1855 (Davids 1855, 208). Already by 1858, Chinese created a distinct Chinatown, or *barrio de los Chinos,* in Havana. The Qing Commission estimated that by 1873, two-tenths of the Chinese population had obtained legal residency to become cooks, laundrymen, and peddlers (China 1970, 110). According to the Cuban census of 1872, 24.1 percent (14,064 out of 58,400) of Cuba's Chinese population had received status as free residents; 2,254 free Chinese resided in Havana (Pérez de la Riva 1967, 6). Urban life must have beaconed to coolies grimly toiling on sugar plantations.

Cubans often debated about whether coolies would disrupt, or ameliorate, existing racial tensions. The coolie system introduced the idea of an alternative labor system to slavery, and to some degree, Asians upset existing social structures through their interactions with black slaves (Scott 1985, 106–7). According to the Cuban elite, Chinese opium smoking and gambling disrupted public order (Narváez 2010, 299–300). Given growing violence against Chinese workers in California (Pfaelzer 2008, 7–16), the plantation class may have anticipated that a floating population of free Chinese would potentially incite social unrest. Despite promises of gradual reform, the plantation class systematically delayed abolition and wage labor in Cuba (Scott 1985, 109, 130; Schmidt-Nowara 1999, 138).

The Qing's weaknesses, manifest in the Treaty of Tianjin ratified by China in 1860, coincided with what historian Arnold Meagher (2008, 209) describes as a "radical change of heart toward the Chinese as colonists." In August 1860, Captain General Francisco Serrano suggested, unsuccessfully, an end to the coolie trade (Wakeman 2009, 8). With significant numbers of contracts due to expire, the administration established the Comisión Central de Colonización (López 2013, 88). Madrid issued a Royal

Decree on June 6, 1860, mandating that, after eight years of indentured servitude, the Chinese must reindenture or leave the island within two months, or otherwise face imprisonment and corvée labor. Plantation owners welcomed the new law as a cheap means to retain coolie labor without having to pay for new shipments of workers (Meagher 2008, 210). In 1862, Madrid clarified that the new law applied specifically to those who had arrived after February 15, 1851 (China 1970, 74, 78, 127, 149; Hu-DeHart 1994, 46). This law had far-reaching consequences for strengthening the almost inevitability of recontracting coolie labor on sugar plantations (Yun 2008, 123).

The Cantonese men from Cienfuegos felt the brunt of the 1860 law. Their contracts terminated in the days and months after the cutoff of February 15, 1861. Guards threw them into jails for runaway slaves. There the Afro-Cuban supervisor whipped them until many neared the point of death (Petition 23). This detail is important as one among many examples of tensions among the Chinese and Afro-Cubans during the slave period (e.g., García Rodríguez 2011, 24–27, 126–27; Yun 2008, 166–67). Plantation owners had introduced Asian laborers in an effort to fragment the majority Afro-Cuban slave population on sugar plantations and, by hiring Afro-Cubans to oversee the Chinese, discouraged solidarity between the groups (Narváez 2010, 31, 154). Despite recognizing their shared plight, the Chinese often lacked the linguistic ability to connect with the majority Afro-Cuban population. Instead, the indentured Chinese often struggled to define themselves as free and different from black slaves.

Because of the large number of runaways, the colonial guards claimed due cause to suspect any nonwhite person. When found without "walking papers" outside of a planation, the Chinese were subject to arrest as vagrants and assigned to corvée labor before recontracting (*Reglamento* 1861; Hu-DeHart 2005, 173; Yun, 119; e.g., MC 1858c). Guards circulated notices describing captured Asian and African men among plantation owners (e.g., MC 1858a; 1858b). For example, after entering the depositary for runaway slaves in Havana, the Asian Vicente recontracted with his former patron, Don Martín de Cárdenas y Legas (MC 1860). Policing mechanisms thus pushed the Chinese back onto sugar plantations. Notwithstanding the legal rationale for detaining suspects, these customs amounted to authorizing authorities to detain any person of color on the basis of racial phenotype alone (Yun 2008, 115; Martínez-Alier 1989, 34).

The example of the Cantonese men from Cienfuegos illustrates how poorly many fared under these laws. Under duress, they signed second contracts for sugar plantations Candelaria (諫爹拉) in Manacas (present-day Cienfuegos) and Juanita (江素簍) in Santo Domingo. To deaden the pain, some Chinese fell into gambling and opium smoking, committed suicide, or ran away (e.g., MC 1863b; Hu-DeHart 2005, 181). Given the violence of the measures taken to confine laborers to plantations, the cycle of recontracting amounted to, from the perspective of the Chinese, a lifetime of forced labor akin to slavery (China 1970, 98). For example, one coolie, Zeng Ashi 曾阿石, begged the Qing Commission, "I pray you to aid me in escaping from a life-time of slavery by procuring for me my freedman's papers" (China 1970, 75).

Despite the importance of paperwork, nineteenth-century documentation lacked the means to track identity, and these problems were compounded by arbitrary renaming practices between Chinese and Spanish (China 1970, 41). Shippers Latinized Chinese names, pronounced in various southern Chinese dialects, and assigned Spanish names. *Chinese* names changed. One possibility is that, on the pretext that coolies were illiterate, Chinese scribes had signed contracts without the consent of the workers (China 1970, 36–41), and the Chinese migrants later signed their own names. The second possibility points to the falsification of paperwork on the part of the immigrant. As often practiced with "paper sons" during the later exclusion era in the United States, some could have adopted another's identity to qualify for naturalization.[7] For example, in his application files, it was especially noted that "the Asian Serapio came to this Island before July of 1860" and the onset of stricter regulations (MC 1866). When submitting a letter of endorsement to the lieutenant governor in 1866, Captain Tirso de Arregui overlooked the inconsistency of Serapio's Chinese signature, which changed from "Lin Yason" (pinyin: Lin Ceng 林曾) on his original contract in 1854 to Huang Ye 黃爺 on all subsequent documents.

Perhaps to guard against falsified identities, the Chinese needed to undertake a lengthy "paper chase" for the application process (Yun 2008, 112–23). Expensive stamps verified each document. It may have been hard for the Chinese, often illiterate in Spanish, to differentiate between falsified and legitimate stamps. Like slaves who could gain manumission through a system of self-purchase called *coartación* (Reid-Vazquez 2011, 21; García Rodríguez 2011, 138), the Chinese also in effect had to purchase freedom. Low-paid mayoral judges enjoyed opportunities, at each stage of the process, to gouge the petitioners (China 1970, 74; Corbitt 1971, 69). Locals also often demanded payment in return for their testimony vouchsafing for the applicants (China 1970, 74–75). The burden fell on petitioners to prove their identity, and colonial guards could easily accuse the Chinese of falsification.[8] Despite Spanish justifications of the legality of coolie contracts, colonial authorities often doubted the authenticity of those very legal documents during the naturalization process.

Without success stories like Serapio's and Ysidro's, who both had holes in their paperwork, it is hard to understand how some Chinese continued to seek legal recourse. Contract laborers may have felt trapped in the coolie system, not by the law but by distortions of the law through kidnapping, graft, and the need for local patrons. Hope in the law, and in the contract's termination, encouraged some to invest in the costly process of naturalization. Those who underwent an arduous application process must have thought that the expense was worth the effort to gain legal status as free residents. Even the Cantonese men from Cienfuegos, upon reentering indenture in 1861, would have had another opportunity to terminate their second eight-year contracts in 1869 and perhaps aspire to enter the ranks of free urban Chinese. Yet, two years thereafter, they would be swept up in larger forces, of imperialism, colonialism, and rebellion.

■ THE INTERVENTIONS OF EMPIRES: MASS INCARCERATION AND DIPLOMACY

As some contract laborers were applying for naturalization, others were joining the ranks of rebel insurgents. When the Ten Years' War broke out on October 10, 1868, rebels promised freedom to slaves and coolies who joined their ranks (Corwin 1967, 224). By 1869, the rebel movement had attracted coolies in Puerto Príncipe (now Camaguey), and then in Cienfuegos and Matanzas (Corbitt 1971, 21). In response, the Cuban elite in 1870 demanded that the Crown deport all Chinese found without proper papers. Madrid complied (Meagher 2008, 211). With a realignment of power in favor of a loyalist plantation class, the Ten Years' War touched the lives of the law-abiding as much as the rebels. Published in the *Official Gazette* (Cuba 1872a, 54), the Royal Order of April 27, 1871, contained instructions to expel uncontracted Chinese from the island (Cuba 1872a, 54; Narváez 2010, 219).

For the uninformed Chinese of Havana, the guards struck like lightning in the dead of night (MC 1872b). On Sunday, September 10, and Monday, September 11, 1871, the colonial government incarcerated "every [free] Chinaman ... found on the streets, their dwellings, or shops" (*Despatches* 1871, vol. 65, no. 539).[9] The Chinese claimed that guards had "indiscriminately" arrested *all* Chinese men, *even* free Chinese with legal papers (Yun 2008, 79; Chen 1985, 664; China 1874, 3:9).[10] Many complained that guards stole their papers in order to throw them in jail, on the pretext of lacking the very *cédulas* just confiscated (China 1970, 95; Yun 2008, 254). Their protests indicate that, no matter what the government motivation for registering dossiers of Chinese men, many workers had labored under the impression that paperwork would confer basic protections against incarceration without due cause.

Many of the roughly fifteen hundred arrested were "peaceable and law-abiding citizens" who had excited "the hostility of the Spanish lower classes . . . by their successful competition" in petty trade (*New York Times* 1871). Stationed in Havana, U.S. consul Henry Hall confirmed that the arrested men had owned "small establishments, shops, fruit stalls, eating houses, etc." He characterized the Chinese as "peaceable, inoffensive, industrious and thrifty" (*Despatches* 1871, vol. 65, no. 539) and thus disagreed with an article from the *Diario de la Marina,* translated and enclosed in his diplomatic pouch. Therein, the Spanish colonial authorities alleged that urban Chinese, "having abandoned their occupations [on sugar estates], have become an element of disturbance" in the cities. The article allowed plantation owners an opportunity to claim their runaways before deporting the Chinese. Hall understood that the laws intended "to discourage their remaining in the towns, in fact to deprive them of all occupations except that of working on sugar plantations" (*Despatches* 1871, vol. 65, no. 539). The mass incarceration thus specifically attacked the Chinese petty bourgeoisie of Havana to reindenture their labor in the agricultural sector.

Colonial authorities were allegedly inciting anti-Chinese and anti-merchant sentiment "to curry favor with the lower classes" during the insurgency (*New York Times* 1872c). These reports may add some credibility to the Chinese claim that the mass incarceration had begun with an anti-Chinese riot in Havana (Yun 2008, 254). Colonial guards confiscated all the material goods of the Chinese (China 1970, 96). In jail, some Chinese died from beatings (Yun 2008, 254). In October 1871, more than two thousand Chinese were sent to Havana, purportedly for more systematic examination of their papers (*Royal Gazette* 1871; *Boston Daily Advertiser* 1871). In December 1871, Count Valmaseda (Blas Villate y de la Hera), who had been sent to Cuba to quiet the rebellion, mandated that all Chinese submit themselves to a government depot for reindenture or expulsion; while in prison, the men labored in government workshops for a salary of four pesos a month (China 1970, 148; *Panama Star and Herald* 1872a). This salary effectively prevented impoverished Chinese from leaving, if they could not already afford a government-issued passport at the price of four pesos (*Despatches* 1871, vol. 65, no. 551). In early 1872, General Féliz Ferrer, acting captain general in Count Valmaseda's absence, suspended governmental review of Chinese applicants for naturalization and prohibited free Chinese from leaving the island (Cuba 1872a, 80–81). These measures further pressed Chinese workers into labor for the

Spanish Crown during its counterattack against insurgents during the Ten Years' War (*New York Times* 1872e). Whereas Afro-Cubans sometimes gained status by fighting in the colonial militia, the Chinese were more often assigned hard labor (Reid-Vazquez 2011, 35–38; Cottrol 2013, 41; Scott 1985, 48–50).

In the following weeks, the Chinese who had escaped incarceration appealed to foreign diplomats for help. They succeeded. In the words of Consul Hall, "the manner in which these arrests have been made, the deplorable and defenseless situation of the Chinamen have excited the indignation as well as the sympathy of the foreign population of the place" (*Despatches* 1871, vol. 65, no. 539). The consuls of England, France, Italy, Holland, Belgium, and Denmark protested against the unjust imprisonment of the Chinese (*Milwaukee Sentinel* 1872a; 1872b). The British and Portuguese consuls attempted to protect those who had come via Hong Kong and Macao, respectively (*Despatches* 1871, vol. 65, no. 539). The Chinese turned to these diplomats for help in the absence of a Qing "representative here or in fact anyone whom they can appeal for assistance or advice in their troubles" (*Despatches* 1871, vol. 65, no. 55). Chinese men like Jian Shiguang 簡仕光 attributed their release to "heroes from other countries" who used "legal justifications" to subdue "local rich tyrants" (China 1970, 95; Yun 2008, 252–55). They felt freed: "Finally, the iron lock was open; the birdcage was broken; we were like swimming fish fleeing from the fishnet, weighing favor from those countries as heavy as a mountain" (Yun 2008, 254–55). According to Su Jinsheng 蘇進生 and others, "the [foreign] Consuls [各國領事官] who had taken pity on such sufferings succeeded in obtaining the release of those who could furnish security"; yet, 160 unfortunate men who could not were sold to plantation owners for one hundred to four hundred pesos each (China 1970, 90; Chen 1985, 2:624; *New York Times* 1872e). Su's account thus suggests that relatively impoverished Chinese had been sent back to the sugar plantations.

The reaction of the local foreign community in 1871 was echoed in the foreign press and became a sounding board for complaints against Spain and Portugal (e.g., *Milwaukee Sentinel* 1872a). Foreign dignitaries increased ongoing criticism of the slave and coolie systems in Cuba (*Sacramento Daily Union* 1872). The editors of the *New York Times* claimed that the "ultra Spanish party [intended] to reopen the African slave-trade and to reduce the eighty thousand Chinese now in Cuba to a condition of slavery" (*New York Times* 1872a). Classifying the coolie system as a Hispanic-run form of slavery, Anglo-American protests increased (*New York Times* 1872d; *Boston Daily Advertiser* 1872; *Standard* 1872; Yun 2008, 38). While complaining to Madrid (*Panama Star and Herald* 1872b), members of the British government also pressured Portugal to suspend coolie traffic from Macao (*Daily News* 1872). The British may have been motivated by pressure from Chinese in treaty ports (Irick 1982, 69), rivalries over Cuba from their base in the Antilles, and competition between British Hong Kong and Portuguese Macao (Helly 1993, 6).

Perhaps in response to international pressure, Count Valmaseda publicized government laws (e.g., Cuba 1872a; 1872b). According to Valmaseda, the incarceration had simply enforced the letter of law of 1860 (*Despatches* 1873, vol. 67, no. 30). Thus the Chinese had been given more than a decade of warning. On October 1872, the Central Committee of Colonization published an article in the *Diario de la Marina* renewing its support for the coolie system as a step in gradual abolition. The problem was that the Chinese "obtain surreptitiously the necessary police documents, or make new contracts with fictitious masters" (*Despatches* 1871, vol. 65, no. 572). Especially in the context of potential rebellion, reliable witnesses were, after all, not young ironworkers like Vicente Cabradilla but sugar planters like committee president Don Julián de Zulueta, the former slave trader who first imported coolies to Cuba (Yun 2008, 46). Because these policies continued to exempt the Chinese who could prove that they had arrived before February 15, 1861, the Chinese had an even greater incentive to invest in legal paperwork.

■ THE CHINESE CIVIC ASSOCIATION AND ITS LIMITS

The mass incarceration led the free Chinese of Havana to organize protection for fellow Chinese. At the private home of Pio Fam Achó, the free Chinese residents of Havana formed an association (Narváez 2010, 451). The colonial government granted the Chinese in Havana permission to organize a body for legal representation on March 20, 1872 (China 1970, 129). Ten leaders of the Chinese Civic Association wrote a historical statement and a set of bylaws (called *condiciones,* or "terms" in the Spanish-language translation) on April 1, 1872 (MC 1872b). While viewing the association's appeal for official recognition, collected in the Archivo National de Cuba, historian Benjamin Narváez (2010, 448) noted that there was no further evidence of the Chinese Civic Association or its effectiveness.[11] Now, the newly discovered association bylaws (Figure 1), in concert with diplomatic records, newspaper accounts, and testimony in the *Cuba Commission Report,* help to explain the fate of the Chinese Civic Association.

The Chinese Civic Association proposed to represent Chinese workers when they faced jail or the renegotiation of their contracts (ANC 1872; MC 1872b; see the author's translation of its bylaws in the appendix). In

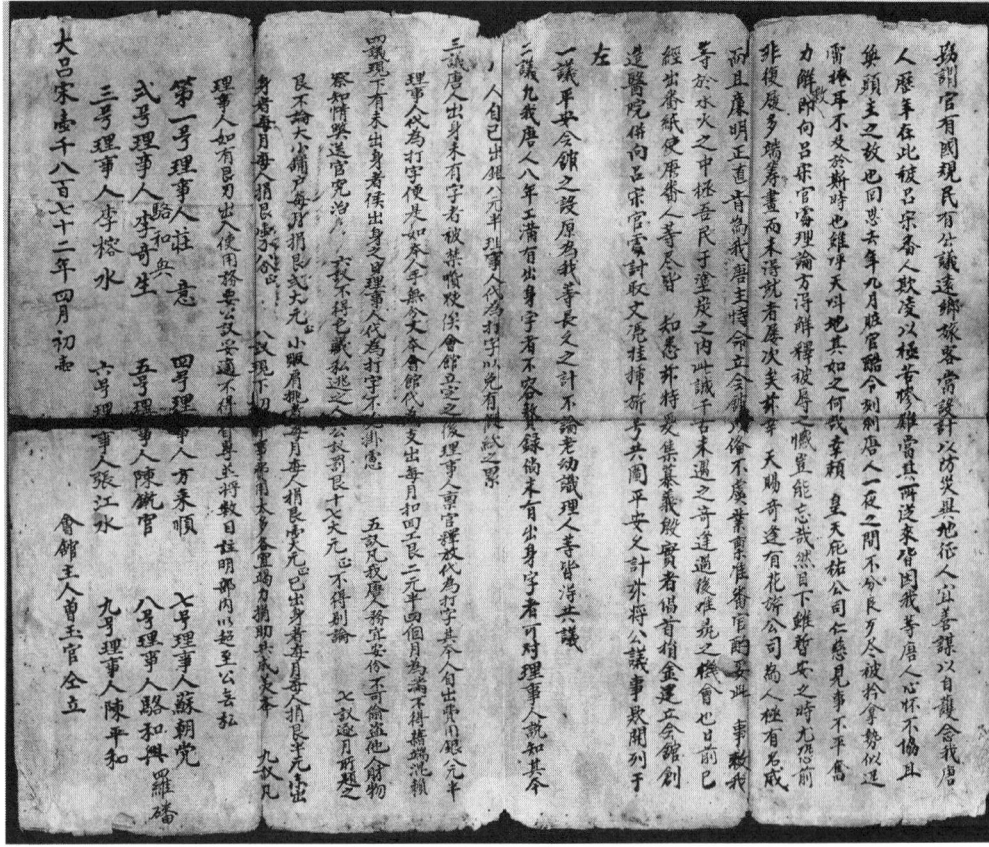

Figure 1. The Chinese Civic Association bylaws include a preamble about its collective history and aims, its rules and regulations, and its signatories. Melikian Collection 1872, no. 370. Courtesy of Chinese Immigrants in Cuba Archive, Arizona State University Libraries.

exchange for a fee of eight and a half pesos, the Chinese Civic Association would draw up paperwork on behalf of members. Such collective processing could allow the Chinese to avoid false paperwork (ANC 1872). By thus guaranteeing the authenticity of paperwork, collective action could allow the Chinese to handle the arduous application process "without anxiety" (MC 1872b). Third-person processing could also help to reinforce the legitimacy of the applicant's claims. The organization would allow more isolated Chinese to tap into larger social networks of free Chinese. According to the *Cuba Commission Report,* "certain Chinese domiciled in Havana and possessed of some means, induced the Colonial Government to sanction, by a Decree dated 20th March, 1872, the appointment of a foreigner resident in that city, as Chief Agent, and of Subagents in the cities of the interior, to act as representatives of Chinese, in cases where interference became necessary to prevent the suffering of wrong through ignorance of the laws and language, and the bad faith of those with whom they were dealing" (China 1970, 129). Regarding a Decree dated May 22, 1872, the Central Colonization Committee also prepared to establish subcommittees at the local level to verify paperwork (Cuba 1872b, 11–13). Here the Chinese Civic Association did not challenge the coolie system but appealed to sponsors to improve applicants' chances of naturalizing. As literary scholar Lisa Yun (2008, 123) notes, the statements of those who continued to struggle for legal paperwork "revealed a troubled complicity within the very system."

Nevertheless, the Chinese appealed to "a foreign resident" rather than a local *padrino* within Cuban society. According to the *Cuba Commission Report,* "Chinese of every class speak in the highest terms of the honor, integrity of the gentleman selected as chief agent" (China 1970, 129). In the bylaws, members thanked an American benefactor for donating funds.[12] In Petition 23, the Cantonese men of Cienfuegos named this "courageous hero" Langluofu 浪羅付, probably a transliteration of "Adolfo." The Portuguese Consulate ascribed Adolfo D. Straus with the honorific "Consul" (ANC 1872), but the Chinese-language bylaws correctly characterized him as a businessman (MC 1872b). As the anonymous correspondent for the *New York Times* (Straus 186?), Straus had sympathetically reported on the mass incarceration. The philanthropy of an American donor (called "el americano Straus" in the Portuguese consul's note to the Spanish government) with close connections to the U.S. Consulate might have made the Chinese Civic Association even more suspect (ANC 1872).

Even while protesting the coolie system, the Chinese Civic Association drew upon similar economic principles to those that undergird the coolie economy. Chinese leaders recognized that most laborers lacked the capital necessary for the application process. The bylaws promised, "Even if the man himself does not have one centavo [literally the smallest Chinese monetary unit], the association's representative will help him pay the fees." The Chinese Civic Association would allow the laborer to defer payment with a deduction of two and a half pesos from his salary every month for four months (thus charging one and a half pesos of interest). The laborer "cannot use an excuse to renege on the debt." (One should note here that the bylaws do not mention February 15, 1861, as a barrier.) Thus, acting as a corporate entity with legal bonds over contract laborers, the Chinese Civic Association effectively offered to indenture Chinese laborers to allow them to escape indenture elsewhere.

Given that the Chinese Civic Association effectively offered contracts of indenture to Chinese of relatively lesser means, one might postulate that the organization attempted to exploit fellow laborers.[13] After all, some Chinese contracted the labor of other Chinese, especially in one-year domestic service contracts (MC 1868b; 1868c). In 1870, some Chinese also led labor teams of recontracted laborers, called *cuadrillas* (López 2013, 66), but authorities, unable to differentiate between Chinese managers and workers, suspected that *cuadrillas* provided safe havens for runaways (China 1970, 86). Americans also suspected that Chinese gangs indentured workers in exchange for passage to the United States.[14] However, the moral rhetoric of the bylaws suggests that the collective trauma of the mass incarceration had intensified Chinese solidarity. One should also note the distinction between the association fees for processing certifications and the commission of Chinese recontractors who skimmed 10 percent in exchange for negotiating second contracts as go-betweens (Hu-Dehart 2005, 174). The Chinese Civic Association simply did not have the means to offer an alternative from the lending system inherent in the coolie system.

Members of the Chinese Civic Association needed to establish trust that the organization would not resell contracts to third parties. The association bylaws called on executives to report their financial transactions transparently, so that all members could ascertain that collective money had been spent wisely for the "public" good rather than for "private" benefit. The difference between public good and private gain had been a long-standing dichotomy in traditional Chinese statecraft, and those terms must have resonated with the educated Chinese leaders as fundamental to good self-governance (Tillman 1994, 1–37). Because members would effectively indenture themselves to the organization in exchange for loans for legal services, it was necessary that they trust the executives to allow them to fulfill and terminate their debt. In the Cuban context, trust was crucial for Chinese to negotiate on fair terms. The association bylaws thus reiterated the need for financial transparency.

Some Chinese contract laborers may not have had access to legal tender without the help of the Chinese Civic Association. The coolie system manipulated wages to trap Chinese laborers within the system of indenture. Wages were often paid not in hard currency but in script redeemable solely at the local plantation store (China 1970, 27). For example, a script for five pesos was granted specifically to the Chinese Constantino, with the date of issue and name of the plantation, where the manager, Gómez, could easily monitor Constantino's spending (MC 1863a). Script limited the exchange value of wages outside of the planation store. Furthermore, the high prices, as well as deductions from pay for infractions, insured that impoverished coolies would remain in debt. Such practices were so odious that a group of coolies rose up in 1873 to demand payment in silver (*North American and U.S. Gazette* 1873).

The Chinese Civic Association offered to protect Chinese men when they encountered legal difficulty, but only with the explicit understanding that the migrants had been unfairly jailed. Perhaps in response to widespread allegations about Chinese criminality, the Chinese Civic Association instructed its members to obey the laws of the land. Article 5 warned Chinese residents to "abide by the law," especially with respect to property. Association leaders were merchants who supported property rights. These leaders struggled to define their association against stereotypes of Chinese criminality, especially gambling and profiteering, which would have defined the organization as a gang (Narváez 2010, 32). Instead, the Chinese Civic Association promised to hand over criminals and rebels to the authorities, in keeping with the function of Chinese voluntary associations, elsewhere, to govern, especially in developing societies (Kuah-Pearce and Hu-DeHart 2006, 9; Lai 1987).

In keeping native-place and voluntary associations elsewhere (Kuah-Pearce and Hu-DeHart 2006, 8), the Chinese Civic Association also promised to provide medical services, through the foundation of a hospital. In China, hospitals were an established venue for charity work, especially for migrating communities (Sinn 2013, 83–89). Chinese doctors enjoyed success in Cuba's Chinatowns, but authorities in Cuba opposed the practice of non-Western medicine (Corbitt 1971, 87; MC 1847). Faced with "no doctors for illness, no graveyards for the dead, no way to send letters home" (Petition 11), the leaders of the Chinese Civic Association hoped to "save our people from [dying in] the waters and fire" and the "mud and dust," imagery classically connected to the disasters of cruel government or barbarian domination (MC 1872b).[15] In this context, the proposals of the Chinese Civic Association would leverage the freedom to engage in Chinese cultural practices, such as medicine, that were not recognized as legitimate by colonial authorities.

The Chinese compared such organizations to mutual-aid associations in China and abroad (e.g., Petition 11). The Chinese Civic Association perhaps built on the groundwork of Chinese clubs, called *casinos asiáticos,* which were established by the first generation of Chinese contract workers from Amoy (López 2013, 105; Narváez 2010, 447–48; Chuffat Latour 1927, 18). The executives of the Chinese Civic Association implied that all such organizations were law abiding and primarily motivated by the initiative of local Chinese. In the aftermath of the Tian'anmen demonstration, historians of China argued about whether such associations were "official-merchant" collaborations that failed to meet Western standards of a true "civil society" (Wakeman 1993). In the absence of local Chinese officials in 1872, the Chinese Civic Association turned to the sanction of the U.S. Consulate. This move is in keeping with the appearance of overseas Chinese associations as transnational organizations (Kuhn 2008).

For Spanish colonial authorities, the Chinese Civic Association would be most readily categorized as an organization for free people of color, such as Afro-Cuban mutual-aid associations, called *cabildos* (García Rodríguez 2011, 32). Government authorities scrutinized these organizations because of connections to insurrections against Spain in the 1830s and 1840s (Howard 1998, 112). Since the Chinese Civic Association coincided with the Ten Years' War, this prior history may have negatively impacted the government's assessment. In the latter half of the nineteenth century, Afro-Cuban mutual-aid societies began to emphasize their role in helping to regulate members (Howard 1998, 133). The *casta* system had long placed relatively more assimilated blacks in positions of authority over free Indians and newly arrived Africans (Cottrol 2013, 37, 40–42), and *cabildos* extended this practice into free society. Likewise, the Chinese Civic Association's promise "never to neglect order and respect for the laws of the government" must have helped the initial endorsement of the Chinese Civic Association (ANC 1872).

Here the Chinese-language bylaws potentially undermined the claims of free Chinese, not to law and order, but to serving the Spanish Crown. In files for *cartas de domicilio,* contract laborers had pledged absolute loyalty to the Spanish throne—even in the event of military conflict with China. In contrast, the bylaws reveal resentment for larger structures of power, especially the "Spanish barbarians" of Luzón, the principal island in the Philippines that served as the major hub of the Spanish colonial government and trade in East and Southeast Asia. As in many coolie testimonials, Luzón was a metonym for Spanish colonization connecting Asia with the New World (Yun 2008, 92).

The documents indicate the importance of Portugal, as the major player that exported coolies out of Macao, and also suggest the hand of Portuguese officials in the fate of the Chinese Civic Association. The Chinese had appealed to the Portuguese consul for protection in 1871. On the back of the Chinese-language bylaws, there is a note that the document was translated by the consul general of Portugal on July 18, 1872 (Figure 2) (MC 1872b). On July 19, the Portuguese consul general remitted a copy of the document, translated by the same interpreters to the gobierno

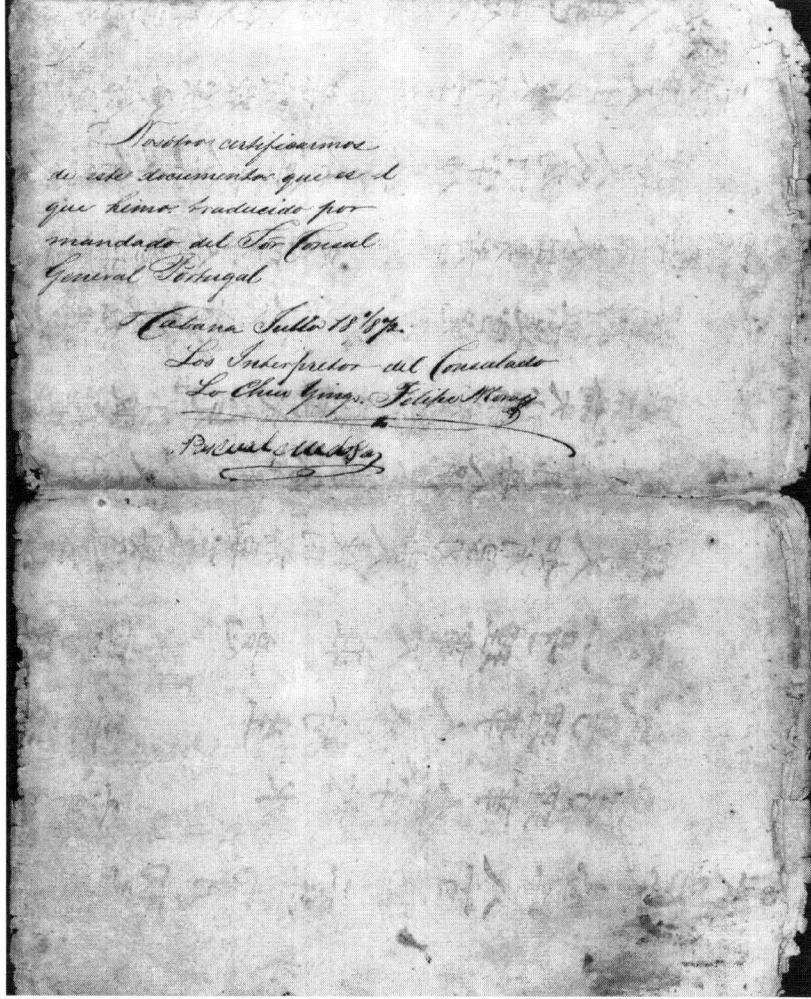

Figure 2. The backside of the Chinese Civic Association bylaws indicates that the document was translated by the Portuguese consul general. Melikian Collection 1872, no. 370. Courtesy of Chinese Immigrants in Cuba Archive, Arizona State University Libraries.

superior civil (ANC 1872). Unlike the Chinese-language document, the translation includes a direct appeal to the Portuguese consul general for aid in obtaining permission from the Spanish colonial authorities and removes some of the emotionally charged language regarding the trauma of the Chinese at the hands of Spanish barbarians. The translation still condemns the mass incarceration of September 1871 as "without just cause, foundation," or provocation (ANC 1872).

In 1873–74, retrospective Chinese testimonies to the Qing Commission suggest that, rather than helping the Chinese, the Portuguese governor general was responsible for sabotaging their efforts. Chinese men accused Portuguese officials of convincing the Spanish colonial authorities that the Chinese were collecting money for rebellion (Petition 11) (Yun 2008, 247). The Portuguese vice-consul allegedly lured the Chinese to Cárdenas to obtain what turned out to be fake papers while also alerting the Cuban authorities to arrest them. According to the *Cuban Commission Report,* in July 1872, due to actions occurring in Cárdenas, the colonial government had revoked permission for a Chinese mutual-aid association for legal representation (China 1970, 129). The translation affirms the interference of Portugal. Perhaps via the Consulate, someone acquired knowledge of the association's collective ability to pay for paperwork and thereby entrapped the Chinese at Cárdenas and caused the Spanish authorities' subsequent disbanding of the organization.

By reaching out to foreign diplomats, the Chinese had attempted to circumvent the local Hispanic society. Not only had contract workers chaffed at working under Afro-Cubans on sugar plantations but free Chinese also probably competed with Afro-Cubans to enter the ranks of the petty urban bourgeoisie. Afro-Cuban *cabildos* had accumulated capital and real estate investments to sustain their institutions (Howard 1998, 28). The government allowed Afro-Cuban mutual-aid associations with the rationale that prohibition would be viewed as racial discrimination (Howard 1998, xvi). Lacking connections to Afro-Cuban mutual-aid associations, perhaps due to the deliberate measures of the plantation class to divide the communities, the Chinese Civic Association overlooked a potential source of support.

The coolie trade continued. With renewed permission from Madrid, sugar plantation owners arranged new shipments of coolies from Asia.[16] On October 23, 1872, in the *Official Gazette,* political secretary Miguel Suárez Vigil also successfully petitioned to suspend laws requiring plantation owners to submit their coolies to government depots for review—and thus facilitated recontracting with original plantation owners (*Despatches* 1872, vol. 67, no. 134). The plantation elite thereby also asserted control over the Cuban petty bourgeoisie who had accepted bribes as *padrones.* These legal measures mask violence. Repeatedly, the Chinese encountered violence while navigating the coolie system: at the termination of their first contracts, during the mass incarceration of 1871, and in the entrapment that led to the withdrawal of official permission for the Chinese Civic Association.

Despite the failure of the Chinese Civic Association in 1872, their voices of protest, via connections to foreign consuls, may have been among those that drew the attention of Western advisors to Prince Gong, the head of China's Foreign Affairs Office (*Foreign Relations* 1871, 149–51; Ng 2014).[17] In 1871, the members of two Peruvian Chinese guilds remonstrated to the U.S. consul, who relayed their reports of abuse to the Qing court (Ng 2014; U.S. Department of State 1872, no. 30, 112–14). In 1873, the Qing court dispatched the Imperial Commission, and "the investigations of the Commission developed nothing startling or different from the statements which have been received in regard to coolie matters in Cuba" (*Sacramento Daily Union* 1874). The *Cuba Commission Report* drew upon coolie testimony as a tactic to gain greater national sovereignty for China in the international arena.

■ CONCLUSION: BETWEEN EMPIRES

In the confrontation of empires in the nineteenth century, international law became a platform for negotiating power. The *Cuba Commission Report* outlines a persuasive argument in favor of China's national sovereignty. Coolie shippers had violated China's laws, which had before 1860 prohibited out-migration; furthermore, the report also pointed to the disjuncture between legal contracts and practices of recruitment. The commission impugned the legality of contracts entered under duress and also challenged labor systems that forever indentured workers. Anglo-American critiques sometimes had the effect of exceptionally reinforcing China's national sovereignty, as when the *North China Herald* called, in 1872, for China to retake Macao to stop the coolie trade. The *Milwaukee Sentinel* (1872b) joined the *New York Mail* in opining that "the Chinese Government has in this order [allowing the incarceration of contract laborers in 1871] a sufficient cause for war upon the Spanish power that perpetrated it."

The commission is an example of the Qing's attempt to employ new diplomatic tools, even those produced by the unequal treaties, such as the Imperial Maritime Customs Service. The Qing court assigned A. MacPherson 馬福臣, commissioner of customs in Hankou, and Alfred Huber 吳秉文, commissioner of customs at Tientsin, to join the investigation (Yun 2008, 39). In Havana, the Qing Commission visited with the captain general, the Comisión Central de Colonización, and the consular diplomats of Great Britain, France, Russia, the United States, Germany, Sweden, Norway, Denmark, Holland, Austria, Belgium, and Italy—many of whom had protested against the mass incarceration of 1871 (China 1970, 32). MacPherson and Huber translated the *Cuba Commission Report* into English and French to reach a wider international audience (Yun 2008, 38; Ng 2014).

In an effort to assert sovereignty, the Qing fixed the identities of a mobile population. The Imperial Commission produced information widely circulated in Chinese through the *Shanghai News* (*Shen Bao* 1873a; 1873b; 1873c; 1873d; 1873e; 1875a; 1875b), and these documents moved among, in literary scholar Lydia Liu's (2004, 110) terms, "troops of equivalence in the middle zone of translation." In 1872, the *Shanghai News* labeled Chinese contract laborers *huayong* 華庸 to distinguish them from coolies (*kuli* 苦力) (*Shen Bao* 1872). The government's term *huagong* 華工 for "Chinese workers" homogenized contract and noncontract migrants (e.g., China Imperial Maritime Customs 1879, 88–96; China 1970, 95). The commission did not translate its findings into Spanish, resulting in incommensurability between the Spanish and Chinese identities of the workers—thus protecting workers from retaliation by the colonial authorities but also obscuring their identity in the historical record. In Cuba, the Chinese had created an "acute classificatory embarrassment" within the established *casta* system because the Chinese were technically labeled as colonists (Martínez-Alier 1989, 76–81). Chinese Cubans welcomed Qing diplomatic measures to improve their status, such as certificates of citizenship issued by the Qing Consulate in 1875 (*Shen Bao* 1875c; 1878a; 1893; *Sheffield Daily Telegraph* 1879; e.g., MC 1880).[18] The commission suggests that the Chinese saw the political representation as an important venue for legal protection, which Chinese Cubans had been actively seeking in the association. Nevertheless, free Chinese had willingly pledged allegiance to the Spanish Crown and reached out to the U.S. Consulate for protection. These actions suggest a politically flexible search for personal rights and an understanding of their vulnerability at the intersection of imperial powers.

The events of 1871 had provoked international condemnation precisely because the Chinese in Cuba were tied to global capitalism. Often indentured against their will, Chinese coolies had always been pawns of the forces of global capital, but what is remarkable is that consuls implicitly recognized the Chinese as economic allies against the Spanish colonial empire and, even more broadly, Hispanic power in the Americas. Historian Evelyn Hu-DeHart (1980, 284) has argued that despite increasing anti-Chinese sentiment at home, the United States protected Chinese migrants as economic allies beyond its borders. In the case of Mexico, locals attacked Chinese petty merchants who served the invisible forces of global capital reshaping their society (Hu-DeHart 1980). Even though overseas Chinese had achieved relatively less economic success in Cuba, Cubans were also ambivalent about urban Chinese and their international connections. As one U.S. consul to Spain noted, "loud protests have come from Cuba against what is called an American intrigue to deprive planters of Chinese laborers by means of an unfavorable report to be made by the investigating committee" (U.S. Department of State 1875, 857). Perhaps the Chinese had been incarcerated to contain not so much their criminality as their success, as aspiring petty bourgeoisie with connections to global capital.

The Chinese Civic Association bylaws reveal the limits of the coolie system, especially as enforced by legal contracts alone. While reiterating the legality of contracts, Spanish authorities doubted the authenticity of the paperwork that released the Chinese from indenture. Chinese could bribe godfathers to reinforce the validity of the paperwork. Technically indentured, many Chinese struggled to distinguish themselves from the enslaved Afro-Cuban population, who had to purchase their freedom if they were to become free; the Chinese expected instead that their indenture would expire through tenure of service. Instead of easing into Cuban society in a position alongside upwardly mobile, free Afro-Cubans, the Chinese appealed instead to foreign merchants. In this particular instance, the Chinese upheld the legal enforcement of the termination contracts and the definite universality of those terms (independent of local social capital or other legal regulations).

In their attempts to abide by the letter of the coolie system, the Chinese Civic Association indirectly exposed the incongruities between indenture and slavery: release from indenture could spark urban commercialization rather than buttress slave-based agriculture. Anglo-Americans saw in the incarceration an effort to maintain Cuba's slave economy rather than transition into a commercial economy. Reports fed into the U.S. conflation of coolies with slaves in the late nineteenth century and thus the threat that near-slave indenture might pose to wage labor (Jung 2006; Redman 2010). Members of the Chinese Civic Association supported the contract system as an alternative to slavery and forced recontracting. After abnegating the possibility of naturalization, the revised coolie system thus conflicted with the neoliberalism that had justified contracts of indenture and thereby exposed the limits of the coolie system.

Simultaneously, the Chinese Civic Association drew on patterns of loan from within the larger system of indenture. Lacking the capital of the Afro-Cuban societies, the leaders of the Chinese Civic Association needed to establish trust within their own ranks through promises of full financial transparency. The association bylaws thus reveal some of the complications of solidarity, both within the Chinese community and between the Chinese and Afro-Cuban communities. By proposing to establish a law-abiding association for the upward mobility of coolies, the literate (in Chinese) and free Chinese shopkeepers of Havana continued to support existing legal systems that protected private property and, as such, exposed the fraught complications of attempting cross-class solidarity. Even when faced with conditions of near-slavery, migrant Chinese in Cuba could represent the face, at the ground level, of global capital threatening the stability of colonial labor systems enforced by Spanish imperial power.

■ APPENDIX: THE ASSOCIATION BYLAWS (MC 1872, NO. 370)

Everyone says that officials have national regulations, and the people have [the right] to public discussion. Travelers far from home should have plans to guard against calamity. As sojourners in an unfamiliar land, [we] should prepare good strategies to protect ourselves, considering we Chinese have, for many years in this place, been bullied and insulted by the Spanish colonists to the extreme point that [we can] no longer bear the suffering and hardship. The reason all that has happened is because our Chinese people lack the heart to unite and furthermore because we lack leadership. Thinking back to September of last year, corrupt officials [issued a] cruel order to oppress the Chinese people. Within one night, everyone—the law-abiding and criminal alike—was arrested as quickly as a thunder-clap strikes, without time to cover the ears. At that time, although we called out to Heaven and Earth, it was of no use. Fortunately, thanks to august Heaven, a benevolent U.S. businessman witnessed these unjust events and strove to save and release [the Chinese prisoners]. The businessman approached the official colonial government to appeal and petition and finally obtained the release [of the Chinese prisoners]. But our laments for these insults, how could we forget? However, presently, although we are temporarily in a period of peace, we still worry about whether the previous calamity will occur again. We planned many strategies, and have failed each time. Recently, Heaven fortunately bestowed an extraordinary encounter with a U.S. benefactor, ["Langluofu," 浪羅付 or Adolfo D. Straus], of renown and authority, who is furthermore extremely honest and upright, and was willing to act on behalf of us Chinese. With his backing, we are establishing the Chinese Civic Association to prepare against future misfortune. Already [he] has reported these matters for consideration and obtained approval from the barbarian [Spanish colonial] officials in order to rescue our people from [dying in] the waters and fire, and to save our people from utter misery. This truly is an unprecedented encounter, and if we pass it up, we will not find it again. A day ago, the barbarian [Spanish] officials already issued official documents to inform all Chinese and barbarian people [about this matter]. Now, we especially convene those who respect what is just and those with resources to lead in donating money to establish the association, to found a hospital, and furthermore, to petition Luzón [i.e., Spanish] officials for a permit to install a plaque [for the formal establishment of the Chinese Civic Association], and collectively to strategize a plan for long-term tranquility. Now, we list below the following items [that arose from] public consensus.

First Article. The rationale of establishing the Association was originally a plan for long-term peace. No matter one's age, all people of reason have the right to discuss [these matters] collectively.

Second Article. It is unnecessary to discuss those Chinese who have already gained manumission after fulfilling their contracts of eight years. If one has not gained manumission, he may tell the board members [of the Association]. If a man has not redeemed himself, he may tell the board members, and he needs to pay eight and a half pesos for the executive board to draw up the paperwork on his behalf, in order to avoid any problems with fake documentation.

Third Article. When Chinese people without registration numbers are arrested, they may be re-contracted. After the establishment of the Association, the board members will report to the Spanish officials to release that man, and handle the paperwork on his behalf. The man himself pays the expenses of eight and a half pesos for the board members to draw up the documentation for him. Even if the man does not have a centavo to his name, the Association will advance the fees for him. Every month, two and a half pesos will be deducted from his salary [to reimburse the Association]. The man will not be allowed to find an excuse to renege on the debt, and after four months, it will be repaid in full.

Fourth Article. From now on, those who have not yet been released from their contracts, upon fulfilling the terms of their contracts, [will have the option of allowing] the board members to handle documentation on their behalf, so they need not worry.

Fifth Article. All we Chinese people should abide by the law, and should not steal other people's property. Upon discovery of such crimes, [the association will] send [those criminals] to the authorities to be tried and punished.

Sixth Article. One should not protect or hide fugitives. According to public consensus, those [who do] will be fined seventeen pesos exactly. There is no room for further discussion.

Seventh Article. As to the aforementioned monthly contribution, every shop—no matter large or small—needs to contribute exactly two pesos every month. Each peddler contributes exactly one peso every month. Those who have already fulfilled their contracts must donate half a peso every month, but those who have not yet fulfilled their contracts must only pay eight centavos.

Eighth Article. Recently, [two missing characters] the expenses [to process paperwork for legal residency] have become exorbitant; everyone should try his best to donate and to contribute to accomplish this great deed collectively.

Ninth Article. If any board member incurs expenses or financial discrepancies, [he] must disclose [the discrepancy] to settle it properly. One should not act arbitrarily, but should clearly note the monetary amounts within the association records in order to attain the public good and selfless altruism.

[The undersigned:]

First Executive Zhuang Yi 莊意 [Chon Yeck in the document in the Archivo National Cuba]

Second Executive Li Qisheng 李奇[奇]生 [name stricken, presumably replaced by] Luo Hexing 駱和[興] [Lok Woo hing]

Third Executive Li Rongshui 李榕水 [Leo Yun Sui]

Fourth Executive Fang Laishun 方来顺 [Fon Lay Sun]

Fifth Executive Chen Long(guan) 陳乾[19]官 [Chun Kin]

Sixth Executive Zhang Jiangshui 張江水 [Cheong Kan Sui]

Seventh Executive Su Chaodang 蘇朝党 [Soe Chevo Ton]

Eighth Executive Luo Hexing 駱和興 [here, not written in shorthand, as previously; presumably, when he replaced Li Qisheng, he was replaced by] Luo Pan 羅磻 [Loo Pun]

Ninth Executive Chen Pinghe 陳平和 [Chun Ping Voo]

Association President Ceng Yu(guan) 曾玉官 [Chang Yu]

The Great Luzón [Havana], April 1872

Margaret Mih Tillman is assistant professor of modern Chinese history at Purdue University.

■ **NOTES**

This article is indebted to James and Ana Melikian and Arizona State University librarians Ralph Gabbard, Melissa Guy, and Qian Liu for access to materials; Margaret Moore for access to the National Library of Congress; Benjamin Narváez for sharing archival notes; Natalie Mendoza for copying archival material; and Zhang Yibing and Gu Chengrui for access to a typed transcript of the original petitions compiled by the Qing Commission in 1874, now housed in the National Library of Beijing. Qian Liu provided consultation for Chinese translations and Melisa Galván and Elizabeth Ashcroft Terry for Spanish-language signatures. The article benefited from insightful feedback from Erica Fox Brindley, J. Peter Escalante, Jennifer Foray, David Foster, Sally Hastings, On-cho Ng, K. Lynn Stoner, Hoyt Cleveland Tillman, and anonymous referees.

1. The Chinese referred to their organization as a *huiguan* 會館, or mutual-aid association (MC, no. 370, "Association Bylaws," not yet cataloged, 1872); the Portuguese Consulate refers to the organization as "la Agencia de Asiáticos de Straus" (ANC 1872). To distinguish this particular organization from other clubs, I use the gloss "the Chinese Civic Association" to refer to this specific group and to indicate how it projected its function.

2. For the history and estimates of the coolie trade, see Bergad (1995, 248), Pérez de la Riva (1978, 57), and Yun (2008, 16).

3. For the economic impact of coolie labor, see Hu-DeHart (1994) and Helly (1993). Given labor shortages on Cuban sugar plantations, the coolie trade was highly profitable, with an average investment of 30,000 to 50,000 pesos for a shipment of five hundred coolies but yielding an average of 100,000 to 120,000 pesos; see Yun (2008, 16–17) and Meagher (2008, 142–43).

4. For an example of a contract laborer called a *colono,* see MC (no. 199, "Death Record," http://hdl.handle.net/2286/R.I.19467, 1862). For views of the Chinese as temporary workers, see López (2013, 88).

5. See, e.g., China 1970, 82–84, 95. According to the commission, the Chinese repeated the phrase "sold as slaves" 賣作奴 (Columbia University 2014; *Shen Bao* 1872). For scholarly debates on their status, see, e.g., Jiménez Pastrana (2000), Hu-DeHart (1989, 106–9), Scott (1985, 30–31), and López (2013, 50–51).

6. For an example of forced baptism, see Columbia University (2014, 14); for government monitoring, see García Triana and Herrera (2009, 124) and MC (no. 508, "Complaints." http://hdl.handle.net/2286/R.I.23748, 1867).

7. In the Confession Program of 1956, more than thirty thousand Chinese Americans admitted to having come to the United States with false papers. See Lee (2003, 18–19).

8. E.g., China 1970, 86. A comparison to the case of Afro-Cubans, who were granted opportunities to gain gradual abolition under the Moret Law after the Ten Years' War, may be illustrative; former slaves who had illegally entered Cuba suffered from insufficient evidence and paperwork (Scott 1985, 146).

9. All citations to the *Despatches* are to Despatches from United States

Consuls in Havana, MS Despatches from U.S. Consuls in Havana, Cuba, 1783–1906, U.S. National Archives.

10. If the document reads as "the tenth day of the ninth lunar month," as Yun suggests, the correct date should be October 23. Because the document used the year 1871 rather than either a reign title or cyclical-dating characters, because lunar dating is hard to ascertain without a calendar, and because it correlates with consular and newspaper accounts, the date is probably September 10, 1871.

11. In e-mail correspondence, dated August 26, 2015, to the author, Benjamin Narváez clarified that the document came from the ANC. All references to this document are drawn from Narváez's transcribed notes.

12. The term for "American" differs in the two documents, with the term 花旂 [旗] used in the bylaws, written by the Cantonese men, and the Mandarin term in Petition 23, transcribed for the Qing court.

13. McClain (1994, 14–15) examines similar charges concerning mutual aid associations in the United States and finds those charges wanting; see also Qin ([2009] 2014, 55–57).

14. According to Ngai (2012), these accusations are based on an unsubstantiated loop of rumors.

15. Original: 數年華人以病無人醫死無地葬寄書跟回國; see Petition 11 (China 1874; Yun 2008, 245–47). Original: 救我 [等] 於水火之中拯吾民於塗炭之內; see MC 1872b (no. 370). Mencius wrote that serving the court of an evil person would be, for the righteous man Bo Yi, like wearing ceremonial robes while sitting in mud and dust; echoing this language, the Chinese condemned local officials.

16. In 1872, Cuban traders contracted 786 Chinese workers to transport from Macao via the *Ambotó* and 1,007 via the *Fatchoy*. See *Despatches* (1872, vol. 67, no. 134), MC (no. 519, "Death Investigation," http://hdl.handle.net/2286/R.A.132160, 1873), and Great Britain and Foreign Office (1875).

17. For Chinese reports of the abuses, see *Shen Bao* (1875c; 1877b; 1877c; 1878b).

18. Chen Lanbin, originally deemed by Chinese scholars a "conservative," has been favorably reevaluated in the light of his contribution to the Cuba Commission (Chen 2005; Xie 2010; Peng 2014).

19. The handwritten character includes the medal radical 金, but this formulation cannot be found among Chinese character variants 異體字.

■ WORKS CITED

Aldus, Don. 1876. *Coolie Traffic and Kidnapping.* London: McCorquodale.

Archivo Nacional de Cuba. 1872. *Fondo Miscelánea de Expedientes, Leg. 4151, Exp. Al: promovido por el Cónsul de Portugal remitiendo una circular*

expuesta al público en caracteres Chinos referente á la Agencia de Asiáti-
cos de Straus [Endorsed by the Portuguese consul, remitting a public
circular in Chinese characters in reference to Straus's Asian group].
Spanish translation transcribed and given to the author by Benjamin
Narváez, August 26, 2015.

Bergad, Laird. 1995. *The Cuban Slave Market, 1780–1880*. Cambridge: Cambridge University Press.

Boston Daily Advertiser. 1871. "Cuba, the Chinese Question." September 14.

———. 1872. "Chinese Bondage." January 2.

Chen Hansheng, ed. 1985. *Huagong chuguo shiliao* 华工出国史料 [Histori-
cal materials regarding overseas Chinese workers]. Beijing: Zhunghua
shuju.

Chen Xiaoyan 陈晓燕. 2005. "Guba Huagong an yu wan Qing waijiao jin-
daihua" 古巴华工案与晚清外交近代化 [The case of Chinese contract
workers in Cuba and the modernization of late Qing diplomatic rela-
tions]. *Zhejiang shehui kexue* [Zhejiang social sciences], no. 3: 159–65.

China. 1874. *Guba huagong chengci* 古巴華工呈詞 [Testimonies given by
Chinese laborers in Cuba]. National Central Library, Beijing.

———. 1970. *Chinese Emigration: Report of the Commission Sent by China to
Ascertain the Condition of Chinese Coolies in Cuba*. Taipei: Cheng Wen.

China Imperial Maritime Customs. 1879. "The Convention to Regulate
the Engagement of China Emigrants by British and French Subjects."
Service Series IV. Statistical Department of the Inspectorate General.

Chuffat Latour, Antonio. 1927. *Apunte Histórico de los Chinos en Cuba*.
Havana: Molina.

Columbia University, ed. 2014. *Guba huagong chengci* 古巴華工呈詞
[Survey of Chinese workers in Cuba]. Shanghai: Shanghai Bookstore
Publishing House. Selected republication of China 1874.

Corbitt, Duvon Clough. 1942. "Immigration in Cuba." *The Hispanic American Historical Review* 22, no. 2: 280–308.

———. 1971. *A Study of the Chinese in Cuba, 1847–1947*. Wilmore, Ken.:
Asbury College.

Corwin, Arthur F. 1967. *Spain and the Abolition of Slavery in Cuba, 1817–
1886*. Austin: University of Texas Press.

Cottrol, Robert J. 2013. *The Long, Lingering Shadow: Slavery, Race, and the
Law in the American Hemisphere*. Athens: University of Georgia Press.

Cuba. 1872a. *Colección de las Disposiciones que sobre colonos han sido expedi-
das hasta la fecha para su complimiento* [Collection of the dispositions
regarding the contract laborers who have been issued papers]. Impr.
del gobierno y capitania general por S. M.

———. 1872b. "Decreto del gobierno superior político sobre colonización asiática publicado en 14 de setiembre de 1872 é instrucciones dictadas por dicho superior gobierno para las subcomisiones y delegaciones creadas en 22 de mayo de 1872" [Decree of the Superior Political Government regarding Asian immigration published on September 14, 1872, and instructions issued by that body for the subcommittees and delegations created on May 22, 1872]. Cienfuegos, Impr. de Pabellon nacional. Bancroft Library.

Daily News (London). 1872. "The Chinese Coolie Traffic." February 17.

Davids, Jules, compiler. 1842–60. *American Diplomatic and Public Papers. The United States and China. Series 1: The Treaty Season and The Taiping Rebellion.* Compiled by Jules Davids. Wilmington, Del.: Scholarly Resources.

Dundee Courier. 1873. "The China Coolie Traffic." July 16.

Foreign Relations. 1871. Washington, D.C.: U.S. Department of State.

García Rodríguez, Gloria. 2011. *Voices of the Enslaved in Nineteenth-Century Cuba: A Documentary History.* Chapel Hill: University of North Carolina Press.

García Triana, Mauro, and Pedro Eng Herrera. 2009. *The Chinese in Cuba, 1847–Now.* Lanham, Md.: Lexington Books.

Great Britain and Foreign Office. 1875. *Correspondence Respecting the Macao Coolie Trade: 1874–1875.* London: Harrison.

Hamilton, Gary. 1979. "Regional Associations and the Chinese City: A Comparative Perspective." *Comparative Studies in Society and History,* no. 21: 346–61.

Hao Musheng 蒿目生. 1875. "Lun Guba huagong yi ling fu Meiguo shou gong" 論古巴華工宜令赴美國受僱 [On the question of relocating Chinese–Cuban contract laborers to the United States]. *Shen Bao* [Shanghai news], November 26.

Helly, Denise. 1993. *The Cuba Commission Report: A Hidden History of the Chinese in Cuba. The Original English-Language Text of 1876.* Baltimore: Johns Hopkins University Press.

Ho, Ping-ti. 1962. *The Ladder of Success in Imperial China: Aspects of Social Mobility, 1368–1911.* New York: Columbia University Press.

Howard, Philip A. 1998. *Changing History: Afro-Cuban Cabildos and Societies of Color in the Nineteenth Century.* Baton Rouge: Louisiana State University Press.

Hu-DeHart, Evelyn. 1980. "Immigrants to a Developing Society." *The Journal of Arizona History* 21, no. 3: 275–312.

———. 1989. "Coolies, Shopkeepers, Pioneers: The Chinese of Mexico and Peru (1849–1930)." *Amerasia Journal* 15, no. 2: 91–116.

———. 1994. "Chinese Coolie Labor in Cuba in the Nineteenth Century:

Free Labor of Neoslavery." *Contributions in Black Studies* 12: 38–54.

———. 2005. "Opium and Social Control: Coolies on the Plantations of Peru and Cuba." *Journal of Overseas Chinese* 1, no. 2: 169–83.

Irick, Robert L. 1982. *Ch'ing Policy toward the Coolie Trade, 1847–1878.* Taipei: Chinese Materials Center.

Jiménez Pastrana, Juan. 2000. *Los Culíes Chinos en Cuba, 1847–1880: Contribución al Estudio de la Inmigración contratada en el Caribe* [The Chinese coolies in Cuba, 1847–1880: A contribution to the study of indentured immigration to the Caribbean]. Havana: Ciencias Sociales.

Jung, Moon-Ho. 2006. *Coolies and Cane: Race, Labor, and Sugar in the Age of Emancipation.* Baltimore: Johns Hopkins University Press.

Kuah-Pearce, Khun Eng, and Evelyn Hu-Dehart. 2006. "Introduction: The Chinese Diaspora and Voluntary Associations." In *Voluntary Organizations in the Chinese Diaspora,* edited by Khun Eng Kuah-Pearce and Evelyn Hu-Dehart, 1–28. Hong Kong: Hong Kong University Press.

Kuhn, Philip. 2008. *Chinese among Others: Emigration in Modern Times.* Lanham, Md.: Rowman and Littlefield.

Lai, Him Mark. 1987. "Historical Development of the Chinese Consolidated Benevolent Association/*Huiguan* System." In *Chinese America: History and Perspectives,* 13–33. San Francisco: Chinese Historical Society of America.

Lee, Erika. 2003. *At America's Gates: Chinese Emigration in the Exclusion Era, 1882–1943.* Chapel Hill: University of North Carolina Press.

Liu, Lydia He. 2004. *The Clash of Empires: The Invention of China in Modern World Making.* Cambridge, Mass.: Harvard University Press.

Lloyd's Weekly Newspaper (London). 1856. "The Coolie Slave Trade." April 27.

López, Kathleen. 2008. "Afro-Asian Alliances: Marriage, Godparentage, and Social Status in Late-Nineteenth-Century Cuba." *Afro-Hispanic Review* 27, no. 1: 59–72.

———. 2013. *Chinese Cubans: A Transnational History.* Chapel Hill: University of North Carolina Press.

Martínez-Alier, Verena [Verena Stolcke]. 1989. *Marriage, Class and Colour in Nineteenth-Century Cuba: A Study of Racial Attitudes and Sexual Values in a Slave Society.* 2nd ed. Ann Arbor: University of Michigan Press.

McClain, Charles. 1994. *In Search of Equality: The Chinese Struggle against Discrimination in the Nineteenth Century.* Berkeley: University of California Press.

McKeown, Adam. 2001. *Chinese Migrant Networks and Cultural Change: Peru, Chicago, Hawaii, 1900–1936.* Chicago: University of Chicago Press.

Meagher, Arnold. 2008. *The Coolie Trade: The Traffic in Chinese Laborers to Latin America, 1847–1874.* Philadelphia: Xlibris Corporation.

Melikian Collection. 1847. "Médico Chino." File no. 503. http://hdl.handle.net/2286/R.I.23743.

———. 1858a. "Runaway Workers." File no. 249. http://hdl.handle.net/2286/R.I.19636.

———. 1858b. "Runaway Slaves." File no. 293. http://hdl.handle.net/2286/R.I.19555.

———. 1858c. "Runaway Workers." File no. 875. http://hdl.handle.net/2286/R.I.24117.

———. 1860. "Second Contract." File no. 104. http://hdl.handle.net/2286/R.I.19725.

———. 1861. "Contract Completion." File no. 896. http://hdl.handle.net/2286/R.I.24137.

———. 1862. "Death Record." File no. 199. http://hdl.handle.net/2286/R.I.19467.

———. 1863a. "Check." File no. 200. http://hdl.handle.net/2286/R.I.19584.

———. 1863b. "Permanent Residence Documents." File no. 353. http://hdl.handle.net/2286/R.I.19715.

———. 1866. "Application Documents for Legal Residency." File no. 586. http://hdl.handle.net/2286/R.I.23827.

———. 1867. "Complaints." File no. 508. http://hdl.handle.net/2286/R.I.23748.

———. 1868a. "Naturalization Documents." File no. 860. http://hdl.handle.net/2286/R.I.24101.

———. 1868b. "Second Contract." File no. 940. http://hdl.handle.net/2286/R.I.24181.

———. 1868c. "Second Contract." File no. 941. http://hdl.handle.net/2286/R.I.24182.

———. 1871. "Naturalization Documents." File no. 867. http://hdl.handle.net/2286/R.I.24108.

———. 1872a. "Application Documents for Legal Residency." File no. 513. http://hdl.handle.net/2286/R.A.132137.

———. 1872b. "Association Bylaws." File no. 370. Not yet cataloged.

———. 1873. "Death Investigation." File no. 519. http://hdl.handle.net/2286/R.A.132160.

———. 1880. "Certificates of Nationality." File no. 236. http://hdl.handle.net/2286/R.I.19696.

Milwaukee Sentinel. 1872a. "The Coolie Trade." February 6.

———. 1872b. "A Havana Correspondent." February 20.

Mörner, Magnus. 1967. *Race Mixture in the History of Latin America.* Boston: Little, Brown.

MS British Cabinet Papers, 1880–1916. 1907. "Coolie Emigration from Hong Kong and China Ports."

Narváez, Benjamin. 2010. "Chinese Coolies in Cuba and Peru: Race, Labor, and Immigration, 1839–1886." PhD diss., University of Texas.

New York Evangelist. 1860. "The Slave and Coolie Trade at Havana." November 8.

New York Times. 1871. "Cuban Affairs: Arrest of Chinamen—a Crusade against the Celestials in Cuba—Protection 'with a Vengeance'—the Insurrection." September 25.

———. 1872a. "Cuba: The Liberties of the Chinamen, Wholesale Enslaving Planned." February 17.

———. 1872b. "A Talk with Kin." March 3.

———. 1872c. "Cuba: A Practical Revival of the Slave Trade." June 15.

———. 1872d. "Cuba: Horrible Treatment of Chinese Coolies by the Cuban Authorities War News and Miscellaneous Items." August 2.

———. 1872e. "Cuba: Further Outrages against the Chinese Coolies." September 22.

Ng, Rudolph. 2014. "The Chinese Commission to Cuba (1874): Reexamining International Relations in the Nineteenth Century from a Transcultural Perspective." *Transcultural Studies*, no. 2: 39–62.

Ngai, Mae. 2012. "Chinese Miners, the 'Coolie' Question, and the Propaganda of History." Berkeley: Center for Race Gender, University of California.

North American and U.S. Gazette. 1873. "The Latest News." July 21.

North China Herald and Supreme Court and Consular Gazette. 1872. "Portugal and China." November 14.

Panama Star and Herald. 1872a. "Cuba." January 20.

———. 1872b. "Great Britain." April 27.

Peng Leiting 彭雷霆. 2014. "Shoujiu yu quxin: zai shi shouren liu Mei xuesheng jindu Chen Lanbin" 守旧与趋新:再识首任留美学生监督陈兰彬 [Conservativism and innovation—new understanding of Chen Lanbin, the first supervisor of Chinese students in America]. *Baoji Wenlixueyuan Xuebao* 宝鸡文理学报 [Journal of Baoji University of Arts and Sciences] 34, no. 4: 42–47.

Pérez de la Riva, Juan. 1967. *Demografía de los Culies Chinos en Cuba.* Havana.

———. 1978. *El barracón: esclavitud y capitalismo en Cuba.* Barcelona: Critica.

Pfaelzer, Jean. 2008. *Driven Out: The Forgotten War against Chinese Americans.* Berkeley: University California Press.

Powers, Marshall K. 1953. "Chinese Coolie Migration to Cuba." PhD diss., University of Florida.

Qin, Yucheng. (2009) 2014. *The Diplomacy of Nationalism: The Six Companies and China's Policy toward Exclusion.* Honolulu: University of Hawai'i Press.

Rawski, Evelyn. 1979. *Education and Popular Literacy in Ch'ing China.* Ann Arbor: University of Michigan Press.

Redman, Renee. 2010. "From Importation of Slaves to Migration of Laborers: The Struggle to Outlaw American Participation in the Chinese Coolie Trade and the Seeds of United States Immigration Law." *Albany Government Law Review* 3, no. 1. http://papers.ssrn.com/sol3/papers.cfm?abstract_id=1658571.

Reglamento para la Introducción y Régimen de los colonos Asiáticos en la isla de Cuba [Laws concerning the introduction and governance of the Asian settlers on the island of Cuba]. 1861. Havana: Imprenta del gobierno y capitania general por S. M. Bancroft Library.

Reid-Vazquez, Michele. 2011. *The Year of the Lash: Free People of Color in Cuba and the Nineteenth-Century Atlantic World.* Athens: University of Georgia Press.

Royal Gazette. 1871. October 3, p. 3.

Sacramento Daily Union. 1872. "The Curse of Coolieism." December 6.

———. 1874. "Stocks." May 19.

Schmidt-Nowara, Christopher. 1999. *Empire and Antislavery: Spain, Cuba, and Puerto Rico, 1833–1874.* Pittsburgh, Pa.: University of Pittsburgh Press.

Scott, Rebecca J. 1985. *Slave Emancipation in Cuba: The Transition to Free Labor, 1860–1899.* Princeton, N.J.: Princeton University Press.

Sheffield Daily Telegraph. 1879. "General Foreign News." May 12.

Shen Bao [Shanghai news]. 1872. "Xia Yiyuan gongyi fan Huamin wei nu shi kuan" [The House of Commons bans contracts enslaving Chinese]. May 14.

———. 1873a. "Lun Aomen Zongdu huitong jinzhi ban ren chuyang shi" 論澳門總督會同禁止販人出洋事 [On Macao Governor General prohibiting out-emigration to the West]. January 8.

———. 1873b. "Zhongguo pai shi chen chu Guba guo" 中國派使臣赴古巴國 [China sends officials to Cuba]. October 10.

———. 1873c. "Lun Piluguoren yu sha huayong shi" 論皮魯國人欲殺華傭事 [Discussing the aim of Peruvians to kill coolies]. October 16.

———. 1873d. "Chen Gongli qiu pai chong chu shi Pilu Guba liangguo" 陳公荔秋派充出使皮魯古巴兩國 [Chen Gongli commissioned to go to Puerto Rico and Cuba]. *Shen Bao,* November 4.

———. 1873e. "Wang Gubaguo shuiwu ci yi dao Hu" 往古巴國稅務司已到滬 [Service official commissioned for Cuba has already arrived in Shanghai]. November 28.

———. 1875a. "Zongli Yamen kan lie Guba huayong bingci zhailu" 總理衙門刊列古巴華傭禀詞摘錄 [Excerpt of the Qing Imperial Commission to Cuba]. March 13. Continued on March 15.

———. 1875b. "Shu Shichen deng bing fucha kan Guba huayong qingxing bing ce gongjie hou" 書使臣等禀復查勘古巴華傭情形禀册供結後 [After officials investigated the situation with Cuban contract laborers]. March 17.

———. 1875c. "Lun sheguan yu waiguo shi" 論設官於外國事 [On establishing foreign consulates abroad]. October 14.

———. 1877a. "Bian Huagong gong cheng Guba zhuang pian lun" 辯華工供稱古巴撞騙論 [Debate on Chinese contract laborers' claims of being tricked]. May 19. Continued on May 21 and May 22.

———. 1877b. "Guba yongren ku kunag" 古巴傭人苦况 [Miserable conditions of Chinese contract laborers in Cuba]. October 24.

———. 1877c. "Shuben bao shu Guba huayong ku kuang hou" 書本報述古巴華傭苦况後 [After newspapers described the Qing Imperial Commission's Report on Chinese contract laborers]. October 30.

———. 1877d. "Guba huagong tiao kuan" 古巴華工條欵 [Articles for Chinese contract laborers in Cuba]. December 6. Continued on December 7.

———. 1878a. "Lun Zhong Xi gegguan wei zheng qingxing" 論中西各官為政情形 [On the political situation of Sino-Western offices]. January 5.

———. 1878b. "Lun Xibao shu jinri Huaren zai gudang qingxing" 論西報述近日華人在谷當情形 [On Western newspapers describing the current plight of overseas Chinese]. January 9.

———. 1893. "Lun sheguan yu waiguo shi" 論設官於外國事 [On establishing foreign consulates abroad]. November 14.

Sinn, Elizabeth. 2013. *Pacific Crossing: California Gold, Chinese Migration, and the Making of Hong Kong*. Hong Kong: Hong Kong University Press.

Standard. 1872. "Multiple News Items." April 20.

Straus, Adolfo D. 186?. Letter to Frederick Seward. William Henry Seward Collection. Original in the Rush Rhees Library, University of Rochester, Rochester, N.Y.

Tillman, Hoyt Cleveland. 1994. *Ch'en Liang on Public Interest and the Law*. Honolulu: University of Hawai'i Press.

U.S. Department of State. 1872. *The Executive Documents Printed by Order of the House of Representatives during the Second Session of the Forty-Second Congress (1871–1872)*. Washington, D.C.: U.S. Department of State.

———. 1875. *The Executive Documents Printed by Order of the House of Representatives during the Second Session of the Forty-Third Congress (1874–1875)*. Washington, D.C.: U.S. Department of State.

Viraphol, Sarasin. 1977. *Tribute and Profit: Sino-Siamese Trade, 1652–1853*. Cambridge, Mass.: Council on East Asian Studies, Harvard University Press.

Wakeman, Frederic. 1993. "The Civil Society and Public Sphere Debate: Western Reflections on Chinese Political Culture." *Modern China* 19, no. 2: 108–38.

———. 2009. *Telling Chinese History: A Selection of Essays*. Berkeley: University of California Press.

Xie Fang 谢放. 2010. "Chen Lanbin shishi buzheng ji bianxi" 陈兰彬史实补正及辨析 [Corrections and analysis on the basis of historical documents about Chen Lanbin]. *Xueshu Yanjiu* 学术研究 [Academic research], no. 10: 96–102.

Yan, Ching-hwang. 1985. *Coolies and Mandarins: China's Protection of Overseas Chinese during the Late Ch'ing Period (1851–1911)*. Singapore: Singapore University Press.

Yu Heping 虞和平 and Chen Junjing 陈君静. 2013. "Chen Lanbin yu Zhongguo weihu chuguo Huagong quanli de qishi" 陈兰彬与中国维护出国华工权力的起始 [Chen Lanbin and the advocacy of overseas Chinese workers' rights]. *Anhui Daxue xuebao* 安徽大学学报 [Journal of Anhui University] 4: 58–65.

Yun, Lisa. 2008. *The Coolie Speaks: Chinese Indentured Laborers and African Slaves in Cuba*. Philadelphia: Temple University Press.

Zhang Kai 张铠. 1988. "Guba huagong yu Zhonggu jianjiao kaiwei" 古巴工与中古建交始末 [Chinese labor in Cuba and the establishment of Sino-Cuban diplomatic relations]. *Huaren Lishi Yanjiu* 華人歷史研究 [Overseas Chinese history review] 4: 3–11.

CHINA

Research Ph.D. Fellowship | Ph.D. in China Fellowship

The Confucius China Studies Program Fellowships provide generous funding and support for qualified U.S. and international (non-Chinese) students who wish to pursue their doctoral research in China. Funding awards range from one semester to four years.

AWARD PACKAGE INCLUDES:

Grantees will receive comprehensive support during their time in China, including:

- 80,000 RMB annual living stipend
- 20,000 RMB annual research stipend
- Insurance
- Host university tuition
- Roundtrip airfare
- In addition, the Research Ph.D. Fellowship provides financial support for a research visit to China by the grantee's home university advisor.

Applications due February 15, 2017. For more info, including application instructions and deadline updates, visit: **www.iie.org/ccsp** or email **ccsp@iie.org**

Confucius China Studies Program
孔子新汉学计划 | Powered by IIE

New Books from
University of Minnesota Press

Living for Change
An Autobiography
Grace Lee Boggs
Foreword by Robin D. G. Kelley

The remarkable life of an untraditional radical on the American Left—now with a new foreword

"An intrepid and courageous fighter for economic, racial, and social justice, Boggs writes with a passionate optimism that is a true inspiration." —*Publishers Weekly*

$19.95 paper | 328 pages | 30 b&w images

Brown Threat
Identification in the Security State
Kumarini Silva

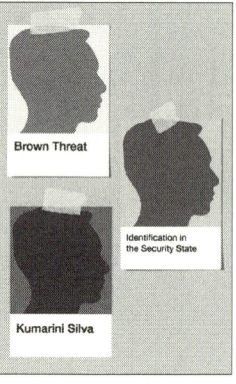

Revealing a post-9/11 America in which a dubious identity concept has become a dragnet for the "deviant"

"An essential text on the contemporary mediations of race in America. Kumarini Silva's analysis fills a critical gap in studies of race, arguing for the work done by the malleability of the racialized category of 'South Asian brown' for the U.S. security state."
—**Inderpal Grewal**, Yale University

$27.00 paper | $94.50 cloth | 224 pages | 9 b&w images

The Book of the Dead
Orikuchi Shinobu
Translated by Jeffrey Angles
With a commentary by Andō Reiji

The first complete English translation of Orikuchi Shinobu's masterwork, *The Book of the Dead* is a sweeping historical romance telling a gothic tale of love between a noblewoman and a ghost in eighth-century Japan. Readers will soon discover that a great deal lies hidden beneath the surface of the story; the entire text is a modernist mystery waiting to be decoded.

$25.95 paper | $91.00 cloth | 352 pages | 9 b&w images